Talking With Celtic

Absorbing, informative, amusing…
a collection of candid interviews with
former players of the Bhoys

Eugene MacBride

breedon books
PUBLISHING

First published in Great Britain in 2001 by
The Breedon Books Publishing Company Limited
Breedon House, 3 The Parker Centre, Derby, DE21 4SZ.

ISBN 1 85983 274 1

Printed and bound by Butler & Tanner, Frome, Somerset, England.
Jacket printing by GreenShires, Leicester, England.

Contents

Dedication

To Zelda who navigated, took photographs, checked
the tape and kept me always encouraged.
In memoriam Minstrel who purred on my lap as I
worked at the PC.

Foreword

THE idea of committing oral tradition to print is not new. It is about 2000 years old at least. Matthew, Mark, Luke and John elevated it to an art form and are the best-selling authors of all time.

It is hardly likely that the sales of this book will outdo those of the Gospels. However, that is to miss the point of how vital it is to record the experiences of players of a bygone age when football was indeed a sport, a game to be enjoyed and not simply, as it has become, a vehicle for people to make money.

The game has changed to distortion point, even in the last ten years and so it becomes important for future historians to have access to memories and experiences of years gone by.

Nowadays we live in an age where the focus is on the star. Everything he/she does or says appears in print or on his/her own website. What he/she has for breakfast is something we must know. The star has been interviewed to breaking point.

In this book, Eugene MacBride has interviewed the foot-soldiers or whom Cantona calls the water-carriers, the unsung heroes whose stories are new to us and who provide aspects of football history from a different angle. To a Celtic fan, any player who has worn the green and white is a hero. The span of this book covers over half a century. The players interviewed are representative of their generation. Each one was unfailingly courteous, hospitable and willing to give of his time. I had the pleasure of hosting the interview with Bobby Carroll and can vouch for the impression he left. This was a gentleman. They were all gentlemen.

Eugene MacBride shrewdly lets these gentlemen do the talking. I am sure you will find them well worth listening to.

George Sheridan
The Celt fanzine.

Acknowledgements

Martin O'Connor for the Johnny Paton interview; Tony Meadows for what it was like to play against Matthews; Bill Millar for reading transcripts; Frank Glencross for photographs and illustrations; Ian Gibson for help on the computer; Marion and Rab of the Campsie Guest House; Jamie and Elizabeth of Craigielea House; George and Marie and the gang at Celt House; Rab and Marianne at the Railway Hotel, Denny; Dom Sullivan for giving us the run of the place; Andy and Carole at Dunblane; Margaret and Mick for house-sitting over and over; Stuart (Hole in One) Weedon, Julie Weedon, Sandra and Linda at the PO for constant interest in the book's progress; the players' wives for those fabulous cups of tea; above all, Anton Rippon at Breedon Books. Have I forgotten someone? I'm sorry.

E.A. MacBride
Grantham, 2001.

Willie Buchan

Inside-right
1933-1937

Willie, when you signed for Celtic is it true that Willie Maley made a dash to Grangemouth to get you?

And Struth did. The pair of them came from Glasgow. Struth was the manager of Rangers.

So why did you sign for Celtic?

Because with Camelon Juniors was a red-headed fellow called Archie MacAuley who had signed for Rangers. I didn't think there was much chance of a game in the Rangers first team. That was the only reason.

Peter McGonagle was at Parkhead when you arrived?

Ah, Peter, aye! You know, we were champion five-a-sides, Celtic. As I say, I loved my football so I used to play all summer. One day we were playing at Hampden in the Sports and Jimmy Delaney and I were the two forwards. And there was Peter McGonagle, Peter Wilson and somebody else but anyway we got beat in the Final. So I hear McGonagle say to Wilson, "Great! We've done it!" You see, beforehand they'd gone and inspected all the prizes and the first prize was some horses' hoofs made into egg stands. Wilson and McGonagle had decided there and then weren't having those! The second prize was cases of cutlery. That was what they were after. So they shook hands and got their prizes and I said to them, "What did you not tell us for?" Peter patted me on the back, "Well, it would look better if some of us were trying!"

Now, Willie, your first game for the Celtic big team was a friendly in Dublin: Free State League 3, Celtic 6 at Dalymount on 30 April 1933. Have you any memory of it?

I'm sorry. No, I haven't at all. The only time I remember playing in Ireland was playing for the Scottish League against the Irish League. We were going across on the boat overnight and I shared a cabin with Jerry Dawson. I always remember there were two penalties and I scored with the two of them. And on the way back, I remember Jerry Dawson said, "Wait till you take a penalty kick against me." He felt he could pick them. And that was due to a five-a-side thing. We were playing five-a-sides down at Largs and we got a penalty. And at that time you had to stand still until the ball was kicked. So this goalie stood over by his left-hand post and I knew he was going to take a flier over to his right. So I ran to put it to his right, he dived to his right and the ball went past him to his left. I practised that sort of thing. The goalkeeper always watched what way your body was going. I used to charge up to stick it one way, then stick it the other.

People wanted a penalty kick to happen so Buchan could take one.

We played over in Copenhagen, I think it was – this wasn't with Celtic – and I got a penalty and I charged up and one of the defenders said to me, "We thought you were going to put the ball out of the park!"

Talking about goalies, Willie, any memories of Joe Kennaway?

Aye, Joe was a Canadian. In fact, I think he got my house after I moved to Blackpool.

He got your house in King's Park. Did you own that house, Willie, or was it a club house?

No, it was a rented house. Up in Croftfoot. Fifty-five – all the fives – Croftburn Drive.

Now Malky MacDonald. You blighted Malky's career for quite a time. Have you got the same opinion of the late Malky's genius as so many other people?

Yes, oh yes. Actually, they used Malky as a defender but in fact he was a great inside-man. A good dribbler. Oh, I liked Malky, aye. He was a great centre-half but to me he was a better inside man or a wing-half. He was a good centre-half but he was wee. He wasn't a great big fellow like Willie Lyon.

His career was more or less re-made when you left for Blackpool?

Aye. They moved him forward. I was inside-forward and he took my place.

Now, Willie, when you were at Celtic, club tradition demanded that the centre-half have an attacking role. Am I correct?

Aye, aye.

Even Willie Lyon was required to go up and support his forwards old-style like the great Willie Loney.

To an extent, aye. Aye.

You see it's a bee in my bonnet that the gap in front of the goalkeeper cost John Thomson his life. Jimmy McStay is reported as not playing the third back game.

I never saw John Thomson.

No, I know that, Willie, but what I mean is, if Jimmy McStay had been playing stopper, Thomson might never have needed to go down at Sam English's feet.

A lot of teams at that time employed the attacking centre-half. When we won the Cup in 1937, Aberdeen had Falloon. I was put through sort of style for the winning goal and he was up the park, the backs were wide apart and there was this big gap I found myself in. As you say, the goalkeeper had to come out. When I scored the winning goal, the two backs were closing in, George Johnstone started coming out and I was seeing less and less of the target. There was just a wee bit of the goals left and I thought, I better hit it now or I'm not going to see the goals at all.

You made your Scottish League debut at Palmerston in a 3-2 defeat on 12 August 1933. Do you remember that?

I remember that.

Happy Feet Charlie Napier was moved out of position to accommodate you. Didn't you feel privileged?

Aye, Charlie was an inside-left. I liked Charlie. It was great playing with him. Mind you, he could be dour. He had a great left foot, you know. Some player, Charlie.

Have you memories of Johnny Crum?

Ah, Johnny. Johnny was a wee Glaswegian. I think he was from Ashfield.
He was a right wee jocular character, do you know what I mean? And a great header of the ball too. I think nearly all Glaswegians of that time were great headers of the ball. I think they used to spend a lot of time playing keepy-uppy, heading the ball against a wall.

Now, Willie, Celtic, including you, play a Chile-Peru XI at Parkhead on 4 October 1933. Celtic win 2-1 but the crowd is mesmerised by the South Americans: brilliant footwork, no third back – just like Celtic! – no encroaching centre-forward, three substitutes stripped, a sensation in 1933! Any memories, Willie?

Aye, I've still got the pennant they gave me. All the South Americans gave each of the Celtic players a pennant. I'll show it to you. I meant to leave it out. The Chile-Peru inside-right presented his pennant to me. Tomas Fernandez.

Was the way they played an education for you, Willie? Did they strike you as something very different?

Actually, they were brilliant footballers, do you know what I mean? Frank O'Donnell scored one of the goals, I will always remember, and they couldn't get the goalkeeper to stand back in the goals. He was crying! He was leaning against one of the goalposts and crying! He was desolate at losing a goal. He lost two that night. I think Frank O'Donnell got both of them. You could see they were a team. They were very agile, wiry, like most South Americans, supple and they enjoyed their game too.

Do you remember Chic Geatons?

Aye, I remember Chic. He was our captain when the Scottish League played the Irish League and I got the two penalties. A nice man. A very nice man. As a matter of fact, I'd taken the first penalty and I was worried about the second one, because of going the same way sort of style, you know? And Chic said, "Ach, stick it in the same place, Willie." So that's what I did.

So you used to worry about these penalties?

No, not really. The only time I ever worried was when I was playing for Hull City against Rotherham and we were the two top teams. We got a second penalty. The first penalty, we had missed it. I had just gone to Hull but the two directors, they had seen me take a penalty with Blackpool reserves when they'd come to look at me. So they signalled for me to take the second penalty. I took the penalty and of course, as luck would have it, I scored. But it was the second penalty and we'd missed the first and that was one time I was really worried about not scoring. That time with the Scottish League was the only time I ever took two penalties in a game and I was worried then.

You were afraid the goalkeeper would suss you?

I was afraid he would suss me. In fact, after I took the two against the Irish League, Bertie

Harrison of Hamilton Accies was the other inside-forward on the day. And of course, like Jerry Dawson, he felt he knew how I took a penalty. So we got a penalty against Hamilton and he went running up to the goalkeeper, Jimmy Morgan and yapped away to him, how I was going to hit it. So I took it the same way and I scored. Morgan went the wrong way so Harrison went running back to him, "I told you so! I told you so!"

When you were taking penalties, did you suffer from the sort of thing that Jim Baxter used to do to put people like Paddy Crerand off, you know, mouth, gamesmanship, what the cricketers might call sledging?

No, no. None of that at all. You see, it's a different game nowadays. There was no one then to pull your jersey or bodycheck you. But see nowadays, it's really bad. They ignore the ball and bump you and impede you all they can and they get away with it.

Two players cannot challenge for the ball but one's holding on to the other by his shirt yet the referee says nothing. It's becoming a legitimate aspect of the play.

That's right.

So, Willie, you began your run-up from the centre circle, kid on, and there was nobody to distract you?

Not exactly from the centre circle. A wee bit to the right.

Now, in April 1934, you went down with appendicitis which in those days was a no-joke operation. You could die as soon as get over it and a lot of footballers did. How did you know? What were the symptoms?

I had pain and I was sick at training. It was Celtic told me I had appendicitis. I always remember the Celtic doctor – I can't mind now who he was – he came and he laid me down on a table and he pressed on me here. Oof! I nearly went through the roof! He said, "You've got appendicitis." They sent me to Charing Cross, private, specialist sort of thing. I wasn't long with it, you know what I mean? Seemingly it's like getting a tooth out nowadays. It's a simple operation now. The danger was always it might burst and you would get peritonitis.

Willie, why did so many footballers of your time go down with appendicitis because bar this boy Rafael that Celtic have just signed, you never hear of a footballer going down with it today and Rafael is just Celtic's luck.

No, I couldn't tell you. We used to be told it was from eating seeds like the pips of an orange or apple pips, you know. I don't know the reason. It wasn't the training or anything like that. The training didn't cause it.

Now, as you say, you came back quickly, because you played in the first Public Trial of 1934. Peter Wilson left for Hibs on 24 August 1934. Can you remember him leaving?

No, but I can remember playing with him. He was my right-half. He played behind me. He did a lot of talking but he was a nice fellow too. He didn't swear or anything like that. He'd help you. You know what I mean. He'd encourage you because you were a lot younger than he was.

Were you willing to listen to these older chaps?

Oh yes! Oh, definitely! Especially the likes of Charlie Napier. As I've said, Charlie – he was getting on a bit too. But Charlie was very dogmatic. Peter was never as dogmatic as Charlie. Charlie would lay down the law.

Would they advise you with regard to players you were coming up against? You're playing against so-and-so today, he's weak on his left side, that sort of thing?

No, no, you had to find that sort of business out for yourself, you know. I can't remember anyone advising me.

Willie, you become a regular in the big team with a 4-0 win over Hibs on 11 September 1934 with Delaney as your winger. Delaney is described as 'dashing about like the fire brigade'. I remember Jimmy Delaney and I think that is a very good description. He had a lot of football brain but he did put himself about. You were his first partner. What was it like playing with Jimmy?

Jimmy was an ordinary individual, kind of style. On the field he was always there when you wanted him. Of course, I used to wander all over the place too. If you were absent-minded you might finish up at outside-left, that sort of thing. Then go back to your position. But no one ever remonstrated with you for being out of place. You were actually working hard, you know what I mean? That's what I liked about inside-forward, you were never out of position really because you could go any place.

All right, Willie. Now, on 24 November 1934, Celtic beat Dundee 4-0 with McGrory at outside-right and Buchan scores 4. The first three were tap-ins but the fourth saw you gain possession 40 yards out, beat 2 men and shoot from well outside the box. Is this you enjoying your football?

Were they tap-ins?

The first three goals were tap-ins.

I remember the first one. I headed it in nearly standing on the goal-line. But the only other one I remember is the last one there. I was away out on the right.

Willie, a guy like you, what small voice speaks to you inside and says the dribble is on?

Well, there was one time I scored a goal against Hearts on 6 February 1937 and to tell you the truth, I wasn't trying to score, I was trying to give the ball to McGrory. I was away out on the right wing and it was one of those heavy days, a really heavy day, you know, and I beat this fellow and I beat another fellow and I was going to give it to McGrory but McGrory's marked, this fellow goes with McGrory, you know what I mean, so I had another couple of strides towards the goals, tried to give it to McGrory again, but still the chap goes with him, I'd to carry on, another few yards, and I end up taking a shot myself and I scored! I was beating fellows trying to give it to McGrory!

And that's a famous goal!

Here's something I made up for you before you came. These are the teams I played for: Celtic, Blackpool, Hull City, Gateshead, East Stirling, Coleraine in peacetime and during the war, Manchester United, Manchester City, Leicester City, Bristol City, Bath City, Fulham, Hamilton Accies and Stenhousemuir.

Willie, that is some list. Can I hold on to it?

Aye, it's for you.

Thank you, Willie. Now Willie Lyon signs for Celtic on 13 May 1935. Would Celtic have landed the 1936 League championship without him?

Who did we have at centre-half before him?

Jimmy McStay.

Well, Willie Lyon was a very strict disciplinarian. When we were playing Motherwell in the Scottish Cup on St Patrick's Day 1937, we were losing 4-1 or 4-2. Lyon got a penalty and that made it 4-3. I went through near the end and made it 4-4. Willie was up but he wasn't up to congratulate me. He said, "Come on, let's get another one now!" Grabbed the ball and away back with it to the centre-circle, you know? And that was a funny thing. I've only had like two sort of premonitions in my life and when I was actually scoring that goal against Motherwell was one of them. I felt this fellow was going to hook my leg as I drew it back. I was going to kick it with my left. I was sure he was going to hook it so I said to myself, "I'll take another stride." I took another stride and hit it with the outside of my right foot past the goalkeeper. To this day, I thought it was a premonition. I had another one, I think it was when I was with Hull City. We were taking a corner kick. I was at the front of the goals and I said to myself, "If I glance this ball up, it'll go over the goalie's head to the far side", and it did. Another goal. I call it a premonition but it was as if there was someone trying to tell me something. That game against Motherwell, if I'd hit it with my left foot, it would've hit the goalie because he was coming out and with me taking this other step there was space past him.

Willie, you're an intuitive genius!

Well, whatever it was!

Okay. Now Happy Feet left for Derby County at 5pm on 12 June 1935. Were you sorry to see him go?

Oh aye.

Did it hit something inside?

Oh aye. Definitely. He was a sort of special friend, you know what I mean? He was a great man for the ladies, Charlie. He'd be telling you about all his conquests.

Was he married or was he single?

I can't actually mind. We used to tell him, "You're a right liar, Charlie! You never did!" He drove a car. I think that was a big draw where the girls were concerned.

Now, Willie, 1935-36 was a Championship year at last but it began with a defeat at Aberdeen in the first game on 10 August 1935. A month later, Alec McNair says he has not

seen such a clever young Celtic team in action for years. How so clever? Was anyone devising tactics? Napoleon McMenemy perhaps?

No, I think it was just 11 fellows who wanted to play a game, who actually wanted a game. You were disappointed if you were training and you never got a game or something like that.

So it was an instantaneous thing? You went out and played and you were happy playing?

That's what I'm saying. And you helped each other.

So there's nobody using a blackboard behind the scenes?

Oh no.

There's no discussion how we're going to beat these people today?

Nope.

So what was Napoleon McMenemy doing all this time? He was trainer. Did he take care of injuries only?

He was more or less in charge of the reserve team. The only actual advice that I got from him or that the young players got from him was to kick a ball against a wall. He used to say the way a ball came off a wall was what happened when you didn't get control properly and the ball went away back off up the park. But if you hit a ball against a curtain, that was control, the way it would drop dead. That's what you've got to do. You've got to use your leg like a curtain, not like a wall. You see them nowadays, they do it ten a penny, they even catch it with the top of the boot, you know? That was the only advice I ever got all the time I was there.

Well, that's interesting. Now, Willie, on 28 September 1935, Celtic beat Hearts 2-1 and I quote: 'Buchan was the best player afield in footwork and scheming'. I know you were a natural, Willie, but would you still maintain you did not work at your game?

I didn't work on it, no. You went out on the park and played.

What was Jimmy McGrory like to play with?

Oh, Jimmy! He was a gentleman! He never narked at you or anything if you missed a pass or anything. He was magnificent in the air. He was breathtaking in the air. He was naturally right-footed but he used both feet. It was a time when players were required to be able to use both feet. I was naturally right-footed. I took all the penalties with my right foot. That's how you can tell what a player's natural foot is when he takes a penalty kick. He always uses his stronger foot.

On 26 October 1935, Celtic gain their first win at Fir Park in 9 years and this is a description of the Celtic play: 'When a 'well forward tricked a man...another at once he had to beat...Celtic could rip things open with a thrust'. To-day's team will be 1937 Cup winners: Kennaway; Hogg and Morrison; Geatons, Lyon and Paterson; Delaney and Buchan; McGrory; Crum and Murphy. They were quote 'as balanced a side as any in the League'. You still say there was no planning, Willie?

No, no planning. There was never any discussion at all, just who was playing.

Now, four days before Christmas 1935 with the lochs frozen over in the Highlands, the Golden Crust passes Hugh Ferguson's aggregate of 364 League and Cup goals in the 5-3 defeat of Aberdeen on a sanded pitch at Parkhead. He walks off with 366 to his credit and convinced he has scored one of the best goals of his life, a dive and butting header at the far post for 2-1. Do you remember that day, Willie?

I know that game was at Parkhead but I can remember one time going to Aberdeen. We used to go by the 10 o'clock from Buchanan Street on a Saturday morning and we got there at two. Four hours to Aberdeen. Every team got that train to Aberdeen. And the train was delayed this day. So McGrory got us to part-strip on the train. I think we saved our boots up for the taxi. So we got the taxi to the ground and McGonagle walks up to the gateman, "We're the Celtic team". The gateman looks at him. "Don't kid me on! Where's your tickets?" We had no tickets. Maley hadn't given us any tickets. So McGonagle says, "Fair enough. There's no game today. If we don't get in, the game's off. You better go and get the manager." I forget who the manager was.

Pat Travers?

Pat Travers, aye. He came. He played hell with the gateman. And that was it. I think we beat them anyway but we weren't going to get in! Three taxiloads of us!

Willie, did you know that in 1950, Raich Carter reckoned you one of the best penalty-kick takers in Britain?

Well, when I hit them, I hit them quite hard, with my right foot, but with the inside of my right foot. The ball went in the corner of the net. See, I once was a goalkeeper with Grangemouth High School and I knew that once you go off balance – I mean, if you could put a goalkeeper off balance – as I say, if you're running to the right and he automatically starts to go that way and you put the ball the other way, he can't get back. He can't recover his balance.

But did you push the ball right or left as the spirit moved you?

No, no. I always shoved them that way, always the same way. I never shoved them to the goalkeeper's right. I went that way and then I turned my foot and quite hard. It's not true that the ball just bobbled in. It was so that the fellow couldn't get back. He'd committed himself.

Right, Willie. So Celtic won their first Championship in ten years on 25 April 1936 at Firhill, 3-1 against Partick Thistle, two goals from Willie Fagan in a team of Kennaway; Hogg and Morrison; Geatons, Lyon and Paterson; Delaney and Buchan; Fagan; Crum and Murphy. A happy day for you?

Do you know, I can't recollect it. I've got no memory of it. I'm sorry. Was it McAllister played centre-half for Partick Thistle?

Jimmy McAllister, yes, but he wasn't playing this particular day.

Well, there was one game, Jimmy McGrory went off to change his boots or something or to get a new lace and Jimmy McAllister used to mark McGrory so tight he followed him off the park to keep an eye on him. You didn't need the referee's permission in those days. McGrory used to get marked very tight. I've told you the story of my solo goal at Hearts. That was tight marking led to that.

Peter McGonagle got a free transfer at the end of 1935-36. Were the Celts sorry to see him go?

Oh, aye. I mean, to me, he was a wonderful character.

There was a great occasion at Hampden in the Charity Cup Final on 9 May 1936. Celtic and Rangers were drawing 2-2 with Rangers ahead 7-6 on corners and 5 minutes to go. Then Delaney struck for his hat-trick and McGrory made it four with two minutes left. Is it true Mr Maley grabbed Delaney up the tunnel and warned him, Don't let this go to your head!

Oh well, Maley wouldn't have congratulated him, I know that. I mean, he was nothing like the managers nowadays. Do you know what I mean? He wouldn't shake your hand for scoring a goal. The day we pulled Motherwell back to 4-4 in the Scottish Cup he never even said, "Well done", to any of us.

But if you lost?

Oh aye! A different story then! I was never actually very struck on Maley.
I mean, he wasn't a jovial person at all or anything like that. He was like a president, a law unto himself, what I say is right.

What about his boss, Tom White? Did you see much of him?

No, we saw a lot more of the other one, Tom Colgan.

The *Celtic Handbook* for 1936-37 claimed Kennaway and McGrory should both have played at Wembley in April. In 38 League games, Joe had conceded 33 goals only, less than one a game. Must it not have been great to have had him as your last line and McGrory getting the goals at the other end? Did Kennaway ever lose a soft goal? I've got no record of it.

Well, I wouldn't say a soft goal but do you remember we played Motherwell in the League after the Scottish Cup Final in 1937?

The 8-0 game?

Well, as I had been a goalkeeper with Grangemouth High years ago, when Kennaway was injured, I had to take over. In those days there were no replacements, you played on with ten men or nine men. Anyway, Kennaway went off injured. By the way, they reckon he was injured when he played in the Cup Final. So he went off injured and we were getting beat 4-0. John Morrison had already gone off injured so we were left with nine men and me in goals and they were coming through in droves! So we got beat 8-0. So as I came off at the final whistle, he said to me, "Some goalkeeper you are, lost eight goals!" I said, "Listen, you lost four of them in the first quarter of an hour with a full team in front of you!"

When Celtic took the park that night, Kennaway apart, were they fielding a wholly fit team? There were rumours about a party atmosphere. I mean, you were on your way to Wembley for the English Cup Final.

Well, the younger players certainly did not drink. We didn't drink.

Willie, can you remember Celtic trialist, Salim Bachi Khan? He tried out for Celtic in August and September 1936 and I believe for his second game, the Celtic first team filled the Parkhead press box to watch him, on 11 September 1936.

Salim? I just faintly remember Salim, aye. He was from Calcutta. He played in bandaged feet.

Now for the big one, the Scottish Cup Final, on 24 April 1937. I read somewhere you felt like fainting because of the din of noise as the teams took the field.

Aye, well as I say, you had about 10,000 fans that broke in on top of the 140,000 upwards already there. And Hampden is a bowl, you know, the crowd are all round you. With all the cheering for the teams, the sound waves seemed to meet in the middle. And then there was the vibration on your eardrums. I almost passed out and it was just the vibration. Once we got started they could cheer all they liked. I never heard it. I never paid any attention to it.

Did any of the other players experience this?

No, I don't think so. It was just a matter of vibrating eardrums, you know?

Well, despite your eardrum problem, this match went down as Willie Buchan's Final. You were on top of your game 'orchestrating a change of tactics throughout that kept Aberdeen guessing.' And what about later? I believe you headed off for the Bank but that Queen Street was impassible.

Oh yes. I've never seen anything like it for crowds. The bus had to make its way through inch by inch.

Willie, can you fill me in on your side of the transfer negotiations of 15 November 1937?

It was as big a surprise to me as it was to anybody. I would have played for Celtic for ever. I was summoned to the Bank and told Blackpool wanted to sign me. I'd never been in England before but Celtic wanted me to go.
They got £10,000 for me. That was a record fee for a Scots player being transferred to England.

Did Celtic give you anything?

I got nothing from Celtic. I got something from Blackpool. If you were to getting £1,000 in those days, you were a millionaire. That £10,000 was a phenomenal fee. Now they wouldn't pick it up if they dropped it, some of the players. They get about £50,000 a week. You only got £8 in my day, £1 for a draw and £2 for a win. Every player got the same. There was nobody got more than anybody else. It was the same when I went to Blackpool. Matthews was just on the same as us. Otherwise he'd be told to go and get the ball himself! I played with the two greatest outside-rights, Jimmy Delaney and Stanley Matthews. They were my partners.

You weren't long at Blackpool after the war.

Two seasons.

Did you like Stanley Matthews as much as everybody else? Everyone else seems to swear by Stanley Matthews.

Well, he was kind of man wouldn't do anybody wrong. He was such a brilliant player. The way he played, you couldn't tell how he did it.

That reminds me one time we were playing Bolton and they put three players on him and God's truth we couldn't get the ball anywhere near him. And I was getting barracked by the crowd! For not giving him the ball! We were going up the left in droves. We had a free passage. Against Bolton. And I'm getting barracked for not giving Matthews the ball. We were putting the ball out to the left. There was no one there! No defenders, sort of style.

Willie, you broke your leg at Gateshead.

Aye, there was a fellow there – oh, he was a devil! He came right through and he broke my ankle down there, that little bone just over my ankle.

And that was your one serious injury in first class football?

Aye, apart from the time I went down with my appendix with Celtic. It was my one serious injury on the field.

And that's between 1933 and 1955. Willie, you played for a lot of club sides during the war but you also got a got a cap for Scotland at Hampden against England on 17 April 1943. Four-nil for England.

Ah, England were unbeatable during the war and for a wee while afterwards. The next time Scotland met them it wasn't 4-0, it was 8-0 at Maine Road. England had a great forward line. Matthews and Carter on the right wing.

Willie, had you been Nelson Mandela or the Dalai Lama, I could not have felt more pleasure in meeting you. It's a red letter day for me.

Ach well, it's been nice meeting you too.

Johnnie Wilson
Inside-forward
1937-1939

When were you born, Johnnie?

1916. I'm 84 at the end of this month, 29 October. Next Sunday.

Where were you born?

Longriggend. Do you know where that is?

Airdrie? Near Airdrie?

I was born there and my mother died with me. And I went to live in Shettleston with my grannie. I was brought up by my grannie.
In Shettleston. I came up here when I was 12 years old.

So what schools did you go to?

I went to St Paul's in Shettleston. I was captain of the under-12s and captain of the under-14s. As I say, I came up here when I was 12. I went to St Columba's in Cowdenbeath but they had no kind of football team. I played for St Bride's, a little school in Cowdenbeath. Then I played with Cowdenbeath District Schoolboys. That's when I was kind of 12 to 14.

Did you get any Scottish caps as a schoolboy?

Yes. But you won't believe me. I played for the Cowdenbeath and District Schoolboys and we won everything. I left school when I was 14 and my grannie got a letter from Johnny Dougray, he was one of the selectors, he was headmaster of Lochgelly School. He sent my grannie a letter, Send him back to school because he's been picked for Scotland! I went back to the school and another selector said, "No, we're not allowing that. He's left school and that's it." And the boy that was reserve took my place was Jimmy Logie, he went from Lochore to Arsenal. Then I played for Lochgelly Albert, another sad story. I played in all the trial matches, East of Scotland versus West of Scotland and all that carry-on, that was in 1937. So I signed provisionally for Celtic in '37, September 1937 and I got called-up in January '38. I was picked to play for Scottish Juniors but the selectors at that time said then it was no use because I was already provisionally signed. So for that one year, anybody that was provisionally signed wasn't allowed to play for Scotland. And the boy that took my place was Oliver Anderson that went to Celtic from Arthurlie. The Tommy Walker of junior football. So that was two caps I lost.

When did you first go down the pits?

On the pithead, like, 1930. I went underground in 193? iere at Blairhall.

can tell by the haircut." But what the difference was between my haircut and the Glasgow haircut, I could never tell. He was a great pal of Jimmy McGrory's. McGrory went to be manager at Kilmarnock and Kilmarnock were playing Celtic in the Cup at Parkhead. This is 1938. Chic had been injured. He was playing at Shawfield with us reserves. At half-time, Kilmarnock were beating Celtic and Geatons at Shawfield put on his clothes and away he went to Parkhead. He left us with ten men. That was it. Just walked away. He never came back out the second half!

He went off to encourage the first team?

No, no! He went off to see McGrory! To shake his hand! Because they were beating Celtic!

I thought he'd gone off because he was worried about Celtic.

No, no! He went to see his pal, to congratulate him!

What about Willie Lyon?

Willie Lyon. He came from Queen's Park. He was an insurance agent. And every player that signed on for Celtic, he was wanting to cover their insurance. He was getting three or four times more money than the rest of the players because with him being with Queen's Park, he got the transfer fee to himself and Celtic were able to spread it out weekly. That meant about £30-40 a week to him.

What? From the transfer fee? He got all the money?

Yes. From Celtic.

Queen's Park couldn't accept money for a player?

No. No, no. The player walked away free. That was the thing then. People said you were better going to Queen's Park for a season and then going on elsewhere because you got all the money to yourself. Well, that's what he got. He got about £30 a week. That's four times the amount of money that the other players were getting. That would be for a year or two year likely. Then that was it.

How did Willie Lyon impress you?

Oh, Willie was a good player, strong, but he wasn't a centre-half like Alec Millar. Alec Millar was 100 per cent footballer. He had everything. So Willie Lyon was more or less a strong man, headed the ball out, kicked the ball out but Alec Millar was articulate, he had style, he had everything. When Willie Lyon was unfit, Alec came in but as soon as Willie was fit again, Alec went back to the reserves. He wasn't allowed to hold his place no matter how well he played.

What about George Paterson?

George Paterson was a good player. I can mind of old Maley one day. See, they would take one of us reserves maybe one week, somebody else another week, looking after the hamper. This was to give you experience. Well, this week I was there, looking after the hamper and George Paterson, you ken, scored the goal in the first half. He'd gone up the field with the ball and he slammed it in the net. At half-time, old Maley went for him. "Don't you ever do that again," he said. "The forwards are there to score goals. You're there to supply them. If that ball had gone past the post or the goalkeeper had saved it, you're well out of position. Don't ever do that again!" Shows you, eh?

Mr Maley was not a believer in Total Football. What about Johnny Crum?

Johnny Crum was great, a great wee player. He came from Maryhill. When we were on holiday in Ireland, me and Alec Hogg, a pal of mine, we met a cousin of Johnny Crum's. She was talking about Johnny Crum. I said, "I know Johnny Crum". She said, "You don't! He plays with Celtic." I said, "I play with Celtic!" So we went back to training after the close season and Johnny Crum came up to me: "So you were talking to my cousin!" I said, "Aye!" That happened on the Derry Walls.

Johnnie, were you at Hampden on 24 April 1937 when Celtic won the Scottish Cup against Aberdeen before 146,000 people? Were you one of them?

No. Do you know where we were that day? We were at Dumfries that day, playing with the reserves. And by the time we got back, we got a glass of milk to celebrate winning the Cup. A glass of milk! In the Bank Restaurant. But old Maley's great saying was, "It's not an honour for you to win the Cup, it's an honour for the other team to win the Cup. You're supposed to win that Cup! It's not an honour. It's an honour for the other team to beat you." He always said that. He said, "You go out there and get that Cup because it belongs to you." That was it.

Now, as you've said, you were at Ibrox for the Exhibition Trophy Final against Everton, 10 June 1938.

Yes! Sitting beside Benny Lynch.

Do you remember chatting to him?

Aye. Aye. He knew all our names. He knew all our names because he trained with us every day. It was the time when he went to put the gloves on, nobody would go near him bar Kennaway.

Now the outbreak of war in 1939.

I went to Chesterfield. I was only down – I played about three games and then I had to come back home with the war. I went back and I played with Blantyre Vics in 1944 because English players could play junior without getting reinstated. Jock Stein was reserve to me at Blantyre Vics. His father was on the committee. He went to Albion Rovers, then went to Wales, Llanelli. He went there, and then he came back home and he met one of the head boys of Celtic and they said they were needing a boy to look after the reserves. Was he willing to take the job? So he went there to look after the reserves. Jock Stein. Then he went to Dunfermline and his father told him, "Whenever you're at Dunfermline, get in touch with Johnnie Wilson and he'll get you players. He'll help you." I gave him five players and they all walked into the first team. That was Eric Martin the goalkeeper, John Lunn full-back, Pat Wilson my nephew, outside-right, Jackie Sinclair outside-left, he went to Newcastle. Eric Martin went to Southampton, the goalkeeper. They all walked into the first team. That's when he was with Dunfermline.

Johnnie Wilson

Johnnie, you played in a Scottish Junior Cup Final during the war, isn't that right?

Aye, Blantyre Vics versus Glasgow Perthshire. We got beat 1-0.

Now when you say that you kept Jock Stein out of the team, were you still playing inside-right?

No, wing-half. Left-half. Jock was a wing-half. He was never a centre-half, he was a wing-half at that time.

So you knew him quite well socially?

Oh, he was in the house! Every time that they came to the big do in Dunfermline, at East End Park, the St Margaret's pilgrimage. Jock used to drop Jean off in Dunfermline. She used to go on the pilgrimage. And my Ella used to go. She and my son used to go. And Jock would come and stay with me. He would come out and sit with me and we'd give each other all the news about the football. Then he'd pick Jean up later. And then he came and was manager of Dunfermline. He lived in Dunfermline.

Now you played for Berwick Rangers during the war, Dunfermline and Hamilton. How did Hamilton get hold of you?

There were two boys that worked at the pit came from Hamilton. I was playing with Blantyre Vics at the time. And of course they said, "We'll get Hamilton on the job." So Hamilton came, signed me on and I was playing with Davie Wilson. He was the centre-forward and I was inside-right. They thought we were kind of two brothers. They thought I was English, Davie Wilson and Johnnie Wilson.

Because Davie Wilson was English, I think.

Aye. And Frank Swift from Manchester City and England was the goalkeeper. Bobby Reid was outside-left, him with the middle shed. We played against Hibs and Matt Busby was playing with Hibs at the time. He was guesting for Hibs and the wee outside-left – what do you call him again?

Caskie?

Caskie! Jimmy Caskie. Then when I went to Berwick, they were all at Berwick, Jimmy Caskie, Houliston, Juliussen. It was Houliston, Juliussen, and Wilson. And Caskie. All played with Berwick Rangers.

See, I asked you about Hamilton Accies because they were really enterprising when it came to bringing in guest players and Frank Swift is the outstanding example. What was big Swiftie like?

He was great. A nice big man. But I got to know him after that. I played for Chesterfield against Manchester City and he broke two of my ribs with his elbow. That was in 1946.

Now when you were transferred to Chesterfield, were you a Celtic player or were you a free agent?

They made a mistake at Parkhead. The Chesterfield boy came to see me and I said, "I know nothing from Celtic, I've had no word that I've been retained or released or anything. So when I went to Parkhead to get my boots and that, old Maley said, "Where are you going?" I said, "I'm going to Chesterfield." He said, "No you're not!" I said, "I am, because I've had no word about anything." He said it was a mistake. "You're not to leave!" I said, "I'm going." I was never retained for season 1939-40 but he said it was a mistake, I was retained. Now I went to Chesterfield and I played three games and war broke out. I came back home and I went back down again in 1945. I just carried on in 1939 because he was really good to me, this scout, I can't remember his name. He was a boxing promoter and he was doing well. So I went to Chesterfield along with Bobby Sinclair from Musselburgh and another boy that was just a junior, like. I can't remember his name. We went to Chesterfield and I really loved it. We went to Tottenham, beat Tottenham. Went to Blackpool, beat Blackpool. A really good team. A really great team. But Ella came home to have the baby, the son, in 1950 and she didn't want to go back.

But you went back down the pits after Chesterfield in 1939?

Back down the pits.

And you rejoined Chesterfield in 1945?

I was captain of Cowdenbeath. The next season, Chesterfield wanted me back down there. The manager of Cowdenbeath told me, he said, "Johnnie, you'll have to go because if you stay up here, they won't let you play." So for a full year, I travelled every weekend to Chesterfield and went to wherever we were playing, like. You ken, for a year, and then we went back down and stayed there up till 1950.

You got transferred to Oldham?

To Oldham, yeah. It was at Oldham I met the Hangman, Albert Pierrepoint. He had a pub in Chadderton, just next to Oldham. I'm trying to think of the name of the pub, something to do with hanging! He used to take the wee case down to Manchester, down to the jail, like, whenever there was going to be a hanging, like, the wee case, then back home again. Albert Pierrepoint.

Now you managed Blairhall Colliery football team for 22 years!

A long time. And then I was a scout for Charlton, a scout for Wolverhampton and then I packed it up.

That must have been some life, you know, Johnnie, being a full-time manager for 22 years. Being a manager is not an easy life!

Nup. It's not an easy life for the wife either.

But you carried on and you stuck with it. They must have given you a gold cup or something when you finished?

I got nothing. I took coal home for the fire every week. Football was in my blood. And I put four or five players to senior every year. Every season! Sent them away to Hearts, Aberdeen, Dunfermline, Alloa.

When you transferred a young player, were you always sure you could replace him?

That's right. I'd usually be able to pick up a replacement from the schools.

Did you have a network of people scouting for you?

I did the looking myself. Just myself. I knew that they wouldn't be able to win a lot of things because of young players, but the senior scouts used always to flock to Blairhall because they knew it was young, talented players that was playing with Blairhall. I mean, we'd win the odd Cup, the Cowdenbeath Cup, but as far as the Scottish Junior Cup went, we'd no chance. Eric Martin's mother didn't want him to sign for Dunfermline because if he left Blairhall that was the end of her getting coal from the pit. She came up to the house here. John, she said, "See that he doesn't sign or we'll get no coal!" Dunfermline fell out with me when they were playing Celtic in the 1961 Cup Final. I said to Jackie Sinclair, "I wish you all the best but I hope Celtic wins." I was still Celtic daft, you see. I was barred from East End Park for a month. Jock Stein was in charge of Dunfermline then but he had nothing to do with it. My son had a trial for Hibs the same day as Peter Marinello but he wasn't interested. He was studying for the university at that time. Last story: I mind of Jock Stein when he took over at Dunfermline as manager. At Oakley, they used to have a different man in every week to speak, a lawyer or a union boy or an expert on something or other. Anyway, it was Jock Stein's turn to come out – to talk about football. So I'm sitting at the back, like, and he got up on the stage and they introduced him as Jock Stein, manager of Dunfermline. And the first words he said, "I don't know why you sent for me to give a talk on football when you've got a boy at the back who knows far more about football than I do!" That's what he said! "There's a boy sitting at the back there knows far more about football than I do!"

And did they all look round?

Oh aye! They all knew me! Some boy, Jock. Because he could play none. He wasn't a good player. He was a very ordinary player. I mean, you wouldn't have picked him out. But he was a great manager. He got the breaks at the right time, Celtic, Dunfermline, Hibs, Celtic. And a terrible gambler. He'd have gambled on two flies going up the wall.

Johnnie, if I send you the transcript of this talk, will you be able to check it?

Ella will check it. I've been registered partially blind. That was in August. I mean I can see outside and that but letters and figures and that – hopeless! I have to leave it to Ella. She reads my *Celtic View* to me.

Johnnie, thank you very much.

Thank you very much! Thanks to you!

Jackie Watters

Inside-Forward
1937-1947

Jackie, you were at Ibrox on the day John Thomson sustained his fatal injuries.

I was. I was only about 14, I think. They reckon he had a hole in his head as big as my fist. Poor fellow.

Now, Jackie, did you start to play football with St Aloysius or had you been playing football before that? Were you a street footballer?

Well, it was all street football in Glasgow. But at St Aloysius we had a very, very, very good team. We won everything. Yet we were a very small school. It was the Jesuites, you get me? I had represented Glasgow Schools about five times, you know, Glasgow versus London, played at Craven Cottage. There was 18,000 at the game! Glasgow Secondary Schools against London Grammar Schools. But I enjoyed these games because there was a great wee player used to play behind me, Adam Little, went on to play for Rangers. A great player he was. He and I had a great understanding. So we were always the prima donnas.

How did Celtic contact you?

Well, I came back from London after this schools game at Craven Cottage and there was an old scout came up to the house. He said Celtic would like to sign me provisionally because I was only about 15 or 16. My father said no. He's going to do PE. I was going to do PE at Jordanhill. The scout said that was no bother. We've got two players at the moment. One's doing Medicine and the other's doing a BSc. That was John Fitzsimons and Matt Lynch. So that was the introduction. So then I signed provisionally which meant I was trysted to Celtic and I couldn't sign for anybody else. And in actual fact, I got a nice little weekly wage. And I didn't kick a ball. Willie Maley was the manager then so I used to go down to the Bank Restaurant in Queen Street in Glasgow every month to collect a little brown envelope which was very nice. And from there they sent me to St Roch's, a junior team, and I played there for one year. I was 17 then and I signed for Celtic, professionally.

What was that like, going junior with St Roch's?

Hard. Oh dearie, dear. Even the district St Roch's was in. You know, Garngad, even the cats used to go about in pairs, it was that bad. Rough. It was very, very, very rough. But we had a lot of rough players and they looked after the boys like me. The one thing that sticks in my memory was when I played in the Celtic first team, you know, for the first time. I can remember the whole week before that, you see, because I'd played against Motherwell reserves and I'd gone nap, a nap hand, five! Then Malcolm MacDonald went down with his appendix. In those days the team was picked on a Thursday night. My father was away down to the newsagent to get the Friday morning edition. So he walks in and he was like a Cheshire cat. He was wreathed in smiles, eh? So that was the run-up to me getting into the team. Was it against Hibs the first game I played?

No, it wasn't.
Arbroath?

Arbroath. It was against the Red Lichties up at Arbroath. Celtic won two-nil. But we're coming there. We're coming there gradually. What I want to ask you, have you any memories of the 1937 Cup Final? Were you there?
Oh yes, I was there. I was a signed player since the January of 1937. I wouldn't be with the official party but while I was still a reserve I was at the 1938 Exhibition Cup final against Everton. I was in the party for that, about six of us. I was at the 1937 game, definitely. But the great memory is the Exhibition Cup Final of 1938, one of the greatest games I ever saw.

But we're coming to that. You don't seem to have played in the pre-season trial of 1937 but I want to run through the teams just in case the mention of a name prompts a memory. I'm always on the look-out for wee stories. Are you ready?
Ready.

The green and whites were Kennaway, Hogg and Morrison. Geatons, Lyon and Paterson. Delaney and Buchan, McGrory, Crum and Murphy. Against: Tom Doyle, John Boyle and John Doyle. Dawson, Millar and Duffy. Anderson and Carruth, Murray, Divers and Fitzsimons.
I remember a wee story about Doc Fitzsimons. I always remember he came into the house once. He was just in passing, you know, and he had been playing against Partick Thistle and there was this lull in the crowd as you get sometimes, you know, same as in boxing, the crowd goes silent for a moment, and in this lull, this shout comes from the terracing, "Hey, Fitzsimons! Are you nationalised or just paralysed!" That would be about 1948 when Nationalisation was coming in. So he said, "I'm going to hang my boots up." There was another of the reserves Mick Davitt and it's funny, I can tell you about him. I was on the *Warspite*, the battleship, during the war, and I went ashore, and I went into one of these places – it wasn't the Salvation Army – whatever it was, it was to get my head down for the night, anyway. It was for servicemen, so I went in there and I met Mick Davitt! He was two beds away from me. He was in the Guards. In the Guards. Big, strapping lad he was. Came from Bridgeton. He played centre-half.

You play against Rangers reserves on 4 April 1938, 1-1 at Ibrox. The Celtic team is Doherty, Boyle and Doyle. Lynch, Millar and Davitt. Dawson and Anderson. Carruth, Watters and Fitzsimons.
I remember that game well. Because I missed a goal in the dying minutes. And I don't think – I hit a pigeon! And I was only about ten yards from the goal. There was nobody either side of me. From a corner kick. I remember that well.

You put it over the bar?
Yeah. I hit a pigeon.

Is that a metaphor? You mean a real pigeon?

A real pigeon. I remember that game. I've often quoted that game. It was a corner kick and there was nobody near me at all. It was as if I had a number eight niblick in my boot. It was harder to put the ball over the bar than to put it into the goal. And the ball hit a pigeon.

So a real pigeon! Now your memories of the Empire Trophy Final, 10 June 1938. I think you've got some vivid memories.

Oh, that was great! There were 22 men on the field and every one of them was a class footballer. It was 0-0 at full-time and they played 15 minutes each way extra time. And funny enough, I met that big centre-half of Everton again.

Tommy Jones?

When I was with Sunderland, he was still attached to Everton which made for long-term continuity. Crum put the ball through his legs and scored. The modern terminology is, he nutmegged him. And I always remember that we went down to the Bank Restaurant for the meal afterwards. And on our table there were two bottles of champagne. There were four of us at our table. There was Kennaway, the goalkeeper, Crum, Joe Carruth and myself. So Kennaway takes this bottle of champagne and he looks at Carruth and me and he says, "Boys, you are too young to drink. This is for Mrs Kennaway." So Crum takes the other bottle and says, "This is for my wife too!" But that was a great night. And they got blotto! Absolutely! I remember Bobby Hogg, he played right-back. He was reserve about 45 times for Scotland. Yes, it was a great game! A great game that! A great game!

Now on 9 August 1938, you played at Parkhead for the Greens in the pre-season trial in this team: Doherty, Davitt and Doyle. Lynch, Millar and Duffy. Kennan and Anderson. Carruth, Watters and Fitzsimons. You lost to the big team 5-3.

I remember a pre-season game and there was a lad called McLaughlin. He went to Aberdeen later. Joe McLaughlin.

That would be pre-season 1939.

Well he was playing against me. I was inside-right and he was left-half, the old style. He was marking me. Now straight in front of the stand, he grassed me. He shouldered me out of touch onto the shale, the running track. But not dirty. We didn't play dirty. A shoulder charge. But in the second half I went to head the ball backwards and Joe was coming forwards behind me and I caught the bone here above his eye with the back of my skull. He was gashed. I think he needed seven or eight stitches. But when I went in, he was away. So I was going in to tell him I hadn't meant it despite the fact that earlier he had grassed me. So anyway, to use a Scottish expression, I plunked my classes on the Monday morning to get up to Parkhead. I was a full-time student so I just fitted in my training with my classes. Pre-season was always easiest because we were on holiday. Anyway on the Monday I went up and he came straight across to me. There was a billiards room there, a billiard table so he comes right up and he says, "You would never come and ask me how I was." He says, "I knew I was going to get it, you know!" I said to him, "Do you think for one minute I would do that to anybody?" What you have to remember, the Glasgow kiss wasn't in vogue in those days. Not even my backwards version.

the way I was running. I wasn't running free, you know. She didn't know who I was, by the way, she didn't recognise me. But we came in and we had a wee cup of tea and she said, "No, Jackie!" I said, "Aye, Jackie! She said, "Where have you been, Jackie?" I said, "In the war."

So how did you eventually get to Sunderland as physio?

I applied for it. I was in Barnsley. I was group superintendent over three hospitals. It was one of the staff. He said he was putting in for this job at Sunderland. And I used to go away to Leeds and that with a lot of amputees on outings so I put in for it as well. And I got the job which is another thing.
Twenty-eight years I was there.

Twenty-eight years! And you spotted Jimmy Montgomery?

There was a friend of mine that was a teacher. Jimmy was playing in his school team, you know. I don't think they had much of a team and every time they were playing, it was Jimmy Montgomery versus 11 others. So he kept on telling me, you want to get this boy to Roker Park. Anyway, I met him and he told me, "It's too late, he's gone to Burnley." So I saw Allan Brown, Burnley manager and he said, "Go up and see him." So I went up and saw his mother. Oh, she said, "I'll 'phone him." So he was back the next day and fixed for Sunderland.

He was the Wonder Goalkeeper of the 1973 English Cup Final.

That was a great day, that. Oh, a great day! When you're playing football you absorb your adrenaline, you absorb it, whereas when you're watching the game, you're not absorbing it, you know. It was a funny thing about when the game finished, 1-0 to Sunderland. We'd beaten Leeds, a great team, must have been one of the best teams in the world at the time. Bob Stokoe was our manager. He ran on. Then what's his name – Arthur Cox , that went on to help the England manager – he ran on. There was another fellow there, Billy Elliot, he ran on. And the next thing is, like sheep again, I ran on. And when I got on the field, I said to myself all of a sudden, "What the hell are you doing on here?" And as it happens, I've got a tape of it, a tape of the game. Porterfield who had scored the goal threw his arms round me and he said, "You played a great game, John," so that kind of settled me. So I made my way then to the dressing-room and they all went running round the field.

Jackie, thank you very much and Mrs Watters for that lovely tea. The water certainly tastes different up here on Wearside.

Thank you. I hope that tape's all right. I've been watching the wee red light.

Ah, the old light emoting diode? So have I. It'll be okay, I'm sure. Thank you, Jackie. Thank you very, very much.

Seton Airlie
Centre-forward
1939-1947

You were from a big family, Seton?

I was. Three sisters and six brothers. I was the seventh. I was born in Carmyle. I wasn't short for brains but I had to leave school at 14 in 1934 to help bring money into the house. I started my working life as a tea boy to Irish navvies laying sewers on the housing developments going up everywhere round Glasgow at the time. After that, I started my apprenticeship as an engineer with Stewart and Lloyds at Tollcross.

How did your football career begin?

I started with St Mungo juveniles at Garngad. I was paid two shillings to sign for them. My first game was against St Pat's at Coatbridge. We changed in iron huts and we were told to run for the trams at the end, our clothes would be all collected. There must have been a crowd of 2-3,000. We won 3-1 and made a beeline for the tramcar as soon as the final whistle went.

Seton, what happened between 1939 and 1942?

I'd gone up to Greyfriars juniors from St Mungo. We were playing in the Langbank Smyllum Cup final at Parkhead on 16 May 1939 against St Roch's and before half-time I was carried off with a heavy ankle injury. So the manager of Celtic, it was Mr Maley then, came in at half-time, and just looked around, while the physio was attending to me and he just had a general chat about me, concerning my ankle. Then after the game, Jimmy McClone, Mr McClone who was the secretary at St Anthony's, said Mr Maley was waiting to see me before I left the ground. Both of us went in and then he asked me to come into the Bank Restaurant in Glasgow the next evening, 17 May, where I signed a provisional form for £2. And then the war started of course, but I was told to report for night training twice a week. You had to go in and train evenings, and, of course, the full-time players, they were training also, so I just carried on doing that really until, I think, early 1942 when I was playing for St Anthony's. Jimmy Gribben had asked me to go and play for St Anthony's, to get a bit of experience or something. Then Motherwell came along. Bobby Ferrier, the manager, got me to play against Hibernian, funny enough, a great team at that time. We hadn't won for ages and we beat Hibernian. And of course, Celtic were up in arms: They had put me at St Anthony's! I was playing for them! I was training at Celtic Park! I was a Celtic player! So the next week they offered me a game at Parkhead with Jimmy McStay watching and I signed a form and that was me a full-time Celtic player. So I really signed for them twice.

Now, your first game for Celtic was on 17 January 1942. You break into a very famous forward line: Delaney and MacDonald; Airlie; Divers and Murphy.

They were all heroes of mine but I'd been training with them. Johnny Divers was a really brainy footballer. He taught me to head a ball. I just fitted in, I played with them, unlike a lot of young players that came to Celtic after me.

Seton, when you say you learned from a player, was he actively coaching you? On the park?

No, not necessarily. It's just that a lot of players have got good habits, like Malcolm MacDonald. Malcolm always seemed to have a lot of time to do things. But I remember Jimmy Delaney telling me odd things like when I had the chance of a shot, not to hit it off balance, to take that few seconds to get myself on target. He used other words but that was the gist of what he meant. When I was a young fellow with St Mungo, I used to go up to Celtic and watch Johnny Divers at corners. He lurked outside the penalty area as if he wasn't interested in the action and then he would run full pelt to meet the ball, to head it, so that was one of the first things I learned from him. And little Johnny Crum was moving around doing his decoy. Then Johnny Divers would start his run into the box, a great header of the ball. Poor Johnny Crum, he'd come to training from a full shift in the shipyards, still in his overalls. And Johnny Divers too, to Parkhead, straight from a full shift. Malcolm MacDonald was my real hero as a Celtic player and I used to be a bit in awe of him really but the rest of the players, they were all down to earth people, even Willie Lyon. Before I went to Celtic, I used to think he would be a bit of an aristocrat, he was such a proper gentleman. I don't think I ever played with him. I just remember seeing him in the dressing room. They were all smashing fellows. One time I went up with the centre-half, I think it was Frank Brennan of Airdrie or some big fellow, and my instructions were to head the ball on when that happened. So I headed it on and before I reached the ground I heard the roar of the crowd. Delaney had scored. He said to me, "Well done, it's your goal." That's the kind they were.

Now you're called up when your Celtic career is hardly started and you end up in the Honourable Artillery Company. Saving your reverence, Seton, how did you manage to get into such a posh mob? And such a London mob?

I was posted to Bushey Hill Park in London which was the HQ of the HAC. I think they took me because they were down on numbers.

Did you ever bring a plane down?

Ah, there were a lot of them brought down over London but you couldn't say of any one, that was us that did that. You just couldn't tell. We were based at Chigwell and other places, even Hyde Park, and we patrolled London, places like Tottenham, White Hart Lane and planes were brought down but you could never say for certain we got that one.

And when did you first meet your future Prime Minister?

I met him, in Ghent, in Belgium. He was just like all the other officers and people that I had to deal with so I didn't really sort of take any special notice. I just knew him in the Army, you know, and I was surprised really when he turned up in politics.

But Ted Heath was 1944, 1945. Let's go back to 1942. How did Chelsea get on to you?

Well, I was stationed at a little place called Thames Dittton in Surrey. The sergeant of the guard came down to tell me there was somebody wanting to see me in the guardhouse. So I went up there and it was Mr Birrell, manager of Chelsea and he told me he had permission from Celtic that I could play for his club. Yeah, Billy Birrell, he came from Kirkcaldy.

And you loved it at Chelsea!

Oh yeah! Then it was all open terraces then and they used to get enormous crowds. I used to go from Esher in Surrey to Clapham Junction because I used to meet two players there, a chap called Dickie Foss and Peter McKennan of Partick Thistle. He had been there quite a while. And we used to get the tram to Fulham Broadway, I think, and then we'd walk to the ground. We used to have hundreds of kids following us! Chelsea were a really friendly club. The supporters were fantastic. They gave you a lot of encouragement. I think I played one game or two games for Derby County because I was on a course in Derby. They asked me if I'd play for Derby. I was up there for less than a fortnight and I played one game for them at West Bromwich. George Paterson was playing for Derby at that time. I got dropped off the Derby team bus at New Street station in Birmingham. Massive queues. I didn't have a travel pass but big Jackie Stamps, the Derby centre, was with me. I said, "I'll get the tickets." He said, "I'm older than you... I'll get them." So he went away to get them. I can't remember how it worked out, but it was only when we're pulling into King's Cross I discover we've been travelling on platform tickets valid for New Street!

Now you were home on 5 September 1942, in the Glasgow Cup first round at Ibrox, 2-1 for Rangers after extra time. You are quoted as saying, "We had them groggy." Can you remember that game?

Funny, I've got cuttings of that game. I never really kept cuttings myself. I was usually on my way back to the unit when the paper came out but my brother used to send me little things out of the press, just little things, so maybe I was a bit foolish really, you know. Looking back on it now, I should have kept things but you don't realise at the time, you think today is going to last for ever.

Well, on 5 September, according to the papers, George Young did not know what to do with you. You were the dashing Airlie, the commando-like Airlie, and to score Celtic's equaliser, you beat Young with great dexterity and a low header past Jerry Dawson. But Seton, you played in a dreadful game for Celtic, your first Ne'erday fixture at Ibrox 1943, Rangers 8, Celtic 1. Have you got nightmares of that one?

Oh, terrible! Yeah. Well, Matt and Malcolm were sent off. It seemed very harsh, both of them being sent off. We were overrun, you know. When you look back there wasn't very much anybody could have done about it when you lose two players. As I say, you always think the referee's against you. This one was probably. I always thought most of the referees in Scotland were very good like little Bobby Calder. No, I always found the referees in Scotland very fair.

What was the experience like for you, playing against Rangers?

Well, I never got the chance to play against Rangers at Celtic Park. I played against Rangers four times for Celtic and every time it was at Ibrox. Somehow or other it was just like playing at home really. The Celtic had marvellous support there because in those days, as you know, it was no tickets, it was all pay at the turnstile. You could get vast crowds into both grounds. You felt a little bit nervous before the kick-off and that, funny enough, as soon as the game started you seemed to forget that, you know.

There was a game at Goodison on 4 December 1943, Army in England versus Army in Scotland, a 2-2 draw, Seton Airlie versus Stan Cullis.

Aye, it was just like an England-Scotland game, they were most of them internationals. Before the match, our captain, that great player, that well-known player, Tommy Walker of Hearts – we had a discussion before the game, sitting in the hotel, the Adelphi Hotel in Liverpool – that when a ball was picked up, it would be sort of hit over the full-back's head and I'd to go for it but without any qualms and as soon as I got it, I'd to cross it and there'd already be someone there waiting for me. And all during the game there were things like that happening but this particular time the ball was played off Archie MacAuley and he got the ball over the full-back's head. I ran on to it and without any hesitation, I hit it hard across the area. That was the idea but Stan Cullis came in and the ball hit him hard in the face. He got concussed and had to stay overnight in hospital in Liverpool. He lived not far from here, the other side of Malvern. I met him at a local match at Malvern Town. He remembered the incident. We had a bit of a chat. That was some great player, Stan Cullis. It was this match every time I got near this bit of the touchline, I was getting all sorts of abuse from this serviceman for being a Celtic player. I had words with him. I said we were both in the same Army, for God's sake. Hitler was his enemy, not me. It was a representative game so we were introduced to George VI. Jimmy Carabine led him down the Scottish line. He shook each player's hand and when he reached me, he asked me, 'Where do you come from?' So, I said in a broad Scottish accent, "Glasgow, sir." He said, "Ah, Gloucester, I know it well!"

Seton, Normandy D-Day, 6 June 1944. You went into Europe, I think, a day or two after?

No, I think it would be seven days or something.

You sat – you told me once, Seton – you sat in a field, September 1944, and you watched the gliders coming in over Arnhem – trying to take A Bridge Too Far.

Yeah, I couldn't tell you exactly how far we were from Arnhem but the gliders were going into Arnhem. We could see them coming down because they were mostly shot down. It was a disaster really. You know it's a shame, you're sitting there and you can't do anything, really. A lot of troops were stationed round there, hoping they were going to do something but of course it didn't work out.

Yeah. Now, when the war ended, did you stay on in Germany? I mean, did you go home on leave or what?

No, when the war finished, it didn't mean that all the troops could go home. You had to take your turn and all that. You were in what they called the Occupation Army now and I had to wait my turn and be demobbed like everybody else. Everybody wanted to go home, we all wanted to go home, but you couldn't really.

Because you played in a match to remember, on 17 October 1945, in Hanover: Combined Services 6, Rangers 1 and you scored three that day, if I'm not mistaken. Ma Ba' McKennan got the other three.

The trouble with that game is, I'm not on the official team sheet, me nor Eddie Hodgkinson of Leeds United but we both played. It's like that Stan Cullis game you were talking about. I don't think the team lists quoted today are totally correct. I think Crozier of Brentford was our goalie in 1943, not Moodie but Moodie gets quoted.

But you did play against Rangers?

I did play. But the way the programme reads I'm not on it. The Combined Services team really, it was to entertain the troops. Every Thursday, sometimes a Wednesday, they'd bring out a team from Britain like Arsenal or Rangers.

Or Queen's Park.

Or Queen's Park. Funny enough, Celtic never came. But most of the big teams from England came. We played mostly all the big cities of Germany, like Hanover, Munster, Berlin, Hamburg and we played to vast crowds because they used to allow the German lads in to foster good relations, I suppose. And someone like Billy Steel, he learned a lot there. Billy was in the Signals. We played into Europe as deep as the Ukraine. We were stationed in Hanover as a team really but we were all over the place otherwise. We used to fly from a place called Celle. We used to fly to Poland, you know, places like Warsaw, then after you played there, away down into Katowice and Krakow. Some of our teams have played there in recent years. I think we had three games there but one was a one hour flight from Katowice to somewhere, God knows nowadays exactly where, in the Ukraine, I've got the name somewhere, but most games were played in Germany obviously. We played over in Switzerland – four games in Switzerland. Billy Steel played against Poland at the Olympic Stadium in Berlin. Nine-nil for the Combined Services. Can you imagine that when you think of nowadays? The game with Billy Steel when I first met him, that was in Berlin, with Reg Lewis and Les Compton of the Arsenal, Billy Hughes of Birmingham and Wales and Billy Bly of Hull City who was our goalkeeper. That was the first time I saw Billy Steel. It was to entertain the soldiers in the big cities. Somebody had to keep the soldiers entertained. I played for Osnabruck as well in the Bundesliga and it was funny enough. I was stationed in Osnabruck. You sort of work at keeping up the training and all that. The war's finished and you look out the local football club and of course I went round there and trained with them. The Bundesliga, just like in Britain with the war on, they carried on playing, same as over here. So I joined them. They used to get good crowds. I never took any money or anything, I used to like playing for them. I think I only had six games altogether in the Bundesliga, six league games and a couple of friendlies, I think it was.

Were you the only British player or were there others?

No, no, there were others. Stan Rickaby, I think he was with Munchengladbach.

Stan Rickaby of West Brom?

Middlesbro' and West Brom. He married a German girl. I'm not right sure but I think Tim Ward played. I might be wrong here with Tim Ward. It could be either Tim Ward or another Derby player. They played for Munster. But I should imagine that some of the British lads stationed in the big cities probably did. I can definitely remember Stan Rickaby, you know, playing. There were about five of us.

Now when was demob?

I was demobbed in November 1946.

And you were home in December 1946. You scored two goals against Clyde on 14 December in the revived Scottish League and the forward line read Evans and Kiernan; Airlie; McAloon and Hazlett.

Well, as I say, I was coming back from the Army, and compared with the Celtic team I'd left and the Celtic team I was just going to play in, it was like darkness and light. But I'm not blaming the lads that were in the team. They have suffered what I feel is very unfair criticism because most of the Celtic players before the war, they were sort of eased into the team. These young lads, they didn't have that, you know. Good people like Pat McAuley, big Duncan McMillan that went to Grimsby, Jimmy Mallan, a lot of good, good young lads, they never got that experience of fitting in with good older players. Because all the older Celtic players like Bobby Hogg, Johnny Divers, Malcolm MacDonald, Johnny Crum, Jimmy Delaney, they were all more or less at the same time. They came and they left about the same time. Jimmy Delaney was a wonderful person. I got to know him really well. We used to leave Celtic Park together with Pat McAuley and walk up to Parkhead Cross to get the tram together. I tell you who else was some player – big Joe McLaughlin. Joe had a shot to burst the net and he sometimes did. Did he go to Aberdeen?

He went to Aberdeen because he was fed-up with Celtic playing him all over the park. He won a Scottish Cup medal in 1947.

Another good boy was Dunky McMillan. I knew him in Glasgow, great centre-half. Jimmy Sirrel was a good pal of mine. He lived in Springfield Road near Celtic Park. Anyway, we started off. I think it was a draw in that match in December?

It was 3-3. Clyde were 3-1 up at half-time and then Airlie led the fight-back.

Clyde were a very good team then, you know. I don't know if it was that game or another but we had a wee thing at Celtic, when the centre got the ball, he'd hold it up, then push it into the path of the inside-forward coming through like McDonald Bailey. So this time I held it up for Gerry McAloon. Gerry arrived what seemed like a few minutes later. I said to him, "I timed you. Gerry, you took 25 seconds to get here then. "He said, "Oh forget that one, Seton." Poor Gerry, he was struggling after ten minutes.

On Christmas Day, Joe Rae was centre and Airlie inside-left. Were you happy at inside-forward because Celtic didn't half move their specialist players about sometimes?

Oh yes, I didn't mind really. I used to play inside-right for St Anthony's. Funny enough, I played inside-left at St Mungo's so it didn't matter all that much really. I played inside-left against Poland in Berlin.

And then, it's 1-1 against Rangers at Ibrox again on Ne'erday and the next day, 1-5 against Aberdeen at Parkhead, a crushing defeat. I still remember the shock. And that, Seton, is your last game for Celtic.

Yes. You see, I was – it's very hard to say.

You told me once you didn't want to know any more, your legs didn't want to know, you'd had too much football.

Yeah. When you came out of the Army, you were looking forward to it. But after I'd played at Tynecastle, you know, coming back on the bus, I thought, well, I was on a loser, because I just – I didn't – it's terrible the way you can feel, you know – I didn't really want to play football any more. But I was never like that, even when I was in the Army, I always wanted to play. Whether it was me coming out of the Forces, I can't say. I did ask the manager if I could sort of rest and not play. It was silly really. I carried on playing. My season finished on the second day of January. And funny enough, I could have gone to Chelsea, back to Chelsea, and then I had an invitation from Aston Villa to play, to go there. But in the meantime, Cannes Football Club, they came in for me, a chap from Kilmarnock, he was an agent for them. It wasn't like the agents in these days but he had a house in Golfe Juan which was near Juan-les-Pins and he was well in with the Cannes people. He told me – he asked me – if I'd like to go, sign for them.

Seton, were you a free agent or did the transfer to France have to be negotiated with Celtic?
Yeah, I'm not very sure about that. I think they contacted Celtic first. There was money changed hands. All I know is that other clubs wanted me not for that time, '46-47 but for the next season '47-48 and although I would have liked to have gone to London, maybe it was a mistake really, going to France. Because, like say, Jimmy Sirrel, he went to London, he went to Brentford, and there's more clubs there and I'd probably have been better looked-after privatewise, but there was a sum of money. I think signing for an English club, it would have been £20. That was the maximum. Signing for Cannes was £650.

Riches untold in 1947!
So I opted for that really.

After that Aberdeen game, Seton, what was your status? You were still a signed player, you were out of the Army, so what were you doing on Saturdays, were you playing for the reserves or what?
No, I just stayed – I was actually – I felt that bad about the state – I won't say the state I was in – I think I let it go another fortnight or something like that. I was contacted by Jimmy McGrory, a lovely man, like all the managers there, Jimmy McStay and Willie Maley.

So you were more or less on sick leave?
No – not sick leave. I was just fed-up with football.

And Celtic accommodated you?
Yeah. And really, at the back of my mind, to be honest, after being around London and other parts of the world, I thought, although I loved playing for Celtic, London was in my mind until I got this very, very good offer to go to Cannes. I mean you could buy a four-bedroom house in those days for £650!

So what was the standard of French football then?
Oh, really surprising. It's just like now. Before France won the World Cup in 1998 I think everybody thought French football was a joke. When we went it was a better standard than British football or on an equal standard. Scottish football was always hard and English football, I always thought, a fair standard, but French football was right up there with the best in 1947.

So how did you travel? I mean, suppose you had a game away up in the north of France, did you go by bus, did you have an aeroplane or what?
No, we had two long coaches on the train reserved. It used to take us in those days, if we

played in Paris, it was 14 hours on the train, 14 hours roughly from Cannes to Paris. There were four teams in Paris in those days. The biggest of course was Stade Français who are now Paris Saint-Germain. Places like Lille, Strasbourg, we went by train. Our local derby in those days was Marseille, about three hours from Cannes. That was the local derby. We stayed in Golfe Juan. It was a small hotel, the Hotel Napoleon. The hotel suited us because we got our meals and all that. They looked after us.

You had one famous fan?

Yeah, he lived in Golfe Juan, you know, the same wee village as us near Juan-les-Pins. He was just the same to me as probably the 60 people that made up the population then, not counting the children. Other people knew him. He was a Spaniard, he liked his football. All Spaniards are football mad really, you know. I think he thought we footballers were great. We had a Spaniard playing for us, Jesus Ramous, so I just knew him from a football point of view, really. We all lived in the village. We saw him every day.

He used to greet me. He'd say, "Ça va, Airlie?" and I'd say, "Ça va, Pablo!" But then it wasn't just me, he greeted everybody. He was skint then. A pleasant wee man. We used to gave him a lift with his stuff. We'd talk in pidgin French and pidgin English. He used to go up to a place called Vallauris. He was working on painting little pots. At that time I – like all the other players there – you never dreamt of asking for something. You thought there were other painters around a hundred times better. Maybe I thought I could do better myself! Ellen, my wife, she'd sort of heard of him. He told me he'd been in Glasgow in 1935 at the Kelvin Hall, that he'd had an exhibition. But when I knew him, he wasn't very well-off then. Of course it was soon after the war and it probably took him years later, in the Fifties, to start selling his paintings. It was a long walk along the beach to get to Juan-les-Pins from Golfe Juan. We were isolated and we all knew each other. Picasso was just another one of the villagers, really. It was only after I got back – all I can really remember is, looking out of the window of the hotel, no cars in those days, and he'd maybe be walking past and he'd look up, "Ça va, Airlie?" and I'd shout back, "Ça va, Pablo!" It's only after you come home that you realise. I used to see some of the paintings and I'd say to Ellen, I didn't really understand them, you know.

You weren't into Cubism? Now, Seton, a famous wedding?

Oh yes. Yeah, they lived at the end of Golfe Juan, a big house, you could see it from our hotel in the distance. Yeah, all the Cannes players were invited to the after-do of the wedding. They had the wedding in Grasse-Cannes and the reception in Vallauris, about six kilometres up the mountain. That was Rita Hayworth and Aly Khan. The atmosphere was great. There was a great big square, you can imagine, like George Square in Glasgow, you know, with all these trees and tarmacadam, tables all set out. As soon as you walked in, the bride and the groom were there, shook hands with all the players, invited us to partake of the feast. Aye, it was a great day.

So Seton when did you join Worcester City?

It was 1949-50, I think.

Were you coming home to a job?

Well, Tommy Kiernan, that I'd known at Celtic, he was playing at Gillingham who were non-

League then and I accepted Gillingham's offer because Tommy was there. It was a house, £8 a week, a job. And on my way to Gillingham from Glasgow, it was that warm, I got off the train at Crewe, just for to get a drink because I'd plenty time to go to Gillingham. We had about three days before training started. I had at the back of my mind, I'd like to see my brother. He lived near Birmingham then, at Bidford-on-Avon, so with that in mind and the thirst, I got off the train but at the same time I was thinking, suppose I get the next train for London, have a look at London again? I was in two minds. But the next train to come in was for Birmingham, not London, so that clinched it, and with the leeway before training, I thought that does it, never mind London, I'll go and see my brother. So I went to see my brother in Bidford-on-Avon. But the thing is, I'd already had an offer from Worcester. The manager had travelled up to Scotland to interview quite a few players and as you know, quite a few Celtic players have played for Worcester like Hughie Long and other ones. He had already interviewed me so I played a trial match and at half-time he offered me the same terms as Gillingham and I accepted. So I've been here since.

Now to go back wee bit, to 24 April 1937 and 146,000 spectators at Hampden for the Scottish Cup Final, Celtic two, Aberdeen one. I believe you were part of the unofficial attendance?

Yeah, me and my brother. Somebody gave us the wrong directions and we walked all the way from Shawfield to Cathkin and over to Hampden. When we got there, the gates were shut but then two of them were forced and we were part of the crowd outside that poured through. I think there must have been near 150,000 at that game.

Seton, leaving yourself on the bench, what is your all-time Celtic team?

I think I'd have to go for Kennaway; McGrain, Gemmill, Malcolm MacDonald, McNeill, Geatons, Delaney, Dalglish, McGrory, Auld and Frank Murphy.

Seton Airlie. I wish you'd stayed with Celtic. Thank you very much.

My pleasure. Thank you.

Johnny Paton
Outside-left
1942-1949

Johnny, your dad was also a Celtic player?

That's right. He was born in Cardonald on 31 March 1898. He played for Shawfield Juniors before Celtic. He was an inside-forward so he never had a chance at Celtic. McInally and Patsy Gallacher kept him out. But my grandfather on my mother's side had also been associated with the club. He had been connected with Celtic since its inception. He held season ticket number two.

Two?

Two! He had a confectioner's in Abercromby Street right opposite St Mary's church and he supplied cakes and biscuits to the original Celts at their deliberations in St Mary's. He witnessed the birth of the green and white in Glasgow. He used to take me to Parkhead when I was a wee boy, lift me over the turnstile, take me up to the stand to watch the likes of Jimmy McGrory, Peter Wilson and Jean McFarlane from the seats directly behind the directors' box. Willie Maley, Tom White and the Kelly family were like everyday faces to me in the Thirties. We used to call Willie Maley 'The Boss'.

Johnny, you made your debut for Celtic in a Summer Cup match versus Partick Thistle, 30 May 1942.

That's right.

I want to remind you of your teammates: James Culley in goal, Malcolm MacDonald right-back.

Malcolm, yeah.

Harry Dornan, left-back, Matt Lynch right-half, Willie Corbett centre-half, big Joe McLaughlin left-half; yourself at outside-right.

John McPhail.

John McPhail inside to you.

Jimmy Delaney.

Jimmy Delaney, centre. Bobby Fisher of the Royal Engineers inside left.
And Riley.

And John Riley, outside-left. You remember them?
I remember them. Oh, absolutely. I remember my debut. I was a junior photographer with the *Scottish Daily Express* and they were training me to be a press photographer and I used to sit behind the goal at Celtic Park taking photographs of the game. Of course, one week I was sitting behind the net and next week I was trying to score goals into it.

Right. So what's it like then going into the Celtic dressing room and suddenly mixing with the likes of John McPhail and Jimmy Delaney?
The system in those days was if you were good enough, they put you straight in the team, and having an international reputation as a junior, I signed for Celtic on the Thursday, with Jimmy McStay, and I went straight into the team on the Saturday. Now I was quite in awe of fellows like Jimmy Delaney. Delaney was my hero. I mean, he was my idol, you know, as a boy, watching him. I thought he was the greatest ever and I felt quite self-conscious, as a matter of fact, that they had to move Delaney out of position, to accommodate me at outside-right. I was so reserved I hardly had the courage to talk to him or the other players like Malcolm MacDonald and that. I hadn't the courage to actually speak to them in the dressing room. In fact I think I played for Celtic for at least half-a-dozen games before I said hello to Jimmy Delaney. I wasn't a very forward boy. Jimmy was very helpful, you know, generous, making compliments for what you'd done well. It was me that was backward coming forward but as soon as we got on the park it was different. When I was on the park, 100 per cent confidence. I knew what I could do, I knew my position and I knew the game. In the dressing-room I minded my own business. But I played with Jimmy Delaney all during the war. When I was on leave from the RAF I went up and played for Celtic a lot all the time. Jimmy Delaney in my opinion was the greatest inspiration I've ever played with. To me, he was a Celtic phenomenon. He was a giant in that wartime team. I always felt personally that if Delaney was on the field you could win the match irrespective of the score. You could be two-nil down, five minutes to go, but if Delaney was on the field, you could win that game. That was the inspiring feeling he gave you.

What was he like on the field, was he a general, telling you what to do?
Well, he was a little bit. He led by example on the field, Delaney, you know. He wasn't aggressive in his shouting, but he inspired you. I have never experienced anything like it with any other player. Jimmy was the greatest team player I've ever played with. And he carried Celtic on his back during the war years, game after game.

What about Gerry McAloon?
Gerry McAloon was my best partner ever. We were like bacon and eggs. He knew my talents and he played to my strengths. I was a speed merchant and Gerry and I struck up a great partnership. His passing made it simple for me to score goals. He got the very best out of his winger. Same as Pat McAuley. And my father taught me I had to be a good crosser of the ball, not just with my right foot but with my left foot. When I was at Brentford, we played the overlapping full-back in the early Fifties, long before 4-3-3. We had a left-back called

Roddy Munro, a good left-back, and he was instructed to start overlapping. So big Roddy would gallop down there like a wild elephant and he would get into a good position for crosses but he couldn't cross! He'd get the ball and put the damn thing miles away behind the goal! And then he hardly had the puff to run the 80 yards back into his position! And I used to say, What good is that? You know? I mean, unless Roddy comes out with me in practice matches and in training and practises the art of crossing the ball, well, that's going to be no good to the team. So that was us!

Tell me about Malcolm MacDonald.

Ah well, Malcolm was something else, wasn't he? Celtic supporters adored him. Malcolm was the coach at Brentford so I came under Malcolm's influence again, you know, and he was a very, very, good coach, Malcolm. But he was a wee bit strict, he was a bit dour. But very fair. I remember an incident in the dressing room once, after a match at Brentford and I was just getting dried. The assistant trainer came to Malcolm, "There's somebody at the door wants to speak to Johnny Paton." Malcolm says, "What! You know the rule, nobody comes in here! Whoever it is, he'll have to wait. Who is it anyway?" So the assistant trainer says, "It's Alex James." So Malky says," Alex James! Why did you not say so in the first place! Bring him in!" So, I mean, Alex James is a god, isn't he? So Alex comes in. "Hello, Johnny," he says, "how's your father?" Alex and my father were mates, but this was an excuse, you see. "Oh," I said, "he's all right." But I was overwhelmed, meeting a man like Alex James. What a privilege! "Listen," he says, and he drops his voice, "could you tell me something? Who scored the second goal and how did it happen?" I said it was Jackie Goodwin and how it came about. "Ah," he says, "thank you, Johnny." Do you know what he was doing?

Reporting the game for one of the papers?

For the *News of the World*! I don't think he had seen half the match! By the way, I met Malky at the VE Cup celebrations at Parkhead in 1995.

Tommy Kiernan?

Tommy. I'll never forget Tommy Kiernan. Now Tommy was a very, very good inside-forward. He was strong, a good shot on him, a well-built, good all-round player Tommy, no question about it, but sometimes his work-rate was very low. Tommy thought he was a forward, therefore all his work-rate should be going forward. And in the dressing-room at half-time – I think we were getting beat – the players were voicing their opinion and one of them – I think it was Pat McAuley – said to Tommy, he said, "Listen, you want to chase back and give us some help more than you're doing. You're an inside-forward, you're not supposed to be just up the field." Do you know what Tommy said? He said, "Have you never heard of the Conservation of Energy?" Can you imagine? The Conservation of Energy! An absolutely classic statement. I remember it to this day. McAuley says, "Conservation of Energy! You get back out there and give us a hand! God, we're getting overrun here and you're lying up the park!" In other words he was telling him he was a lazy player.

What was big Jackie Gallacher like?

I met big Jackie in 1995 at the reunion and I know he's dead since, but big Jackie was such a loveable fellow! And an outstanding potential as a centre-forward! A great header of the ball and away from football, what a wonderful singer! Scotland's Frank Sinatra! We never tired of listening to Jackie singing on the bus to away matches, you know. I don't think he got the full potential out of his talent at Celtic. That's the way I felt.

Okay. Now on 1 February 1946, Delaney is about to go and Celtic sign Tommy Bogan from Hibs.

I will always remember an incident with Jimmy and it was so sad. I was in the dressing room again, after training, out of the bath, and Jimmy walked in. Alex Dowdells was there and Jimmy says to Alex, "I need my boots, Alex." So Alex says, "What do you want your boots for, Jimmy?" He says, "I'm leaving. Mmm…I've just been transferred to Manchester United." I was so shocked. Delaney was half the team as far as I was concerned. So Dowdells went and got his boots and he gave them to Jimmy and Jimmy says, "Have you got a bit of brown paper to put round them, Alex?" So Jimmy got his boots wrapped, put them under his arm, and walked out. While we're on this, I can tell you a little story about Matt Busby and Celtic. I happen to be involved in it only because I was there. Nothing to do with it, I was just there. Now, in the first team dressing room, the pegs started at Willie Miller's, number one, and round to Johnny Paton's, number 11, which was nearest the door where you got the draught. There was a knock on the door. This is training time, not on a match day. "Who's that at the door? Go and open that door, Johnny," somebody shouts to me. I've got my towel round me. "Answer the door, Johnny! It might be somebody, you're the nearest!" Another knock, he's persistent whoever it is, so I open the door and there's a soldier standing there. "Yes," I say, "can I help you?" He says, "I'd like to see the manager, Mr McStay." "Oh," I say, "I don't think he's here today." In those days, Jimmy McStay spent a lot of time up at the Bank Restaurant, Willie Maley's place in Queen Street. That was like his office and you only saw him on a Friday to pay the wages. And then on a Saturday for the team! Alex Dowdells was in charge of the players' training and all the keep-fit stuff such as it was. You more or less looked after yourself in those days, you kept yourself fit and in training. So I went across to the treatment room. I said, "Alex, there's a soldier out here says he wants to see the manager." Alex says, "Ask him what he wants, ask him what his name is." So I went back over, "Excuse me," I said, "What is it you want?" He says, "I want to play for Celtic." I say, "Could you tell me your name, please?" He says, "I'm Matt Busby." So I go back to Alex and I say, "It's Matt Busby. He says he wants to play for Celtic." Alex says to me, "We don't play guest players, you know that, Johnny. Besides, the manager's not here. Tell him he'll have to come back on Friday or Saturday." And that was that. Matt went to Hibs, he captained them, they beat Rangers 8-1, and he went on to play for Scotland, captained Scotland. If Celtic had taken him that time, I think it could have transformed Celtic. Things could have turned out very different for post-war Celtic.

Now Johnny, you went to Chelsea in 1946 until the start of the 47-48 season and at Parkhead on 30 August, you beat Rangers, I think for the first time in your experience as a Celtic player, 2-0, and you scored a wonder goal to put Celtic two up.

Did I?

You did.

I'm joking. I do remember that. I can remember that goal.

You came in from the left, walked the ball through the Rangers defence and then just let fly.

That's one of the few goals I can remember scoring, to tell you the truth. The other thing jumps to mind about playing Rangers was in the following season and this was the early days of Charlie Tully. Charlie was wonderful, full of tricks. But, up to the Rangers game, he hadn't made a big impression. Now in this game I'm talking about, against Rangers in the League Cup, on 25 September 1948, when we became 3-1 up, Charlie started showing all his tricks. The whole Rangers defence froze that day and Charlie started doing his tricks from midfield. I thought, I've never seen a player take control of a match, take control of a whole defence, and freeze them, and make them frightened to come near him.

Johnny, but going back a few months before the arrival of Tully, on 17 February 1948, Celtic sign Jock Weir.

Jock, aye. Ah, what a boy! What a boy! Jock, in those days, 1948, Celtic were paying us £8 a week. Jock used to come in with a new suit on nearly every other seven days. From the Fifty Shilling Tailors down in Argyle Street. This is 1948! Where do you get those? What do you do with them? He was a good dresser, a snappy dresser and an eye for the ladies, Jock, you know. A bit of a playboy, Jock, but was he fast! Boy, him and Bogan, and he was a good player, a real good player. I remember he saved Celtic from relegation when he scored three goals against Dundee.

Now you yourself put Motherwell out of the Cup 1-0 on 21 February 1948.

There's a story behind that.

A suspicion the goal was offside?

I used to live in a Celtic club house. I paid them rent. So I was earning eight quid a week and I think I was paying them 30 bob rent and paying insurance and that. I think I had £6 or something left in my wages. And I had a wife and kiddie, you know. I mean, you know, in those days, you weren't earning anything. People thought you were well-off, you know, walking about with plenty of money in your pocket but the truth is you were scraping. I know the working man's wage was probably about £4 10s or £5 a week but I mean, I didn't have much left in my wages after I'd paid rent and insurance and fed myself and the family. I couldn't afford a car. I used to go by tram car to the match and we lived in Giffnock. So I used to leave at 12 o'clock, that'll be time enough for the match. Normally it was, you see. Tram car down to Argyle Street and then the tram car for Parkhead. Well. Because it was a match against Motherwell in the Cup, it was like an execution in Argyle Street. You could not get on a tram! They were hanging on to the front where the driver was! The conductor couldn't move. And there I am standing at my usual stop in Argyle Street and time was going past, thousands of people trying to board and I'm standing there, and I'm playing in the match! So I start getting really worried. Then out of the blue, as it sometimes happens, but not very often, a car came along, a motor car, through all that throng, and stopped, and a voice said out, "Aren't you Johnny Paton?" I said, "Yes." He said, "Are you not supposed to be playing today?" Do you know who it was?

No idea.

It was Alan Breck! Chief sports reporter of the *Glasgow Evening Times*! Out of all that throng, he recognised me! He said, "Do you see the time?" I said, "Aye! I know! Alan, are you going to Parkhead? Can you give me a lift?" He said, "Hurry, get in the car!" So I got there. That's how I got there, courtesy of Alan Breck! And at Parkhead, Alex Dowdells is doing his nut! Everybody is inside stripped but there's no Johnny Paton. Alex is outside Parkhead looking for me and we drive the car right up and I rush in, sweating blood. Alex comes at me, "Bloody hell, get changed! Wait till McGrory hears about this!" I say, "Listen, Alex, don't worry about it," I say, "I'll tell you everything later." So I got in and I got stripped and I think I got the goal, didn't I? Alan Breck wrote his report for the Saturday and then for the Monday and he claimed the victory was his against Motherwell. "If I hadn't spotted Johnny Paton standing stranded in Argyle Street about 35 minutes before kick-off…" It was as close as that. So I'll never forget that. That's one thing I do remember.

And then, on 17 April 1948, the game at Dens Park, the game Celtic have got to win to be sure of avoiding relegation, so they said. What sort of a state were the players in? Was there a lot of nerves?

I can only speak for myself. I never suffered from what I call nerves. I was always keen to get out on the park and play and I mean, you have to have a certain amount of tension in you to play well. I mean, talking about nerves, when I was at Chelsea, one of the most famous Scottish footballers of all time was there. The whole of Scotland thought he was the coolest man on the park when he scored with a penalty kick in the last minute against England at Wembley, a few years before the war, in 1936, and that's Tommy Walker. Now Tommy Walker was playing inside-right in the Chelsea forward line I played in – a great forward line, nearly all internationals and Tommy Walker was one of the most nervous chaps before a match I've ever seen. He just was.

Nerves apart, were you really so badly paid, Johnny?

Players were grossly underpaid. You were on what was called a slave contract. You were contracted from 25 July to 1 June. That was your contract. You got paid that wage. If you didn't re-sign on 1 June, when the season was finished, you never got paid. Do you know, when I left Celtic, they never paid me for the last six weeks I was at the club. I wouldn't re-sign for Glasgow Celtic because they dropped my wages on a sliding scale from £8 to £6 in the summer. But you see, I wasn't on a sliding scale. My contract wage at Celtic, let's see, 1947-48-49, was £8, winter or summer. And I was in a club house for which I was charged rent. And I had a wife and child into the bargain. I couldn't afford a car or anything like that so when they put the sliding scale offer to me, I said to Jimmy McGrory, "Jimmy, you've made a mistake," I said, "my contract is £8 over the whole year". "I'm sorry, Johnny," he said, "that's the new contract." "Well I'm sorry, Jimmy," I said, "I won't re-sign for that." That's the reason I left Celtic and there were five other players in the team felt the same way. Jimmy Mallan, Pat McAuley, Jackie Gallacher and another and we were five first team players. Now I was representative of the Players' Union at Celtic. Jackie Gallacher said to me, "Look, you're the Union Representative. Why don't you do something about this?" I said, "What me, Jackie? Do something? The only thing you can do is not re-sign for Celtic." So I got the five players together. We refused to re-sign. So there it was, half the team not re-signed. It was all over the papers, *Daily Record, Evening Citizen, Evening Times*. They were full of it, the players who would not re-sign for Celtic. And Paton the ringleader, so they said. They didn't know the true story, the papers, at all. They were blaming us, you see. And Celtic were giving their side of the story, "After all we've done for these players…" you know. "They say they've got the club at heart," you know, "but we never expected this," you know. "How can we start the season with a depleted team?" I said to the boys, we had a meeting, the players, and I said, "Well, I'm a man of principle," I said. "I don't think I'm an unfair person," I said, "But once I say I'll do a thing, that's it with me, I do it. I am not going to re-sign for the club until they restore our contract to £8 throughout the season, winter and summer." So they all said, "No, Johnny, you're quite right. We're the same. It's the old contract or nothing." So we all parted. Every week I would pick up the evening paper and read, "McAuley re-signs for Celtic. Mallan re-signs for Celtic. Jackie Gallacher re-signs for Celtic." And I couldn't give my side of the story because in those days you were forbidden to go to the press as players. The system was different. So McGrory comes to me and he says, "Look, you're letting the side down, Johnny. You're the only outside-left we've got," which I was. "Look, we're playing Rangers twice, Johnny, in the League Cup in the first two or three weeks of the season. You can't let us down!" "Jimmy," I said, "I'm as anxious to play as you are. I'm dying to play for the club. My heart's in Celtic. God, I've been Celtic through and through since I was a boy. But this contract is unfair, Jimmy. I want to speak to Bob Kelly, the chairman." So I spoke to Bob Kelly but he was adamant. He said, "Johnny, we decided that's the contract. That's it." "Well, Bob," I said, "I've decided I'm not going to re-sign on those terms." Well, on the Tuesday or the Wednesday – we were playing Rangers in the opening match on 13 August 1949 – on the Tuesday or the Wednesday – there came a telegram to my house in Giffnock: COME TO THE BANK RESTAURANT 2 O'CLOCK, or whenever it was, WEDNESDAY. I said to my wife Eileen, "Everything's all right! They've come to their senses!" So I went to the Bank Restaurant. McGrory had the contract ready. He said, "There you are, give us your signature, Johnny." So I took a look. I said, "You haven't changed that, Jimmy. It's the same contract I rejected. No, no, no." "Come on now," he said, "You're on good bonuses." True enough, the bonus was good moneywise. I said, "No. It's the contract wages. They're still the same." He said, "Well, I'm sorry, Johnny." I said, "I'm sorry too, Jimmy, but I'm not signing." So on the Saturday, I sat in the stand. They played Mike Haughney, a right-back, at outside-left. A right-back! And McGrory said to me, "Do you realise", he said, "you're upsetting the whole team?" I said, "That's not my fault. I want to play in this match as you well know". But I had to sit in the stand and you can imagine how embarrassing it was. The fans were booing me and as far as they were concerned I was anti-Celtic. Very embarrassing.

Celtic won 3-2. Haughney scored.

I had to go to the matches, you see. I sat in the stand and watched the first six matches. Can you believe that! So I said to Jimmy McGrory, "You'll have to put me on the transfers, Jimmy. It's six weeks now and I haven't been paid a halfpenny." Because in those days you didn't get paid if you didn't re-sign your contract until they blew the whole thing open through Jimmy Hill. So I said, "Right, transfer me and get the money for me." "Right then, he says, "you're on the transfer list." So I said to Eileen, my wife, "Don't worry, we'll be all right as far as I'm concerned." Eileen's from London, you see – Greenford. I wanted a London club. And nothing happened. So I went to Jimmy McGrory and I said, "Haven't you had any enquiries?" He said, "Not one, Johnny. Not a single one." I said, "Not one? I mean, you've circulated all the clubs?" He said, "Oh yeah." I said, "Right!" I went straight into the town to Renfrew Street where the Scottish League offices were. I went in there and I said, "My name is Johnny Paton, Glasgow Celtic. I'm on the transfer list. Can you tell me exactly when I went on and what price they want for me?" So they looked it up. They said, "You're not on the transfer list." I took the bull by the horns. I marched straight back up to Parkhead, demanded an interview with Bob Kelly and I went onto the transfer list. Straightaway I lifted the telephone and I called Bernard Joy in London. I said, "Bernard, it's Johnny Paton speaking from Glasgow." I said, "Listen, Celtic have just put me on the transfer list. Could you put a bit of publicity about me in the paper?" So he did that, gave me a puff, and I went to Brentford the next week – £5,000.

But Celtic had attracted such huge crowds in 1948-49. They were generating an enormous amount of cash. Where was all the money going that they could be so niggardly over £8 contracts? Where did it go? There was so much money pouring into football after the war. Why weren't the stadiums rebuilt?

Because of the shareholders and directors! I remember Charlie Tully when he first signed for us. We were out training. I remember jogging around and Charlie and I were chatting. He was a great boy for, you know, larking about, telling jokes but suddenly he came over all serious and he says to me, "Who's that away up there on the terracing?" So I looked up. "Oh," I said, "that's another Charlie, old Charlie, another Irishman like yourself." Tully says, "What's he doing?" I said, "He's the maintenance man here. He looks after the stadium." Well, I'll tell you what old Charlie did. He used to go round with a wooden box full of nails, and he'd go round, especially after a big match with Rangers, when there had been a massive crowd, hammering these big nails into the crush barriers on the terracing. That was the maintenance man. That's what Celtic were spending on ground development in 1948, a hammer and a box of nails.

Johnny, we've covered the end of your time with Celtic but what about Leslie Johnston?

Oh yeah, another one, Leslie. Leslie Johnston, whenever we played Clyde, he used to beat Celtic on his own. He was that kind of player when you played against him. He was a wonder player. He never quite turned on those performances for Celtic. He was smaller than me, and I remember, by Jove, when we were playing Clyde, it wasn't Clyde we had to beat, it was wee Johnston, he was that good. He played some great games for Celtic but he was never the wonder player that he was at Clyde. He was another playboy. He and Jock Weir used to team up together. The two of them used to mate up on the coach and all that kind of thing. Stay in the same room together on tour and that. So I mean, he was no shrinking violet. Put it that way.

You know, Johnny, I have a vivid memory of you and Tully playing together at Parkhead, Tully on the ball, all the semaphore with his arms and you waiting for the pass that might never come.

Oh, Charlie. I remember once we were practising something. I don't know if it was with Chic Geatons or Jimmy Hogan, it was to do with throw-ins, tactical moves at throw-ins. This was during the week. We practised these moves over and over again. And one of the moves I can remember, one of the moves I was involved in, Charlie used to take the throw-in. Charlie used to want to take my corner kicks! I used to say, "Bloody get out the way, Charlie, I can take my own corner kicks." He used to take free-kicks, he used to try and dictate the whole game, Charlie. And he was good enough to do it. Anyway, we were practising this throw-in and the idea was, I would lie away back and then, I would run towards him, you see, and the idea was he would shy the ball 12 or 15 yards over my head and over the head of my marker. I would wheel round quick, get the ball in space and straight in on goal. So he goes to take the shy and I'm muttering, "Okay, Charlie?

This time, Charlie, okay?" He's got the ball poised over his head. I come towards him. I wheel to go round but he doesn't throw it into space for me! I think, What's happening here? Do you know what he does? He throws the ball off my back, takes the rebound and goes dashing into space himself! That was just one of his tricks. He was an instinctive fellow, Charlie. Charlie could do a thing instinctively on the park. You didn't need to practise it. Charlie didn't know he was going to do it himself. But, boy, had he a bundle of tricks! He took a big trick with the supporters.

Johnny, putting yourself on the bench, how would you nominate your Celtic All-Stars XI?
Post-war?

Post-war. Fine.
Miller; McGrain, Gemmell, Murdoch, McNeill, Evans, Johnstone, Bobby Collins, Delaney, Dalglish, Lennox.

Johnny, thank you very much.
I had no idea I could talk so much.

Ah, but all good stuff. Excellent stuff. A-1, Johnny.
Thank you. Thank you very much.

A LETTER FROM JOHNNY'S WIFE, EILEEN, 7 FEBRUARY 1999:

…Regarding the dream I had: I dreamt very vividly that Johnny would break his leg so in the morning I decided to tell him in order to 'break' the dream. He laughed about it and went off to the match. On his arrival home, he looked quite upset. When I asked him what the matter was, he said: "You will never believe it but you know that dream? It wasn't me but Frank Walsh has broken his leg" (17 April 1948).

In a lighter vein, an amusing incident happened which you may or may not be interested in: when Johnny was at Bentley Priory in Stanmore, Ted Heath and his Band used to entertain them and also play football matches with the RAF. There were several professional players at Bentley Priory at that time. In return, Ted Heath used to invite us to the Hammersmith Palais as his guests. I cannot remember all the members of his band but I do remember Jack Parnell was drummer, plus Kenny Baker, Johnny Gray and I believe his singer was Paul Carpenter.

When Johnny was transferred back to Celtic from Chelsea and just after we were married, Ted Heath and his Band were booked to play at the Glasgow Empire so Johnny invited the whole band to a Celtic match. After the game, the band had tea but one member was missing. He had been invited into the Board Room and as you know, even the players in those days were never invited into the sanctum of the Board Room. The missing musician who was invited in, made a fuss of, and offered drinks, was Johnny Gray, a classic case of mistaken identity. The Celtic directors all thought this was Raymond Glendenning, the famous BBC sports commentator. If you saw Johnny Gray in those days, you would understand why. He wore the same large moustache and really did look like R.G. Johnny Gray went on to form his own band and a while back was in the news nationwide. (I believe it was all about not being able to get medical treatment from his local NHS hospital because he was too old!)

Kindest regards, Eileen.

Jimmy Sirrel
Inside-right
1945-1947

Okay, Jimmy, so the first thing I want to ask you about, did you play a lot of schools football?

Och, I've been playing football since Day One. My father told me that I wanted the brass balls off the bedstead because I wanted them to play with. I learned to play kicking a ball with a balloon in the room. You know, you kept it up, didn't you, handy? We had a two minutes silence playing in the street between the lamps posts at 11 o'clock, the day John Thomson was buried. 9 September 1931. I was nine then. So I was always playing football.

Did you watch Celtic much as a boy?

Yeah, I used to go to Celtic Park because my relative was Tommy Drummond and he used to take me. Shall I tell you a story about going to Celtic Park? We used to play in Kerrydale Street. There weren't many motor cars in those days, you understand? We had a fellow called Murray from a big family. And this fellow had lost his leg, the bottom bit. So he plays in goal with a crutch and we call him Stilty Willie. So on this Friday night, St Roch's are playing a Cup Final at Parkhead and we were up on the wall, you see? And we lifted Stilty up. But his stick, the crutch, never made it up and next thing we see is the bloomin' polis coming! They hadn't seen us but we'd seen them. As soon as we saw them it was panic stations, we were down and off and away like down the street there. But Stilty's still up there, this boy with only one leg and no crutch in sight, sitting on the wall to watch the game and they've no idea how he got up there and now he can't get down! Laugh? I'm telling you. No, the only thing we knew was playing football, wasn't it?

What about your own junior career? I've got you with Renfrew Juniors and Bridgeton Waverley. Is that right?

Yeah, I started at Renfrew. I was 16 and my father never saw me play football. So he came to me and he said to me one day, "James, were you playing for Renfrew Juniors?" I said, "Aye!" He said, "I thought it might be you because a man that I work with came to me and said, 'Does your boy play football?' I said, 'Yes, he does nothing else.' He said, 'Renfrew Juniors've got this boy Sirrel playing and that's such a strange name, I thought it might be your son.'" When the war came it suited me to go and play next door in Bridgeton, on London Road with Bridgeton Waverley. I think Celtic train there now. In those days we had one galvanised bath for the whole team. So they filled it up with hot water and you had to make it in kettles. That was for the team! God, you wouldn't believe those days! My first game for Celtic was 2 January, I think, 1946, at Queen of the South. And Tommy Kiernan was the big man – he was the star. In those days, you never knew whether you were playing until they read the team out at 2.30 or whenever, you understand? And I was listening. And cripes! Next thing I know, I'm inside-right and Kiernan's not! And I'm playing with Jimmy Delaney! I think I got £60 for signing.

What was it like playing to Jimmy Delaney?

Well, you know, you must remember, I don't have any experience. I could understand what Delaney wanted, you know, the ball through or whatever, here or there, and I never gave a lot of thought about it, you know. He's picked me and then I go, don't I? All I can remember, it was icy and snowy, whatever, you know, slushy. Then I played at Motherwell and I had my accident. What happened was, I used to say to Matt Lynch, "Now, Matt" – he was outside-right – "when you get up there, you make sure you cross it and I shall try and be at the end of it." So this time he's in at the back, he's whacked it in, and I went in and I missed it. And I turned and Redpath knocked me on my behind and I damaged my sciatic nerve. But that was the end of the game for me. It took me weeks to get better. The treatment in those days was such I could no longer run like I used to but saying that, I played-on a number of years but we went away on the bus, I couldn't sit on it, I couldn't sit in the pictures, I couldn't sleep. After Celtic I never was the man I was before. It was a sporadic thing but at Aldershot I could not push a brush.

What about the two Victory Cup semi-finals against Rangers, Saturday, 1 June, 1946, at Hampden, a glorious day, and the replay, Wednesday night at Hampden again, 5 June? The first match was 0-0 and Willie Miller had a magnificent game. He defied Rangers at every turn.

I threw the first game away. What happened was, we were as good as them but Rangers were better than us because of Willie Waddell. We could handle Rangers but not Willie Waddell. But what happened in that first game was, somewhere during the game, I don't know what time, I was right through and I'm running against Brown, you know, Bobby Brown, and I can beat him if I whack it. So I need to whack it but I feint and I put it to his other side and he saves it. So as a result it was a draw, hence the Bottle Party, the game on the Wednesday night. What happened was, Glasgow Rangers got an offside goal in the first half and we protested against it.

So in the second half, when they got this weak penalty, we wouldn't let them take it. I finished up in hospital. The next day I went to hospital, up to the Royal, I think. At the end of the game I've got to get from outside-left here, to the tunnel there, right across the park. I thought, cripes, and I'm dragging a leg, eh? I'm lame totally, totally lame and the bottles are flying. Here the police surround the place, don't they, eh? In those days the bus would take you over there, to Hampden, but then you went home on your own, you understand?

This is you with your gammy leg?

This is me limping out of Hampden after the game. When I come out, there are all kinds of fights going on, you understand? So my wife Cathie says to me, she says, "This little fellow was making a complaint," she says, "so I just got up and hit him one with the handbag!" Because she was at the game, you see, she was in the stand. You mentioned Willie Miller. He was my friend, Willie Miller. Willie Miller was a tremendous goalkeeper and it's interesting this, he and I became very friendly. He used to say to me, "Jimmy, what are you doing this afternoon?" So I used to go back to Parkhead in the afternoon with Willie. Now, I could kick a football with the right foot. I could hammer this football, make no mistake about that!

That's why I've got a bad knee now. So he used to throw this ball out to me and I would run in and whack it and he would save it and I would get bloomin' angry, eh? He would laugh at me! But Willie and I were great friends. I was great friends with Willie Miller. Do you know someone else I got to know well?

Who?

Tommy McInally. A relative of mine ran the Naval Club up in Elmbank Crescent and Tommy used to go up there. Big Chocolate Tommy! That's his name, isn't it? Chocolate Tommy! He used to go in with us for a drink because he was a friend of my relative, Frank Brogan, who used to run this place. So I knew Chocolate Tommy. He called me Young Sirrel. Young Sirrel, will you buy me a drink? Lovely big man, lovely character. I don't remember too much about how he played football but he was absolutely excellent, eh?

The Apostle of Direct Action.

Is that what they called him?

When he saw the goals – bang! Jimmy, do you remember, you as one of the finest exponents of the inside game in Scotland, being ordered-off with Jimmy Watson, another great inside-forward. Do you remember that?

Did I hit him?

Did you hit him?

I bloomin' didn't half! What happened was, Watson and I were friends! You see? And wait till I tell you. He had a relative was a bookmaker in Uddingston. He was telling me, he couldn't see too well, could Watson's relative, the bookmaker, a street bookmaker, illegal in those days.

Standing up a close?

Aye. Watching out every minute for the polis. So he had a magnifying glass hanging round here, round his neck, but this magnifying glass was dual purpose, eh? Aye. One minute he used it to read the punters' lines and the next minute to light his cigarettes.

How? The sun?

The sun, aye. It saved on matches. Dual purpose. So what has happened is, we're playing this game and I learned a lesson that day. I don't know if I'd learn it today but I learned it that day. What happened was, McAuley and Watson were fighting, you know, McAuley and he, and they were knocking each other all over. Pat was like that, wasn't he, lovely man, Pat, you know, with his bad hand? I can't remember too well today but I think he'd lost a finger or a thumb or something like that, you understand? And he and Watson, they were having the real battle. But then Watson comes over and he bloomin' slaps me, knocks me over. So I just get up and I whack him! So I learned my lesson. I'm ordered-off. You know? And I go in and I walk off there and I sit down and I say, "Jimmy, this will never happen to you again. You'll never get ordered-off again. Jimmy, you never do this again!"

This is you in the dressing-room?

I'm in the dressing-room. But I learned a lesson that day. If you and I are quarrelling, I'll get you. If you're running, I could run on the back of your heel. If you're giving me trouble, I'll turn and knock you accidentally. "It was an accident, ref, I never even knew he was there!" So I learned I could sort the villains out. If you did me – I went three years chasing a goalkeeper in England. I was going to break him in two because he'd done me! So if he gets the ball, I'll just miss the ball and catch him. Smack! So you've got to have that bit of the beast about you which I never had at Glasgow Celtic. I was young and inexperienced. But I learned that day, you don't get into trouble. Whenever I was getting into trouble with the referee, I'd just say, "All right now, ref?" The referee might say to me, "Now Jimmy, behave yourself or I'll book you. You understand?" Because you could talk to them, couldn't you? And I would say, "It's all right, ref, just a misunderstanding, I'll have a wee word with him. I'll sort it out!"

Now you went down to Leeds on 27 May 1947, to play a benefit for the widow and children of Major Eric Stephenson. He'd been killed in Burma. Leeds had some guest stars playing like Jock Dodds at centre, Peter Doherty inside-left and ex-Celt Johnny Kelly outside-left. Can you remember that game?

Yes. I think I scored two. What about Peter Doherty! He and I were friends, argued for years when I'd meet him as a manager and a trainer, whatever, big arrogant so-and-so! Peter knew everything about it so I'd tell Peter what I think. He wouldn't believe it! Yeah, a lovely man, Peter Doherty.

Okay. Now what about the vital relegation match at Dens Park, 17 April 1948? Did you go there?

Yes. I was there. We were in trouble at the bottom of the League and we travelled to Dens Park. And as I told you earlier – Tommy Docherty used to do this also at his clubs – you'd come in at two o'clock and you don't know whether you're playing or not and at half-past two they'd tell you the team. So I was due to play that game. To all intents and purposes, I was playing. So when he read out the team, I wasn't playing. He played Bobby Evans instead of me. And we got a draw, I think, wasn't it?

No. 3-2 for Celtic.

We got a result?

Jock Weir scored a hat-trick. Now, Jimmy, the '48-49 season, Celtic sign on Jimmy Hogan. What are your memories of Jimmy Hogan?

Oh, he and I were great friends! Oh cripes, he and I got on well! Jimmy Hogan had come from abroad, done tremendous things abroad but at Glasgow Celtic I don't think he got on with the players. He got on with me. I respected him. I enjoyed things he used to work at, eh? He was an old man. Hogan, never got through to the players. The modern Hogan is this Dutchman, Weill Corvaer. But he's in Saudi now, I think. He's teaching them out there. But back to when I got ordered-off with Jimmy Watson. I've got fined a fiver. See? I'm not going to pay it! I'm not going to pay a fiver for getting ordered-off! McGrory said to me, "But you've got to pay it!" Because he was a lovely lad, wasn't he? And he liked me and I liked him. But I said, "I'm not paying that!" And it went on and on, "You've got to pay it!" Do you know who paid it in the end? Celtic paid it!

Jimmy, you claim you discovered Bobby Collins?

Well, what happened was this, that I was at football every night in the week, you know, in the summertime, watching the tournaments. I went to these and I knew where all the players were. So Chic Geatons says to me, "Jimmy," he says, "you're at football every night, have you seen any players? Can you recommend anybody?" I said, "Look, Chic, there's two good players, both called Collins. There's one playing for Bent Royal Oak, a Lanarkshire team. He's a big fellow, six feet, and cripes he can play! And there's a little rascal playing, 14 years of age, maybe 15, and he plays for the Polmadie Hawthorn. Bobby Collins. So have a look. Wee Collins is playing first class juvenile, age limit of 25 years. Collins is a boy playing with grown men." So I saw him play then. Anyway, they never signed him. He went to Pollok Juniors and Everton bought him or signed him from Pollok. And he went to Everton with his father on a Saturday and there was nobody at the ground, as I understand it, so he came home and he signed for Glasgow Celtic so maybe they had been looking at him, maybe not, do you understand? Anyway, they signed him. Then it went to the SFA and Collins didn't want to go to Everton any more because of their treatment possibly, do you understand? So Glasgow Celtic as I know, got fined £500 but they got the player. And a lovely little boy was Bobby Collins, eh? Strong as a bull, eh? Good right foot, could kick that football and as hard as blinkin' nails!

I'll tell you a story that happened to ex-Celtic Dougie Livingstone chasing a young player like Collins one day when he was manager of Fulham. I was at Aldershot where I served my time. And I was standing at the station at Guildford and Dougie was there. He said to me, "Jimmy, I've just been trying to sign this schoolboy." I said, "Have you?" He said, "Aye. I've been over there to try and sign him. I've offered him £8,000 and a motor car for his father." And he said, "They've turned me down. Imagine, turned me down." Do you know who the schoolboy was?

No idea.

The fellow that was manager of England two or three times ago. He signed for Chelsea.

Venables?

Terry Venables! Turned down £8,000 for himself and a motor car for his father. I played in one of these tournaments I'm talking about against a team from Kinning Park. I played for this juvenile team that didn't have many supporters. But this other lot, they've got a good team and they win the Govan League every year. But I played against them and I scored two goals and it's a draw in the tournament. So I'm told not to turn up for the next game.

Warned-off?

Aye, so big Jock Somebody that's in charge of our team asks me will I play in the replay. I look at him and say, "No fear! I'm not playing!"

Because you were threatened?

Threatened? It was a break-in! After the game there was this break-in! It was a Catholic team. In those days, we know nothing, do we? All we know is dancing. Betting, gambling, fighting. I kept out of this most. I was lucky. I could always avoid this. When you went to school you went that way not this way, that was the way for coming back to stay out of trouble. So this Saturday night we've looked at the paper. There's dancing at this Errol Street. We don't know where it is but we get over. And we go up the stair. Now I've been playing for Rutherglen St Andrew's in the afternoon, a church team, over age, any age, and

I play for their youth team, reserves you might call it. And we've just got up the stairs and this fellow Crosbie that I've been playing football with, he walks across to me and he says, "Jimmy, Schnozzle has marked your card!" But we've just got up the stairs. We've just walked into the hall. Schnozzle is the leader of the Beehive, isn't he!

Gorbals gang?

Aye! Oh, Lord God Almighty! Talk about keeping out of trouble, did we get down those stairs and out of there – KAH-BOOM!

Gorbals razor gang?

Aye! Armed to the teeth! There were three of us used to go about together. There used to be four but the other one got killed, the so and so's, they never looked after him, he got killed in a Lancaster. He joined up before the war 39ish, 38. And I very near joined the RAF with him. There was this exhibition in Glasgow, you know, and he joined up but he got killed so now there's just the three of us on the stair. KAH-BOOM! Outside! Run like hell!

Had Schnozzle marked your card over football?

No! I've no right to be in his area, have I? No other reason. And Crosbie. They'd hanged Crosbie's brother. Crosbie's brother had done a post office and there'd been a bit of bother and they'd hanged him. And I now play with the other Crosbie. I'd played football with him all afternoon. And he comes over to me and says, "Jimmy, I think you better be on your way. Schnozzle has marked your card." Talk about moving. Talk about rapid response. Out you go!

You lived a very dangerous life. How was the Navy?

I joined in '43. I was a Petty Officer fourth class. Four weeks from the day I joined we were six or seven weeks at sea and nothing to eat except this Icelandic cod and cocoa. Nothing else. Oh no! We had eggs. I spent 13 months down in Somaliland and then we came home. That was when Cathie said "I want to marry you" and there were four of us sharing a room and kitchen, you understand? When I was with Renfrew I lived in a single end with a broken ankle, dragging it about the place.

I lived in a room and kitchen, father, mother, four kids. I could draw it for you.

Of course you could!

How did you cope with the pressure of being a manager?

I never had any pressure! I could always handle whatever it was. I could always deal with things because I'd served my time. I could understand people, eh? Now if you talk about how do I handle this or how do I handle that, at one stage here in this area here, I'm the manager of Notts County. Your man, Allan Brown, he's the manager of Nottingham Forest. McLintock is the manager of Leicester. And Docherty is the manager of Derby. And we've all been brought up under the same system. Starvation! Having nothing, eh? Dealing with bits and pieces.

Were you never intimidated by players?

Of course! Cripes, I've thrown one across the floor and he hit his head on the bloomin' door!

I thought, for God's sake, Jimmy, if he goes to the polis, you're in trouble! Yeah, I've had my moments! That was because they upset me! It's just an individual thing, eh? When I want to create trouble, I want a big one to create trouble with i.e. one of the stars of the team. I can handle the apprentices, eh, the pussycats who are in the reserves. We go up the country on a Saturday and we've lost. I pick my team for next Saturday. Sitting on the coach. So that's one problem out the blinkin' window, isn't it? If they haven't behaved, they know where I stand. "I want you in on Sunday morning." "Oh, but Boss, I'm taking the wife out for a meal tomorrow, you understand? Oh but Boss, I've got relatives coming, I can't come in." I don't give a wee hoot! "You're in tomorrow morning and if you don't come in then please your bloomin' self because I shall deal with you!" So there's a bit of fear in this, isn't there? So sitting here, we are now doing business with a football club. I've got a 'phone in here and a 'phone up the stairs. So the 'phone rings and it's the other man or whoever. So I say to Cathie, "When I go up the stair, you put the 'phone down." She says," Jimmy, I'm your wife!" And I say, "I know you're my wife. But when you go to the Co-op on Monday morning, eh, they cannot say to you, or whatever morning it is, 'What's happening down there at the County?' Because you know sweet Fanny Adam!" So I could handle this.

Were you happy as a manager, Jimmy?

Oh cripes, I loved it! That's not saying I loved being a manager as such. There's nothing better than going in among your footballers. What you must have at your football club is a smile in your dressing room. You must have a smile, eh? Now I know if you're not winning, you're not happy and everybody laughing! Cripes, you're not going to have a Christmas party, are you? So you go in there and you say, "Let's work this out, let's get on with this! We lost again but that was yesterday."

Did you groom Howard Wilkinson?

I didn't groom him. He never was manager of Notts County. When I was the manager of Sheffield United, Howard worked for this area as a coach, you know, an area coach. So he and I got friendly. What happened with Howard was this. Going back years ago, when I was the manager of Brentford, Howard was a quick little outside-right. At Brighton. And I tried to sign him. So I knew about Howard, didn't I? So I don't think he would have left his job as an area coach unless he came to me. So when I came here to Notts County and I was looking for a coach, I agreed that he joins me. And we were very successful because he was a very thorough fellow whatever you read about him in the newspapers. He's not the person that you read about. We got on very well and what happened with Howard was this. The chairman said to me, "Jimmy, why don't you become a paid director?" And he said, "We'll make Howard manager." And I said, "Yeah, all right, I agree with that." He had nothing to do with my team. He trained them up to the way I wanted them. You understand? A good trainer, a good coach. Full of brains. But I picked the team. I asked him on a Monday morning will you do this, that and that and I may take over but he was the only coach that ever I had that I allowed to work. So what's happened is, Mr Dunnett and I have agreed to offer him the manager's job and I said, "Yeah." So we're on Malta and I got a 'phone call because I knew Howard was going to London to meet Mr Dunnett. So Mr Dunnett 'phones me and he says, "I've had Howard in and we've agreed terms in London." You know? So next morning, because when I go to Malta, in those days, they knew where I was because I was always working at football. I was always working at it so they knew where to get me on the beach where Cathie and me where. So I get a call and I go up. It's Howard. He says,

"Jimmy, I'm sorry to inform you that I've joined Sheffield Wednesday. He says, "I'm sorry about this because I'd agreed to join Notts County, but when I got back to Sheffield, the directors and that, they wanted to meet me, so I went and I've joined them." So I said, "Good luck to you!" So that was the way it happened. So when you read that Howard was the manager of Notts County, he never was the manager of Notts County. Do you understand? He was the coach. But back to what you said to me. We had a great relationship. As a matter of fact his darling wife knocked my teeth in a couple of years ago! "Oh," she said, "Jimmy!" and hit me here. I'd to go and pay a lot of money to get them sorted out.

What went wrong, at Sheffield United?

We had no money. I never looked at a balance sheet! I made a mistake. They were so short of money it was unreal. So I sold Currie, because we had no money, to Leeds – £175,000. And when we got back with the money, there was no money coming to the club because the Value Added Tax people wouldn't allow any money to come to Sheffield United. They took it all. So no money went to the bank so we never made a penny on the sale of Tony Currie. So the situation was, the chairman had a place in one of these continental areas and he was on holiday, I can't remember the name of it, he was on holiday, and the vice-chairman had to face up to facts. He couldn't sort anything of it out. So then we had a board meeting. And the bank manager came to the board meeting. So the money that we got for Currie represented no money. But I sold Currie and I bought a winger, a good winger, from Aston Villa, for £30,000. So I got £30,000 from £175,000, I've got a stadium with 16,000 people who want to come every week, eh? And we're getting nothing, eh? I just got fed up with it. They never sacked me. I sacked them! And I didn't have a job. What happened was, this team here, Notts County, weren't doing well so the chairman came and he met me. He said, "We're not doing well, will you come back? "Cripes," I said, "I don't have a job!" So from then on, we went to the First Division. We did well. We handled it with very few people coming in. Listen, before we finish, talking about managers. No matter how you handle footballers, you must have their respect. If you don't have their respect, you are dead! They might not like you because all of the time you are dealing with problems with them, thousands of problems. You deal with all kinds of problems, the young ones getting married, looking for houses, the older ones, but when it comes to the football, when you start talking about football, if they respect you then you've got a chance. The only way they'll respect you, forget about winning and losing – it's difficult to win a football match no matter who you're playing. When you walk in among your players in the morning and they respect you, no matter what you ask them to do, climb a mountain, they'll do it. If they don't respect you, you've got no chance in football.

Was Jimmy McGrory a football manager?

I don't know about that. I couldn't say one thing or the other about Mr McGrory from that point of view. Chic Geatons couldn't handle players.

Couldn't he?

As training coach, no. So this is the reason why they brought this foreign man in, Hogan. That's why they tried to be different, eh? See when you're going to work tactics, you're working tactics, you've got to ask the fundamental question, When is the ball dangerous?

It's football we're talking about! Do you understand when the ball is dangerous? I don't want to suggest that you would know because you're not a football man. When the ball is up there and we're attacking, it's not dangerous. But when you play Liverpool, when they had better players, and they get it, the ball's not dangerous yet, you can come away, you run away. But don't go in there where they'll pass it and isolate you and destroy you. You go in here, because if you go in here, they've now got to go through you. You've got to stop the ball getting dangerous.

I follow, Jimmy. Listen, did you miss Celtic at all?

I tell you what I missed. I missed the Centenary Celebrations in 1988. I got my invitation and I put it there in that pile where I put your letter. By the time I found it again, everything had happened and I missed it all. I really regretted that. I'd have liked to have been there.

Jimmy, I've run out of tape and you're going to watch Notts County. Can I ask you to settle an argument? Is your surname spelt with one ell or two?

One ell. It's a long story. It used to be two but we lost one during World War One.

Sirrell became a casualty of war?

Something like that.

Jimmy, thank you very much. I wish today Celtic or Scotland had gone for you as a manager.

I think I might have made a go of Celtic. Too late now.

Thank you very much, Jimmy.

My pleasure. Thank you.

Frank Walsh
Centre-forward
1947-1949

Frank, you started off at St Ignatius School in Wishaw?

Yes, as a schoolboy. I'd be 11 years old at that particular time. My mother died just before I was 11. I can always remember that. Shortly after, I started playing for the school team. For some reason or other, I always seemed to be captain and centre-half. The centre-halves were supposed to be the good players. I captained the school team and from the school team, the next thing of importance was that I became the first player from St Ignatius in years to be selected for the local schools, the Cambusnethan schools. And I can always remember the Headmaster coming in proud as a peach that one of his boys – he didn't know who I was – had been selected to play for Cambusnethan Schools and they were playing Glasgow RC on the Saturday. So we went into Glasgow – we were taken in by special bus – and we beat Glasgow. We'd a great side, a good side, and we won about 7-1. The great thing was that after the game, they took us into the Bank Restaurant. You know who the Bank Restaurant belonged to? That's right! Willie Maley! Manager of Celtic. I can always remember looking at the walls and all these photographs of players, all these old players. Well, that was the start of my football career.

Was he there? Was the Grand Old Man there?

No, he wasn't there. But just imagine what schoolboys, just under 14, the thrill it was for them to go to the Bank Restaurant. I knew what the Bank Restaurant was then. My father, he was a referee, and I seemed to be – oh, it was all football after my mother died. He used to bring in friends, other referees and they would sit and talk football, football, football. I knew the rules of the game backwards when I was only 12, 13 years of age. I could have been a referee then as far as the rules of the game were concerned! My father would drop me off at Parkhead Cross on his way to a game in Glasgow so I could go and watch Celtic. I was often the first spectator in the ground when the gates opened. So, unfortunately, when I became 14, I was taken away from school and went to work in the pits to start with. The Headmaster that had run the Cambusnethan Schools, he was very disappointed. There was a possibility I could have played for Scotland, for Scottish Schoolboys. But it would have been difficult when you think of the forward line for the Scottish Schoolboys in that year: Gordon Smith that went to the Hibs; Ian Proudfoot that went to Third Lanark; Buster Brown that went to Motherwell; Bobby Combe that went to the Hibs and Johnny Aitkenhead that went to Queen's Park, Motherwell and the Hibs. Smith and Combe played for Scotland. So you realise that the standard was very high. So, shortly after that, with leaving school, I started playing with Wishaw Boys' Guild. Then Mossend Boys' Guild came along and they asked me to play for them. I was only 16 at the time. So I played for Mossend for two seasons, 1940-41-42. We cleared the boards. Next I moved to Wishaw Juniors, 1942-43. In between times I got called up to go down the pit as a Bevin Boy. I was sent down to a place in Ayrshire I'd never, never heard of before, Dalmellington. My father was friendly with a Hughie McAuley, the secretary of Ardeer Recreation. He wrote to Hughie and he asked if he could give me a game. This was 1943. So I got invited to Ardeer. At that particular time they had about eight or nine ex-seniors, all in the Ardeer factory, reserved from the Army.

Making explosives?

Yes! That's Ardeer Rec. The town is Stevenston. So, I arrived. They were playing a team at Somerset Park, home of Ayr United, so I met Hughie McAuley and he said to me, "Where would you like to play, Frank?" I said, "I'll play anywhere." So he said, "Do you fancy playing centre?" He said, "I've got good players, Arthur Rodman that played with Kilmarnock and Hugh McLaughlin that played with Chelsea," he said, "but we need a centre." And as it turns out, they were the tops in Ayrshire. Every Saturday it was goals, goals, tremendous feeling. Anyway, just coming on Christmas 1944, he came to me, Mr McAuley, and he said, "Kilmarnock wants you to play a trial on 2 January against Third Lanark reserves." So I went along and played. Jimmy McGrory was the manager of Kilmarnock at that time and shortly after the game he asked me to sign for them and I signed for them but I stayed with Ardeer until the end of the season and got called up for the new season in August 1945. Rugby Park was all re-turfed. The Army did it. In those days you couldn't take a day off, so to get off on a Saturday, I had to work. I had to go down the pits on a Friday morning early, about six o'clock, and I didn't come back up again until ten o'clock at night. But that was the way I got the Saturday off to play football. But it always seemed, everywhere I went, everybody was so kind to me. I can always remember, our trainer, he was a wizard, Jimmy McWhinnie, and the season was starting, we were playing Queen's Park, 1945-46, at Hampden, the first team, and I didn't know where I would be playing so I can always remember saying to him, "Where do I go on Saturday?" "I'll give you a rub-down on Thursday night," he said. "Just you go to Hampden, and we'll meet you there at Hampden." So that's where my first game was, at Hampden.

You stepped out at Hampden on your debut!

And playing against players that previously I'd only read about in the paper! But I'd never had any apprehension of playing against players who were so much more experienced than I was, the likes of Geordie Young or Willie Woodburn. I remember one experience when I was playing against St Mirren. Davie Lapsley. A hard ticket. The game was only started and we clashed together in the first minute. He said, "I'll break your leg before this game's over!" To put the fear of God in you, see? So the next time, we clash again. No more problems. He was only wanting to frighten a young laddie. He would have had a nice quiet day if he'd succeeded. So that was the start of my career at Kilmarnock. It was a slow start. For the first three or four games, I never hit the target. And then, we happened to be playing a friendly, against a local junior team. I scored a hat-trick I think it was, and after that I couldn't stop scoring. And like all other centres in the world, as soon as you get the knack of scoring, it just seems to come easy. Like Larsson at the moment, it's coming in threes for him. It seems to be that you just can't stop. Everything just runs for you. But when it goes the other way, oh dear!

I remember Mitchell Downie, a fine goalkeeper during your time at Kilmarnock.

He came from Hibs and he was a great golfer. But he was a bag of nerves. Oh yes, very temperamental. I remember we were playing at Tynecastle this particular game, 1 or 2 January – I scored three that day! Malky MacDonald was playing left-half. Mitchell was a wee bit nervous. Malky had a brilliant game, his ball control was superb. There was a ball came into the goal area, Malky trapped it, rolled it up his shin, called, "Mitchell!" and lobbed it into the goalie's hands. That's the type of player Malky was! But he was a very good goalkeeper, Mitchell Downie. And a very nice person.

Now Celtic centre-forwards in 1947-48, Frank, and remembering that you joined in November: Tommy Kiernan, Jackie Gallacher, Joe Rae, Joe McLaughlin and believe it or not, Bobby Evans.

I dislocated my shoulder against Celtic at Parkhead and after that I was in and out the Kilmarnock team, it was me or Ralph Collins at centre-forward. There was one particular week I was playing with the reserves at Leith on the Saturday and I scored a hat-trick. We played Edinburgh City on the Tuesday night and I scored four. They decided – we were playing Raith Rovers on the Wednesday night – so they brought Collins and me together. So I scored another three. That meant in five days I'd scored ten goals. But once I stopped scoring, I was always the one was dropped.

Now, Frank, you signed for Celtic on 13 November 1947. Can you remember the circumstances?

Oh yes! I was down the street. My father came down to meet me, he'd been out chasing me. This telegram had arrived: "MEET CELTIC PARTY STOP EN ROUTE HAMPDEN STOP ST ENOCH HOTEL 2PM STOP FAILING THAT 6PM GRAND HOTEL CHARING CROSS McGRORY STOP." Scotland were playing Wales and the Celtic players were all being taken out to the match. McGrory wanted to me at St Enoch's Square before the bus left up for Hampden. So I immediately – I couldn't get into Glasgow quick enough! So I met McGrory, he took me into the bus so we could discuss terms. He wanted to sign me and I wasn't hard to sign. He wanted to discuss terms but they weren't hard to work out. I did quite well. Probably I could have made more money but I wasn't interested in making more, I just wanted to play for Celtic. I went to the match as a signed Celtic player. I couldn't tell you who won.

Wales won 2-1. 88,000 at Hampden on a Wednesday afternoon. Willie Miller was stretchered off and came back on to play heroics.

I know it was a Wednesday. On the Saturday I played my first game at Firhill.

Now this first game, Frank, Firhill was packed to the limit, 32,000, gates closed before the kick-off, a cracker of a game, 5-3 for Celtic after being 3-1 down. You got the fourth. It was the game inspired Colonel Shaughnessy to say Celtic were on their way back. It must have been some game to make your debut in?

Brilliant. Absolutely. But it's a strange thing about Firhill, you favour grounds and I would say Firhill and Tynecastle were my favourite grounds. Even when I was at Kilmarnock, I always had outstanding games at Firhill, I always scored goals at Firhill. Tynecastle was the same. It's a strange thing. There's other grounds, like Third Lanark, I hated the sight of it. I never seemed to strike a good game at Cathkin. A strange thing. Firhill was a dreamy start for me.

Your first home game was on 29 November against Motherwell. 23,000 turned up to see the new centre-forward.

And it was only a friendly.

And a big cheer for Willie Miller back from injury.

The man he displaced was Rolando Ugolini. Rolando Ugolini was one of the nicest people I ever met. He was brilliant as a goalkeeper. He was an Italian from Armadale and his people had a fish and chip and ice cream business and they were bookmakers as well. They were never short of a penny. Rolando was the type that wanted always to be with the boys. And if there were four or five were going to the picture halls as we occasionally would do, like after training – we would go up Sauchiehall Street to go into one of the shows – Ugolini would be first in, paying all the tickets. He was that kind of person. I remember when I broke my leg he came in visiting. He was one of the first in and he used to have lovely gifts for you. He got me a radio in the days when it was still the wireless, a big piece of furniture, and you had to plug it in, no transistors then. He got me this radio, no throwaway gift in 1948. And on the Celtic bus, I didn't bet, but Rolando was the team bookmaker! He was full of life. The unusual story about him is that eventually Celtic decided to transfer him. He was going to Middlesbrough. And the agreement was that he have x pounds plus, it would be tax free. Something like £1,000 I think he got, a lot of money in 1948. It was definitely to be tax free. But when he came to sign the forms and get the money, McGrory had creamed the tax off it. Ugolini just lifted the cheque that was made out for him, just tore it up, put it in the ashtray. Eventually he got his money as had been agreed. He went down to Middlesbrough but his heart was always at Parkhead.

What about Willie Miller?

Well, Willie was the blue-eyed boy of Maryhill Celtic Supporters' Club. That's where he was from. And when I got married to Betty, we were living in Glasgow, in Rose Street, which is not any great distance from Maryhill and I got an invitation so I started going up to the Maryhill Celtic Supporters' Club and all these Celtic Supporters' Clubs in those days were all very, very kind to the players. They always wanted to give you something. Every time you went up you got a canteen of cutlery, a glass dish or something and Willie was the Honorary President or whatever of the Maryhill Celtic Supporters' Club. In a way it embarrassed me. I didn't think it was fair. These people, they worked hard to make money so what did they want to give it to me for? If it was going to help to bring people into their club, then having the players around was okay, as they still do yet, but they don't need to give you a lot of stuff. It was an embarrassment, aye. Talking like this reminds me of a good wee night out at the Govan Town Hall when the Govan Celtic Supporters' Club had a big, big night with Jimmy Hogan. Tommy Docherty, Joe Baillie. All the young lads came with Hogan. Hogan was a great turn, he used to really get the audience going. That night he sang a parody of *Mademoiselle from Armenteers*:

> 'Rangers are up the greasy pole,
> Parley-voo?
> Rangers are up the greasy pole,
> Parley-voo?
> Rangers are up the greasy pole,
> Can't get down to score a goal,
> Inky-pinky parley-voo!'

I mean, it's nothing, it's nothing at all, it's just a wee thing, but imagine the whole hall clapping hands and stamping feet to the rhythm. He was some turn, Hogan. He could fairly raise the people, get the audience going. You know, John McPhail, Pat McAuley, Jimmy Mallan, they wouldn't listen to him. But the young players of that time, Tommy Docherty, Joe Baillie, a young lad called Johnny McGrory – that was the reserves' half-back line – they were prepared to listen. Docherty, McGrory and Baillie. Joe Baillie was a marvellous player. He died very young. Tommy Docherty used to go to these shows, like the night at Govan, along with Jimmy Hogan. They'd go on the stage and demonstrate ball control. Tommy and him would work the ball between them. And talk-talk-talk-yap-yap-yap all the time.

Right, Frank, you're at centre-forward on 13 December 1947, Hibs 1, Celtic1.
Who scored that day?

Hibs were in the lead until the 86th minute and then an instantaneous goal from Paton. He hit the staunchion with such terrific force that the ball came straight back out and people did not even know a goal had been scored! It was the kind of goal, a few years ago, I think in 1980, when Clive Allen scored one like it, it was disallowed in English football. It was too fast for the referee.

And there's a story to that goal. We didn't have very many players' coaching meetings. But we did have this one previous to that game. Chic Geatons was telling us about a move that the Celtic old players, when he played, would try out and it was mostly quite successful. It's a throw-in in your opponents' half of the park. The first man to reach the ball would shy it in. When it reaches you in the centre of the park, you make as if to pass it back. Instead of that, you flick it to the side, and the player – Johnny Paton was the player – has got a yard on the opposition. And it worked that day! A throw-in up at the corner flag, taken quick, I make to give it back, I just head it to the side, Johnny gathers the ball and it's understatement to say he put it in the back of the net! It was the one and only coaching lesson I ever had at Parkhead and talk about successful!

Chic would seem to have been a great man for set pieces.
Aye, but only on a Tuesday – that was the last time you saw a ball. Wednesday, Thursday, you never saw a ball. They wouldn't give you a ball. They were too dear, I think.

But it's not as if you were playing to empty grounds. Now on Christmas Day, you played at Parkhead against Hearts. The score is 2-2 with three minutes to go and Walsh scores for Celtic! Two more minutes and Tommy McDonald makes it four.
I can remember that goal as if it's yesterday.

A great feeling? Doing it for Celtic!
Oh yes!

Now, Frank, Celtic are booked to entertain Rangers at Parkhead on Ne'erday 1948, a Thursday. The game is postponed 24 hours because of surface water and is played on a mudheap before 60,000. The result is Celtic 0 Rangers 4.
Yeah, it was a bad day.

That game is virtually your nemesis as a Celtic player.

Somebody took a dislike to me then and my face never seemed to fit again. I don't know. I always had a feeling it was Bob Kelly. McGrory used to tell me I was playing on the Saturday and then, come the Saturday, there was a change of plans, somebody changed the team. Walsh wasn't in. I remember Gerry McAloon. He used to tell me, "Run like hell for the first ten minutes, Frank, score a goal, then you can take it easy. If you score a goal they can hardly drop you." Gerry was a great joker. I just felt I was never destined to play in the first team again yet I was having some real good games for the reserves. One game against Falkirk reserves, I was outstanding yet it was doubtful for the semi-final of the Scottish Cup in 1948 at Ibrox whether Bogan would be fit so McGrory comes to me and says, "Frank, if Bogan's not fit, you'll be playing." What happened? I didn't play. Then at Dundee, a few weeks later, for the relegation battle, I was supposed to be going to Dundee. For some reason or other, McGrory would tell me, "You're playing on Saturday," but when Saturday came, I was playing with the reserves.

Celtic go full-time at the start of March, training in the morning, lunch in town, specialised activities in the afternoon. What would these be? Can you remember any of these specialised activities?

Aye. Going to the picture hall! Ugi would be leading the queue for the film to go to. We used to go to a restaurant at Bridgeton Cross then eventually we moved into one of the Glasgow ones – I think it was the Bank – for lunch.

For lunch. Before your specialised activity!

We never came back to Parkhead.

I've been told that no matter how full-time you were, the money was always the same.

The history of the money, if you want to come on to the money, when we started up after the war, the going rate was £4 in the first team, £3 in the reserves. That was the going rate when they started up. This was for all teams. I was at Kilmarnock. There was a threatened strike just before Christmas that first season. A big, big, big Players' Union was formed. Alex Millar was made Players' Secretary. The strike was threatened and they immediately put the money up to £6 and £4. We were all part-timers, supposed to be. So we were earning £6 in the first team, £4 in the reserves and £1 a point. At one time at Kilmarnock, £100 paid the week's bill at Kilmarnock for all the players, 25, 26 players, it's not too hard to count, a £5, a £3 and a £2, multiply that to 20 odds and that was £100. That was all to pay the wage bill. Consider that nowadays!

And when you think, that during the 1948-49 season when even Albion Rovers were averaging away gates of 14,000! You know, where's the money all going if you can't even afford a ball for training! The players aren't getting it. It's really something else. Now, Frank, a game that broke my heart although you didn't play in it: the semi-final of the Scottish Cup at Ibrox on 27 March 1948, Celtic 0, Morton 1 after extra time. Celtic so near. I'd never known them so near a Scottish Cup final before.

That's the game I might have played in had Tommy Bogan declared himself unfit. McGrory told me that week, "If Bogan's not fit, you're playing." The previous week I'd had an outstanding game with the reserves. I was really buzzing. I was playing outside-right in the reserves and I was buzzing and he was going to put me in and play me. But Bogan declared himself fit. Whether he was fit or not, I don't know. I would love to have played along with Jock Weir because I think Jock and I would have complemented each other. We were both of the same type. He was fast, all go, nippy, and I was the same type, we might have been a good blend.

Now the relegation battle at Dundee on 17 April 1948?

McGrory told me on the Tuesday I was playing at Dundee. I was told that on Tuesday but somebody else picked the team and changed it.

The chairman?

That was the only man. Bob Kelly. I don't know why because I never had any crossed swords with him. Only once, and it always sort of sticks in my memory. It wasn't really crossed swords either. We had been struggling but I was playing well. I was playing in the reserves and we had a team meeting to discuss things. We weren't winning essential games and Willie Corbett wasn't at that meeting. To me, there was a trend of thought going, that whatever was discussed, Willie Corbett was carrying the blame. And Bob Kelly was talking that way. I was never one for speaking my mind out loud but I felt there was an injustice being done, that a person who wasn't there couldn't defend himself. That if he had been there, there wouldn't have been as much said. So I spoke up and said I thought it wasn't fair, that Willie Corbett wasn't there so it wasn't very nice more or less to put the whole blame on his shoulders. So whether I had rubbed up against Bob Kelly, I don't know. I may well have rubbed up against Kelly because Desmond White – I didn't have much dealings with him – but we got on exceptionally well. After the first game at Firhill, Desmond White took me onto the players' bus. He was all over the moon with the result. But Bob Kelly, I don't know. It's just a feeling I've always carried. There was something. He had lost faith in me. As far as he was concerned, as chairman, he wanted no more to do with me. I don't know. That was the man. McGrory, that particular day, there was the very important game coming up at Dundee and McGrory on the Tuesday had told me, "You're playing on Saturday at Dundee." When Saturday came, it was Weir outside-right, Dan Lavery centre-forward. They changed their mind and played the Irish boy. I always felt I would have loved to have played with Weir on the wing. That was the type of player that I liked playing with, a fast-raiding winger and me, a fast-raiding centre. I would have done well with a player like Weir.

So instead of Dens Park you went back to fatal Cathkin.

No! I went to Parkhead! Fatal Cathkin came to me! Third Lanark reserves. The Celtic groundsman was Pat Docherty. Pat was a very, very nice person, we got on well, Pat and I. For some reason the Celtic reserve trainer wasn't at the match. So Pat was doing his trainer. He was all right for running about with the bottle or the sponge but I knew I had broken my leg. I'd seen it happen before when I was playing with the Ardeer Rec. I saw a lad get the same as I got. In fact it was more severe, it was compound, the bone had come out. I knew what it was and when he came on, I looked at him and I said, "Pat, don't you touch it. Leave it." And then there was another lad appeared and I just knew by his attitude, his way of going about it – he was the Third Lanark trainer – he knew what he was doing. And he strapped me up. They got the stretcher out, I was taken in. There was a doctor at the game that particular day and he gave us some morphine. To kill the pain.

Pat was a nice person, a special person, but no good with broken legs. I doubt if Chic Geatons was all that good either. I was a long time in plaster. Too long, I think. They'd never allow it that length of time nowadays. You know how the limb wastes. The one good thing is that I broke my leg in April and I married Betty in September. I was very good on the crutches, strangely enough. I was greased lightning. I could travel quicker on crutches than I could walk before I needed them. I used to go into Glasgow to the Royal Infirmary on a pass with the crutches. But I was long enough in plaster. Too long. Quite a lot of the lads came out to my wedding, a lot of the young lads. Tommy Docherty was in the reserves, Joe Baillie was in the reserves, they all came out to Craigneuk. We were married in Craigneuk and we're still there. Last year 1998, in September, we celebrated 50 years married.

Congratulations! Ad multos annos!

Well, to get back to the story, I play against Albion Rovers reserves in January 1949, I score five goals. I was outstanding back. Mind you, I was dragging it a little. So the following Saturday we were playing Queen of the South reserves. There was great speculation that week whether they would take me back into the first team or not. There was a toss-up whether they were going to play me. Hogan called me in, they had decided not, to give me a little more time. And I did a very silly thing. I took a block tackle. I should never – I should have shied clear of it – but it being my nature, I was a young chap, I always wanted to play. I went in and that was it – chipped ankle bone! Now that's 50 years ago almost to the day and that ankle bone still bothers me yet. Still there now. And this morning, the strange thing about it, start talking about it and it gets sore.

It knows you're talking about it.

Some people would laugh if you said that. So I've carried that for 50 years. So after I moved on from Celtic, it would be quite normal on a Saturday night for that ankle to be twice the size and they would have to pile on the ice and the hot and cold water until it was back to normal and I could start training on Tuesday. That's what really cut my career down. I could have played on longer.

I read it in a newspaper article, that once you stopped, you experienced a terrible hole in your life, certainly where a Saturday afternoon was concerned.

Everyone will say they experience that. It's something you've got to go through, so what I did, I decided to keep fit. I'd begun to get heavy so I took up refereeing. I enjoyed it. I had some good seasons with the juveniles. I always seemed to be refereeing all the good games, all the hard games. Some of the hard teams, they were good teams, that was the games I got. I seemed to be refereeing them all the time, the hard-to-handle games. My father had been a referee. I didn't need anyone to teach me the rules of the game. I could recognise offside when I saw it. I started refereeing the juniors but I couldn't go any further than that because of the age barrier. Then there was an Irish chaplain – there's always a story within a story – an Irish chaplain arrived in Shieldmuir and we became friendly and he approached me, What about coming and looking after my Boys' Guild? So I looked after his Boys' Guild for a few years – we won a few trophies too – until he moved on. But I found that the first batch of boys I had then, they were outstanding. The next batch that came along, if Celtic were playing, I was short of a team. So I said to myself, This is not for me. But the spirit of this chaplain, Fr Keegans – he retired there, a few years ago, at 65. He kept me going. He retired and went to live in Lanark and a fortnight ago he was going home to his sister and brother in Cork. He got on the train at Lanark and when it got to Carluke he was dead. He was buried last Tuesday, eight days ago today. I enjoyed the coaching, I got a lot out of training the boys. I still go to Parkhead, I've had a season ticket for about 20 odd years, I've got one of the best seats and views in the ground. You'll see for yourself tonight. I'm sitting here and about ten gaps away McCann sits in the Directors' Box. I've had that seat for over 20 years now. I go to see the game. I like to see a good game. The result doesn't upset me. I like to see Celtic win.

Now listen, Frank, before I go, leaving yourself on the bench, name for me your all-time Celtic XI.

Well, pre-War, it's got to be the side that won the Glasgow Exhibition Trophy at Ibrox on 10 June 1938: Kennaway; Hogg and Morrison; Geatons, Lyon and Paterson; Delaney, MacDonald; Crum; Divers and Murphy. Post-War, I'd go for the Lisbon Lions of 25 May 1967: Simpson; Craig and Gemmell; Murdoch, McNeill and Clark; Johnstone and Wallace; Chalmers; Auld and Lennox.

Frank, you retired in 1956. Who was the hardest centre-half you ever played against?

George Young of Rangers.

Who was your best feeder of an inside-forward at Celtic or elsewhere?

Without a doubt, Malcolm MacDonald. He was transferred from Celtic to Kilmarnock during my first season at Rugby Park and we became great friends. A hell of a player, Malky.

Frank, thank you very much. I hope I haven't exhausted you.

Not one bit! Thank you! I need to get packed for Benidorm.

Johnny Bonnar
Goalkeeper
1948-1958

The first thing I want to ask you, Johnny, my father was from Donegal, and he used to be very proud of you. He used to tell me, Bonnar's from the Rosses, next door to where he was from, Gweedore.

My dad was from the Rosses but I've never been there. I went over with Celtic one time and we did a tour of Ireland and we came through Donegal but that was the only time I ever came near the Rosses, in Donegal Town. Packy Bonner was actually born in the Rosses.

But where were you born, Johnny?

Glasgow, but we came to West Calder. My father worked in the pits for years and years and years. He was a ganger and then he was a clerk of works with Wimpey, you know. All the shale pits at that time were out in the East Lothians. And he was in the shale pits, you know?

In 1945 at Polkemmet, you were attracting a lot of attention as a junior goalkeeper. Why did you go to Arbroath?

Because nobody else would sign me. See, what happened, when I was a boy, I wasn't interested, when I was 14 and I left school, I wasn't interested in football at all. Then they started a team in the parish that I came from, St Mary's in West Calder. They started a football team and I began to play again. As a boy, I was always outstanding as a goalkeeper as a wee laddie, and when they started this football team, of course I got interested all over. So the priest started this team in West Calder. They had a Catholic League in that area, the Lothians, and we were in the League. I played with them then I went to a juvenile team, Stoneyburn Wanderers, they called them. I was outstanding there. I was so outstanding, Eugene, that on one particular day, a scout approached me after the game. He said, "Will you play for Rangers reserves on Wednesday night at Tannadice?" At that time, Rangers reserve team were in the North-eastern League. When he approached me, he also approached another two players if they would play a trial, Bertie McWhorren, a mate at work, and a boy called Neil who played for Lanark Air Training Corps. He was to get in touch but I never heard any more. But the other two boys that played the trial, they were signed for Rangers. Now, after that, I had umpteen junior teams wanting me. I played a trial for Bathgate and they wanted me to sign. I played a trial for Polkemmet and they signed me. A month after I was signed, Eugene, I was playing in the international trials for junior Scotland. Now I signed for Arbroath before the internationals or I would have got a caps. In 1945, I played a trial for the Hearts against Queen of the South. The following Saturday I played a trial for Liverpool against Newcastle at St James' Park. They wouldn't sign me. I was too wee. So when I got an approach from Gayfield, I signed for Arbroath.

Celtic signed you because Rolando had moved on to Middlesbro', hadn't he?

Rolando's father had a chip shop in Armadale and he ran a juvenile team, Armadale United and Rolando went to Armadale Thistle, that was the junior team. Rolando's father came to me to take Rolando's place with the juveniles and he offered me ten shillings a game. Now it was unheard-of for a juvenile to be paid! But I didn't sign for him. That was the funny thing about it.

You signed for Celtic and yet you knew you would become probably another Rolando Ugolini, you'd be number two for a long time to Willie Miller.

Wait now till I tell you something about that now. The night I signed for Celtic, £20 I got. There were no agents or anything like that then. You were glad to sign no matter what you got. Jimmy McGrory said to me, "Now you'll get £8 in the reserves." I said, "But when I get in the first team, how much do I get?" He said, "We've got Willie Miller in the first team." But I persisted. I said, "How much will I get?" He said, "Willie Miller's in the first team." I said, "I know he's in the first team but if I play for the first team, how much will I get?" He said, "Oh, you'll get £12." So I said, "That's fine, that's all right, I'll sign." Within a year I'd taken Miller's place, I'd put Miller out and Miller was the top man. Bob Kelly said to me one time, he said, "John, if you had been another one or two inches taller, you wouldn't have got one cap, you would have got 50!" And you couldn't get many caps then because there were only three or four a year. How many caps would Geordie Young have got in the present day?

Or Bobby Evans?

Look at young McStay here from Hamilton. How many caps has he got with your under-21s and under-16s? Caps galore! He can hardly get into the house for caps. Not only that, Eugene, but they didn't even have a reserve goalkeeper. We went to the World Cup in 1954. Celtic took us because we'd won the Double. All the staff, all the playing staff. And Fred Martin was there. Fred Martin was the Scottish goalkeeper. Now, supposing something had happened to Fred Martin?

You'd have been in! Bonnar for Scotland!

A funny thing, a funny thing. A week or a fortnight before the World Cup started, in 1954, the SFA picked a team, Celtic and Partick Thistle, to train with the squad that was going out to Switzerland. And I was picked as the goalkeeper. Charlie Tully was picked. And two or three others. A few of the Partick Thistle boys were picked. And we all went down and we stayed in the County Hotel in Ayr. And every day we would go out to Somerset Park and we would train with the Scottish team. We were all pals at the time. And we played the Scottish team seven times. Andy Beattie was the manager. We beat them four times! We each got a cheque in for £10. That was my reward. But anyway, we went out to Switzerland. Scotland and England were staying in the hotel at the bottom of our hill and we were up the hill in another hotel but we were pals and every night we went down there and the whole lot of us went out together.

Scotland, England and Celtic?

Oh, we used to go out together. One night, I was out and there was, Lofthouse, Nat Lofthouse and Dickinson, Jimmy Dickinson that used to play for Portsmouth, Stanley

Matthews and a crowd of us, and we all put our five francs down on the table. And we were all drinking German beer. Matthews put his money in too but he never touched the beer, he kept to mineral water. We drank the beer. But that was funny, we beat them four times. We beat them four times.

Now do you remember your debut for Celtic, your first game? On 6 November 1948?
Was that against Partick Thistle?

No, against Clyde at Shawfield. You started with a shut-out, 4-0 for Celtic. Willie Miller was playing at Windsor Park. The team was Bonnar; McGuire and Milne; Tommy Docherty, Boden and Baillie; Sirrel and Tully; Jackie Gallacher; Leslie Johnston and Paton.

Some side! Not a bad side. I put up the shutters. The difference in standard didn't affect me because when I was with Arbroath, we got to the semi-final of the Scottish Cup in 1947. We got beaten by Aberdeen at Dens Park but in the quarter-final, we beat Hearts 2-1 at Gayfield and a lot of great players played for Hearts at that time. The best game I ever played was for Arbroath at Easter Road in a Scottish Cup tie. We lost 4-0, a poor result but I turned in a fantastic performance. I had a good apprenticeship. When I went to Celtic I was experienced. I wasn't a wee laddie, you know? So I went there a quite experienced goalkeeper. But the older you get, you know, Eugene, the better you become. Because it's an inherent thing, you pick up, you make mistakes, you still make mistakes when you're older, but you don't make as many mistakes. If you see – take Ronnie for example. He didn't make very many. I said to Ronnie one time, "Ronnie, why do you not clutch the ball?" He said, "John, I can't clutch it now, I just stop them and grab them." And you must remember, it was no gloves or nothing then. And the ball was a helluva slippy. I remember the old goalkeepers, they used to wear ordinary woollen gloves and when you touched the ball or when you touched the ground, of course they were sodden. You were better using your bare hands than woollen gloves. So I had an idea. You know these dress gloves? I got a pair of these. And these were brilliant for gripping the ball. Now. We were going to a friendly against Wolverhampton, floodlight game. And after the game there was always a meal laid on for the two teams and I was sitting with Bert Williams. Goalkeepers always got together, you know. "You were clutching the ball brilliant," he says, "I couldn't get a grip of the ball tonight." So I began to tell him about my discovery. I said, "I'll send you a pair." So a couple of days later, I parcelled up a pair and sent them down to Bert Williams, Molyneux. They were great! He loved them! Now what I used to do, I used to get these gloves and put them on before the game, see, and rub them in resin, to make them sticky and there's no doubt, they helped you clutch a ball. But you look at these gloves they have now, they're absolutely marvellous. They're that big you can hardly put the ball past them! They're big shovels! They're huge! They put inches on you to put a ball over the bar. And it's so easy! My fingers were getting dislocated all the time, putting balls over the bar. See that finger? Three times it's been bent right back. Three times at an angle of 90 degrees. Doctor Fitzsimons used to put a couple of stitches in it, you know? And when it happened in the game, all they did, Dowdells just came trotting on, he just pulled it back into place. I could play but it was bloody sore. My hands were giving me bother at the end.

How did you rate Jimmy Hogan as a coach?
Oh, Jimmy was a good coach. He talked a lot of sense about the game. All McGrory had to

do was to say, Go and play well. McGrory didn't really have any clout. There was ever only one god in Jimmy Hogan's time and that was Bob Kelly. Then when you take into account poor weather, sodden footballs, the kit we had to wear, big heavy boots with high ankles and massive toe-caps greased in Dubbin for so-called flexibility. It was very hard in that era to became continental-orientated. This is to take nothing away from Jimmy. Jimmy Hogan was a very good coach but limited by all sorts of factors at Parkhead.

Johnny, in August 1949, you were in a dispute over terms. What's the story behind that?

Well, when I signed, I got £8 a week but I did so well as I thought that year, I was wanting £1 of a rise. And I wouldn't re-sign because they wouldn't give me £1 of a rise. So they put me out of the game. So I surrendered. And I got one game, one game for the reserves, between then and – I think it was against Ayr United – between then and Ne'erday 1951.

But it was Bonnar went in against Rangers?

Yeah. I'll tell you the story. Right. I was in dispute and I re-signed. As I say, I think I got one game between then and the New Year. Now, I was courting the lady who became my wife at the time. It was Hogmanay and we went up to Shotts. And of course, New Year at that time, they didn't drink a lot, but I was up all night. No, before I start. About ten o'clock, or 11 o'clock, a policeman came to the door and he enquired if I was there. So I went out to see him and he said to me, "You're to report to the Buchanan Hotel tomorrow at 11am." Now I thought that was me getting transferred to Manchester City. So I carried on the festivities. Anyway, I went to my bed at five o'clock on New Year's morning. And I got up and I was going to get a bus or a train into Glasgow. Anyway, I arrived at the hotel and next thing I know, I'm playing. So I played against Rangers after being up all night.

What about Alex Devanney?

Alex wasn't a bad goalie nor was Andy Bell but I can look at a goalkeeper, Eugene, and I can tell if he's a natural or he's not a natural. You're a goalkeeper or you're not a goalkeeper. But my fault throughout my career was height. I was never off my goal line unless I'm coming out to meet a man. I hadn't the height to leave my line. Because I knew I'd get chipped. I think maybe once or twice was I ever chipped in my whole career. I stayed on my line because I knew my weakness.

6 May 1950, the Charity Cup final at Hampden, 3-2 v Rangers. The Danny Kaye extravaganza.

Oh, that was when Danny Kaye went mad before the start. He was making an arse of Shaw, the Rangers player, what do you call him – Jock Shaw! That was Torry Gillick's last game. One of his last games. Torry Gillick got a great goal against me that day, a great shot, probably from about 18 yards. A bullet. John McPhail gave Woodburn a roasting. He beat Woodburn in the air. Big John was brilliant in the air. We played Lazio at Parkhead in September 1950. We drew with them in Italy and they brought them over here and it was a wet, bloody cold night, 40,000 there. All the Italians all over Scotland were there. John scored four goals that night. And his brother Billy was something in the air too. This time we went to Lazio, it took us five days to get to Rome. Bob Kelly would not fly. We met Bing Crosby on the boat from Dover. Anyway, we got to Rome and we stayed in one of the top hotels in Rome. We stayed in Rome for five days. And of course we got an audience, well, it was a public audience, in St Peter's, with Pius XII, but we got seats right near, up near the front, you know. It was

Monsignor Flanagan, I think, was the rector or the vice-rector of the Scots' College, and the night after the game there was a banquet, and of course all the Lazio people were there and Docherty, the Glasgow Assistant Chief Constable. He was there as our guide on the trip and between him and Monsignor Flanagan, they did the interpreter, you know, with the speeches. We came back via Genoa, Montreux, and then we spent three nights in Paris, another night in London and then home.

What about the Flag controversy in 1952? Did that have much impact on the players?

None, none at all. Bob Kelly refused to give in. He refused to take it down and who can blame him? I keep reading letters in the paper about the Eire flag. The flag has nothing to do with it if people can't behave themselves or have a distorted view of history. Celtic were founded by Irish immigrants. And Brother Walfrid. That was one of the reasons for flying the tricolour. But the flag had nothing to do with religion or bad behaviour. They made it a focus then, they make it a focus now and they always will. Celtic were to take the Eire flag down and Rangers' fans could carry on singing the Sash. It was definitely Bob Kelly's finest hour at Celtic. And don't forget Celtic compromised to help the Scottish League committee save face. Rangers supported Celtic because they knew no rule had been broken.

Right. Back to Andy Bell.

Andy Bell was a good goalkeeper and if I was injured, Andy came in. When I was right again. I got my place back. I always got back in the team again.

There was a wee tour of Ireland in the summer of 1952.

We were made freemen of the City of Dublin. All the boys thought this meant a free drink. They took us to the Dail and of course we met de Valera. In the photograph, we're all standing there and I'm standing here and here's de Valera and Charlie Tully. And de Valera shoves Tully aside and says to me, Come on out, son. We can't see you standing back there. I'll never forget Tully's face. Tully wanted a photograph of him standing right next to de Valera. See, I was on the small side and de Valera was a huge man.

On that tour you played against another great goalkeeper whose career was only just beginning. Do you remember the game against Coleraine?

Aye, Harry Gregg? Not very long before the Munich Disaster, we played Manchester United in a friendly, April 1956. It was for the Cheshire Homes. And there was a dinner in one of the hotels after the game. I was sitting with Tommy Taylor all during the meal. England centre-forward. Nice boy. A very nice boy. He was killed at Munich.

You don't remember that game as being rough? Because you came on in the second half after Taylor's attentions to Beattie.

No, I came on after five minutes, ten minutes. Dick Beattie was in goals, I was sitting up in the stand. Beattie had to leave the field and they shouted me down from the stand. I went down and got changed and out onto the park. Beattie had only been on for about ten minutes.

That was Monday night, 16 April. So you could have played in the 1956 Cup Final against Hearts on the Saturday, couldn't you?

If I'd been playing in that Cup Final, truthfully, we'd have won the Cup. I thought a couple of the goals were thrown away. I would find it very difficult to make it look good to sell a game. They must have known that. I was never approached in the whole of my career.

Back to 1953, Johnny, the day the Princess Victoria went down between Stranraer and Larne, 31 January 1953. You were playing at Palmerston and taking goal kicks into an absolute gale and the ball was boomeranging back. And I think you were fielding Roy Henderson's goal kicks in the first half. Do you remember that day?

I remember a game at East Fife. I took a goal kick, at Bayview in a storm, and I don't think it went out past the 18 yards line. It went away over the bar again, over my own bar! You know? But that was true. Now, we got beat 2-1 by Queen of the South the day you're talking about, and we were on the train and we heard about the disaster. But I can well understand. It was a hell of a day. It was the strongest wind I ever experienced.

Now, in May 1953 and you pick up one of those beautiful Charity Cup medals at Hampden on the ninth against Queen's Park, Neilly Mochan's debut for Celtic. Have you still got that kind of medal?

I've got two Charity Cup medals, the Danny Kaye final 1950 and the one you're talking about. I've got a runners'-up Scottish Cup medal against Clyde from 1955. The difference between the winner's medal and the runners'-up, the winner's is thick, the runners'-up slightly thinner. I've got some other medals but they're spread about the family. My son John's got the Coronation Cup medal.

So, it's May 1953, you hear all sorts of rumours, but is it true that at one time you came into the dressing-room looking for Jimmy Cowan, where Celtic were hiding him?

No. Not in the dressing-room. The team met at St Enoch Square to board the bus. It was aboard the bus. I was asking, Has anyone here seen Cowan? It was just a joke. That happened the first game Neilly played on 9 May. We played Arsenal on the Monday night, 11 May and we won 1-0. Then we played United on the Saturday the 16th, won 2-1, and Hibs on Wednesday the 20th. Now before the tournament started at all, there was a dispute about bonuses. We were all called in. It was Tully that started it. We were all called in to Bob Kelly one at a time. Will you play? Will you play? Of course, everybody said they would play. But if Bob Kelly hadn't been there, we'd have all said we wouldn't play. He was the Boss. Anyway. After the games, the SFA had announced that every player that had played in that competition would get £10 a game. So we got our bonus. I got a cheque, no, not a cheque, cash, £104. Celtic gave us £100 bonus and we got £30 for three games played with £26 off in tax. So we got £104 for winning the Coronation Cup. And if you take the gates, 56,000, 73,000, 117,000, it was like getting paid in pennies.

It was a competition that made a huge impact on Celtic. And of course, your name is synonymous with the winning of the Coronation Cup. I've got here 'Bonnar a Jewel of a 'Keeper', and that's against Hibs in the Final on 20 May.

I mean, when you're having a good game, you're carrying a hell of a lot of luck, Eugene. You're carrying luck. Okay, a wee bit of ability but a hell of a lot of luck. A hell of a lot of luck. A lot of luck.

Were you the kind of goalkeeper who organised his defence? Were you chatting to them? Calling out?

All the time. All the time. But big Jock was the greatest organiser. He was good. Great in the air. Jock gets a lot of criticism, he was one-footed. Okay, he was one-footed but he could still use his right foot. You know. Oh, I would make myself heard. Dowdells used to say I used to bawl like a bull.

I had to be like that because I didn't have the height to dominate. I remember we were playing a game and it was a corner kick. Jock said, "Mick, you stand there!" That was Haughney. "Stand there!" Haughney's looking around where to stand. The first game Sean Fallon played for Celtic, I'm organising the defence. Sean's on the front post. I tell him, "Anything your height, Sean, you head it." Over comes the ball. Sean puts it straight in the net. Lovely header. McGrory couldn't have done better.

Into 1954 and it's neck-and-neck with Hearts for the League. It's a 3-1 win against Thistle at Firhill on 20 March and Bonnar is magnificent. Four world-class saves. That's not me, it's the papers.

Aye, I remember that. We won the League at Easter Road.

On 17 April . And that game you had another balmy day.

John Higgins scored right on time. He was a great player. And there was another lad, a Parkhead boy, Jim Sharkey. These were great players but they lacked strength. I don't think the diet in those days was up to it, after the war. I remember when I'd finished playing, I went down to Celtic Park one day. I'd left the club. I'm standing at the bottom of the tunnel and Bob Kelly comes along. So I'm chatting to Bob Kelly and we're watching the boys go round the track. Then they finished training and they were coming up through the tunnel past Bob Kelly and me. So I say to Bob Kelly, "Look at the size of these boys!" He says, "It's the school milk!" But we were all wee boys. The War took its toll and all the shortages. You must get the packing when you're young. You must get well fed when you're young! You can't get it when you're 17 or 18. Look at Matt McVittie. Matt McVittie was a great player but not strong. Dead now. Jim Sharkey neither but Sharkey had something else to compensate characterwise. Sharkey was something special. You've got to have the packing when you're young. You need to get the feeding. I was strong. Fallon was strong. Nowadays everybody's strong. Tall and strong. You've got to have strength on a football field. Matt McVittie had all that skill but he lacked strength.

Now, John, the Scottish Cup semi-final against Motherwell, 1954, on 27 March. Charlie Aitken headed the equaliser in the last minute.

I can remember one of the goals that Motherwell scored. It was a scrimmage in the goalmouth and I was on the ground and I went to grab the ball and big Forrest sat right on top of me. I couldn't move. I was from here to that chair to get the ball, I was going to dive for it but there was big Forrest on top of me. Of course I complained to the referee but he just waved me away. You know. If Forrest hadn't been sitting on me, I'd have grabbed that ball. Anyway, it was a draw, 2-2. Charlie Aitken got this great header at the death. Charlie was a great player.

Johnny, to go back a wee bit, Celtic's trips to Wembley in 1953. You went to see the Hungarians?

And we went to see the Rest of Europe, 4-4 against England. That was a week or two before the Hungarians.

It seems to have been a period of terrific enterprise at the club?

The trip to Switzerland for the World Cup was a reward for winning the Double. I suppose the Rest of Europe game and the Hungary game were for winning the Coronation Cup. We took a lot of the reserves too. In Switzerland we got £30 spending money. The reserves got £15.

Are there any games that stick in your memory?

The first game we saw was Scotland and Austria. It was one hell of a wet night.

What about Uruguay? Did you see the Uruguay game?

Oh yes, they were tremendous! They had a right-back. I never saw a player like this in my life. Wonderful player! Wonderful. And big Freddie Martin – I'd have had three or four of the goals he lost. I hate to say that but I would have. One of the games we saw was England and Switzerland. I can't remember the score, I think England won. But Matthews was playing and Matthews did nothing that day. And we saw the Battle of Berne. Hungary beat Brazil. We came home after that. We didn't see the Final. Truthfully everybody thought Hungary would win it. But Germany beat them. A great team all the same. A great goalkeeper.

Grosics?

Grosics, aye. I thought he was a great goalkeeper. And another goalkeeper I thought was a true great was the Brazilian. He played for years. Gilmar. But the visit to Wembley for the Hungary game was out of this world. Puskas was getting the ball on the half-way line and running at the English defence and he would hit a ball with the outside of his left foot and it would take a curve inside the back and come on to his winger! Talk about putting a bend on it! Brilliant, just brilliant. And then there was a half-back they had, Hidegkuti, you ought to have seen the shots that he scored with that day.

But that's one thing about Celtic, they did take us to these games. Okay, they took you down on the sleeper and then you came back by sleeper.

Now, Johnny, you play in both Scottish Cup Finals of 1955 and you have some very bad luck with an Archie Robertson corner at the end of the first.

Aye, I was going to clutch that ball! But there was a high wind and you know what it's like with a high wind, the ball kind of rises in the air and it kind of rose in the air and I just got the tips of my fingers to it. Now, truthfully, looking back now, if I'd just done like this and put it back over the bar and not looked to clutch it, it would have been a simple save. But you can't go back. I tried to clutch that ball and I would have clutched it. I tried to grab the ball but the swirl took it. See, we played with a split new ball, all these games, and if there's the least wee bit wind at all, the ball is that way, you can't wholly trust it. You see players going for a ball in a high wind and they get nowhere near the bloody thing! And that was just my bad luck against Clyde. Just bad luck.

Did you get a lot of sympathy?

It was a bad disappointment but people understood. But it was a certainty, an absolute certainty in the replay.

Why was Bobby Collins dropped?

I don't know. I truthfully don't know. That was Bob Kelly. It was Bob Kelly selected the team. McGrory was too weak to stand up to him. McGrory had nothing to do with it. You never saw McGrory in a tracksuit. He never even came out to the track! Bob Kelly every morning went to Mass and after Mass about half-past ten, a quarter to eleven, he'd be standing at the side of the track. And Tully would start running.

Did Charlie practise his corner kicks assiduously?

No! I never saw him practise a corner kick in my life. He just had a knack for taking them. I can't truthfully recollect Charlie practising corner kicks. But that game at Falkirk in the Scottish Cup, 1953, that everyone refers to. It is true that he put the ball in the same place in the net twice from the corner and Archie McFeat was a good goalkeeper. That takes some doing. Charlie had all the ability in the world but those corner kicks against England and Falkirk were luck, purest luck on top of a fine ability. He was never looking to land the ball in that spot in the net.

Now, Johnny, you got to the USA with Celtic on the *Mauretania* in the summer of 1957 and you met Joe Kennaway out there?

Joe Kennaway came down to New York and stayed with the team. And I'll tell you something. Joe Kennaway was smaller than me. He was supposed to be 5ft 11ins. He was never 5ft 11ins at all. Of course he was getting older. But he was never any taller than me. You know. A lot of the goalkeepers at that time weren't big. There were a lot of small goalkeepers. Ronnie Simpson. Ugolini. They were all much about the same height. Willie Miller was tall. He was definitely about 5ft 11ins. We went to Rome and the Lazio goalkeeper was smaller than me.

Johnny, leaving yourself out, which is your all-time Celtic XI?

Well, picking them, 2-3-5, I go for Miller; McGrain and Gemmell; Evans, Stein and John Collins; Johnstone and Dalglish; McGrory; Auld and Lennox. But this means I leave out Bobby Collins and that makes me feel very guilty. And Tully as well. Charlie was a wonderful player but he just would not train.

Who was your most dangerous opponent?

Laurie Reilly of Hibs.

Johnny, ten million thanks. Thank you very much!

Thank you. Come again anytime.

Bertie Peacock
Left-half
1949-1961

Bertie, you played in 1949 in the Irish Cup final against Derry for Glentoran. Were you a signed Glentoran player or were you just guesting for them?

I was a signed Glentoran player as an amateur. My first professional club was Glasgow Celtic. I was inside-forward and Danny Blanchflower was right-half. That Final was my last game for Glentoran. I had gone from Coleraine my local club here and I was lucky enough to make the Final, the senior team in my first year and actually that was when the Celtic people saw me.

Is that when they saw you or didn't Peter O'Connor of Glenavon spot you after the Final of the RUC five-a-sides?

No, not really. Peter O'Connor – he died lately there in America, by the way – Peter saw me and another fellow who was actually a Scot and who came after the war to start a business here, the late Jack Donnelly. It was between Peter O'Connor and Jack Donnelly that sort of interested me in going to Celtic. They asked me would I like to go. And then the manager came over for the five-a-sides, the RUC five-a-sides, and I was to play for Glentoran. I met the manager of Glentoran that morning and I told him that there were English clubs, actually Arsenal and Man City were interested at the same time. And I couldn't believe it. I had never been out of Belfast. Celtic or Arsenal or Manchester City, they were all the same to me really. But when I met Mr McGrory I liked him. He seemed a simple, straightforward man and I like that sort of thing. We met in the the Royal Avenue Hotel and I was impressed with him so I said, "Well, I'll tell you what, without any further ado, I'll sign." So I signed professional forms for him. And there was no money talked or anything. So anyway, I reported on 1 July 1949. I had had a skin problem around that particular time and I'd lost a bit of weight. I arrived at Celtic Park after getting off the boat at Merklands instead of the Broomielaw. It shows you how intelligent I was. I got off where the cattle got off. I walked around for a while and then I went to the digs that they had arranged for me. I went down to Celtic Park about half-past nine, ten o'clock, and, lo and behold, the manager said, "Would you like to go out and exercise yourself? It's important." It was something to do, you know what I mean? So I said, "I don't mind." And the first guy I ever trained with at Celtic Park was Tommy Docherty. And he invited me up that evening for tea with his ma, as he called her. So my first introduction to anybody at Celtic Park was Tommy Docherty. I was so glad of somebody to say, "Come on, come and have a meal," that sort of thing. So that's when lads came over from Donegal to Celtic, Sean Fallon and I used to always try and make them welcome. Charlie did it in his own way. He was the softest-hearted fellow that I ever met. He didn't seem like that, you know, when he was playing football, but he was a very kind man, Charlie Tully. In my younger days there, I was apprentice to him and John McPhail.

I don't think I can say anything but good about those fellows. They actually taught me the game, the real professional game because I was just an amateur. I was 19 going on 20. That was young in those days, you know, really. You take the lads that left in my first year such as Jimmy Sirrel, Willie Taylor, Johnny Paton, you know what I mean, good players – and Willie Taylor a great singer into the bargain. It made me think to myself, What am I doing here? But it's funny, you get stuck in and work at it. You can make a career of it and I must say I enjoyed every minute.

Now you made your debut in the League Cup, I don't know if you can remember it, Celtic 1, Aberdeen 3 on the last day of August 1949. Can you remember that day?

I can remember it very well. I was lost actually, in the game. But the thing I really remember about that game was Tommy Pearson, playing at outside-left for Aberdeen. I thought he was a brilliant player. And he had a kind of shuffle. A two-foot shuffle. And all us young fellows were watching him and trying to copy it. That's what I remember mainly about the game.

What about your digs?

Mrs Durneen was my landlady. Mrs Durneen couldn't do enough for you but my mother was sending over the scones and the eggs for fear I might not be getting enough to eat!

Did you settle in okay at Parkhead?

Oh yes. We had Married Men versus Single Men used to be on a Tuesday morning. I don't know whether you remember this wee man, Father Lyon, Father Michael Lyon?

Of Shettleston?

He loved training with us. He'd play in the games with us. Charlie used to pretend to threaten him, "Hey, Father! If it wasn't for that collar –" Then Father Lyon, "Don't you worry about the collar, Charlie!" I would never have spoken to a priest like that but Charlie could do that. Then Charlie would ask him, "Who are you playing for today, Father, the Married Men or the Single Men?" Charlie would light up the morning for you. Training was something else at Celtic. If you weren't fighting with one another, you were having a laugh. It was Jerry Colonna and Tommy Morgan, wasn't it? They were up one time, Tommy had brought Jerry, and the manager was walking them round the track. I'll never forget it. There were the three of them and there was the Boss with his pipe in his mouth and his hat on, talking away to these two top names in entertainment on a quiet visit to Parkhead and there behind the goals were Jock Weir and Jimmy Mallan absolutely knocking hell out of each other! "Ah," says Charlie, "you can talk about your Empires or your Pavilions or your Alhambras but the one place for non-stop entertainment is Celtic Park. Round the clock."

Did you take up with anyone special?

My big pal in the reserves was Chic Cairney. Right-half. He was my buddy. I took up with Chic. His dad was a boxer. He died in the ring. His mum loved him and she loved him becoming a Celtic player. They were from where they would call Blanner and we would call Blantyre. I used to run about with Chic and Johnny Millsopp from Cambuslang who died young. These were the lads I took off with in my early days. I remember them all. The senior players were

Jock Weir, Jimmy Mallan. The rest of us like Pat McCormack in from the mines, we were just there, a crowd of young fellows, trying to make the grade. The wastage in those days! So much depended on Chic Geatons and Jimmy Gribben, how they judged you. Charlie used to say they go down in busloads to England and come back in trainloads. Celtic didn't go into the transfer market. Very, very rarely did they go into it. There was this Maryhill boy hunting out a pair of boots one day till Jimmy Gribben throws him over a pair and says, "Try them on. They've been well-used but give them a try." The boy tries them on. "Are they any good to you?" says Jimmy. "They're great," says the Maryhill lad. "They're a real fit." "Well," says Jimmy, "if you do as well as the fellow who wore those, you'll do all right." "Who was that?" the boy asks. "Bertie Peacock," says Jimmy. The boy glares at him. "If I couldn't play as well as Bertie Peacock," he says, "I'd go and chuck it" – only the word he used for chuck was a bit more colourful and I'll not repeat it here. Charlie and Carrie and John and Jock used to keep on eye out for me when I was still in digs.

Mr and Mrs Tully and John McPhail and Jock Weir?

We had this night-out at a place down in Ayrshire and a few mornings later the Boss wanted to see me. I knew at once what he was on about. It was the drink. He was afraid of me sort of falling into it. "Boss," I said, "I'm delighted with Charlie and John when they ask me out. They've helped me on the field also enormously. If you're worried about the drink angle, I'm a footballer first and foremost so that's the last thing you need worry about." So he took this piece of paper that was in his hand and scrunched it up and threw it in the bin. Someone had seen us and written to him. He said, "If you weren't in the first team you'd be in here asking me why." What he was doing he was reminding me not to drink and it was a nice way of doing it or so I thought anyway. There was no way we got away with murder at Celtic. We had a lot of fun but it was the club first, always the club.

Bertie, can I ask you now, your first really big game with Celtic, the Charity Cup final versus Rangers on 6 May 1950? I mean what was that like for you stepping out before 80,000 rabid Celtic and Rangers fans on what I think was your first appearance at Hampden?

Well, I was very easy-going, thank God, if you understand me. Things wouldn't bother me too much but I was thrilled. But the thing that stands out for me was Danny Kaye. It was the Danny Kaye final, the pipe band coming out and it nearly made you forget about the game, Sir Harry Lauder, Danny Kaye coming out, clowning, Danny Kaye with a big busby on him, the pipe band, the police pipe band, and wee Collins and Danny Kaye kicking the ball about, you know? What a brilliant atmosphere! Then when the game started I got into it right away. I must say I was always sort of half-calm, if you know what I mean. John McPhail and Charlie would be much the same. John Bonnar would be very excitable. That's not to say anything to his detriment. That's what made him perform and he performed brilliantly at times. I liked the crowds.

Now the Scottish Cup at Hampden, 21 April 1951. That must have been another huge occasion for you, was it not?

What I remember most about that – it's a daft thing but I took the 'flu' on Thursday and on Friday, I couldn't run, I was desperate, my legs wouldn't go. I was trying to run and it was hopeless. I remember a wee gentleman called Maxie Benjamin, a Jewish businessman, I don't know if you remember him? Organised the Real Madrid game in 1962?

I went down into Maxie's to give him some tickets. "Bertie," he said, "You don't look well." I said, "Maxie, I'm going home, I feel as sick as a dog." Maxie said, "Take some whisky with you." I took some whisky and I had a sleep. I woke up, felt a wee bit better. And I'll never forget this. This is what I liked about it. I went up to Celtic Park on that Friday. I went out, I started to loosen up. The chairman, the manager and Alex Dowdells were there. They said, "How do you feel today, Bertie?" So I said, "I feel a bit better. I feel a wee bit better." Actually, I was dead. I still couldn't run, you know. I said, "I feel a wee bit better today, honestly." "Well, go home," they said, "have a rest. Report tomorrow morning." Well, on the Saturday morning, I felt not bad but not 100 per cent. "Well, I'm better though," I said. "Well," they said, "we'll take a chance." And I'll never forget that. Things like that, it makes you, it encourages you, especially at a younger age when you're not just a mature man. You know that your place is there if you play well. But that's what I remember. I remember it was the John McPhail Final. Motherwell probably had a bigger percentage of play than we had in that particular game but John McPhail won it for us. He was really at the top of his form at that particular time. And the bonus was great because the bonus was a trip to America.

You picked Gil Heron up out there. Did you actually play against him?

In Detroit. Poor Gilly was from Detroit. Oh dear, oh dear. Two Laps and a Song! He wasn't a bad footballer by any manner or means but he was so cold in Scotland, he was desperately cold. He stayed in the Kenilworth. He didn't want to stay anywhere else. He had his music there. He loved his music. It was company for him, that's where the club put him, in the old Kenilworth. It was also a great meeting-place. There's some memories of the trip to the States. I'll never forget Southampton where we boarded ship. The first stop was the Cobh of Cork where we lifted some people. We met this boy who came aboard on his first trip to America. We met him, we were having afternoon tea in the lounge. And this fellow was all on his own. He was going to make his fortune in the States. So I asked him where he was from. I didn't know the man. He said "I'm John McKenna from the Cutts." I said my father worked at the Cutts and lo and behold he knew my father, Hugh Peacock! There was a leap at the Cutts and he used to fish for salmon. And this John McKenna, son of Dan McKenna, has done very well for himself in the States. But imagine meeting him, both of us on our first time out to America. Isn't it funny how things happen to you?

Do you remember the throng in the Central Station on your return from America 30 June 1951, how it felt to be loved?

Oh, it was good. Charlie, Sean and I were booked to sail home that evening, Charlie to Belfast, Sean to Sligo and me to Coleraine. I forget the hotel we went down into but we stayed there until the nine o'clock Belfast boat from the Broomielaw. You talk about the Central Station. Talk about nearness to the spectators. We were loved then. It was a great tour. It's funny it gave me a taste for New York. I never go to the States but I try to go through New York. I love to go to New York.

You came to Celtic as an inside-left and made your fame at left-half.

Joe Baillie was a very good player, very, very stylish. I used to go out with Joe. Joe was a real friend. He had an unfortunate injury at Broomfield, at Airdrie, and he had to have a cartilage operation. On that particular day, Airdrie had Ian McMillan and Jimmy Welsh, a very good side. John McPhail said to me, "Bertie, drop back to left-half." I dropped back and

taking John Kurila?" So I said, "Duncan, I'm recruiting the players here. What do you see wrong with him?" He couldn't tell me and I tell you once big John was in Canada, he really start to play. He had a rocky first month but then a very good five months. I said to Beattie, "What about Kurila now?" He said, "Aye, he can play a bit." Next thing I knew, big John's career was made with Northampton all the way from the old Division Four to the old First Division under Dave Bowen.

Bertie, thank you very much indeed. You've given me more than enough of your time. I'll let you get back to the golf.

You say you had problems getting into Coleraine. Well, you get into your car now and follow me. I'll show you how easy it is.

Sean Fallon
Full-back/centre
1950-1958

Sean, you taught yourself to use your left foot, is this correct?

We used to go to St Anne's Park and that was within a stone's throw from where I lived. And a weakness – any weaknesses we had – for instance, like not using the left foot, which was a weakness – I used to go up with one football boot on my left foot, a sandshoe on my right and there was a chap named Jack Bonnar, Lord have mercy on him – and Randolph Jenkins, Lord have mercy on him – and myself. We used to just kick the ball to each other with our weak foot. We wanted to improve, you know, the left foot, and I ended up, irrespective of how the ball came to me, able to use either foot.

You joined Celtic from Glenavon. As a centre or as a full-back?

As a full-back. I don't think they would have selected me as a centre.

You'd played centre for Glenavon, hadn't you?

I'd played centre only when they were tight for forwards. I only had about four or five games at centre for Glenavon.

Now you were signed for Celtic on 23 March 1950 and you arrived in Glasgow on the 30th.

That's right. I had a week at home. Charlie Tully was to meet me. I'd never been away from Ireland. They told me that Charlie Tully would make himself known to me on the Scottish boat. So I went on board and I saw the purser – I was told to go to the purser, which I did – a hell of a nice man, very good to us over the years, we could always get a berth any time we were travelling from Glasgow back home. He put out a call for Charlie and Charlie duly arrived and introduced himself and brought me down – the first place he brought me was to the bar. "Well, Sean," he said, "What are you having?" I said, "I'll have a lemonade, Charlie." "A what? A lemonade. Oh, dear God, don't tell me you're one of those." I said, "I'm sorry, Charlie. I'm one of those. I don't drink or smoke." I didn't smoke at that time. So I sat there and I was never as sick in all my life. In the morning. I drank about seven lemonades.

Terrible boats.

Charlie's drink was a beer and a half of whisky. Charlie was lightly-made and I was amazed where he was able to put this drink because, irrespective of how he drank, God, could he play! He was a tremendous player. A tremendous, great player. A personality player. A player that people would come to see. Okay, they'd come to see Celtic play but a lot of them were there to see Charlie Tully play. I was offered digs off Alexandra Parade. I got the shock of my life the following morning. I woke up and I turned over and there was this guy in the bed with me! This chap had four sisters. His dad was dead. He was a painter. Jimmy Hogan it was who had recommended this house. I said to myself, this state of affairs is not for me! Anyway, it was explained to me that, you know, with four sisters and the boy, that was all the room they had. It was the son was sleeping alongside of me. That was the only way they could do it, if I shared a bed with the son. Mind you, they never suggested I could sleep with one of the daughters! Anyway, I moved out. The chairman at that time was Bob Kelly and he heard about this and he came up to the park and brought me out to Rutherglen, to Bankhead Drive in Rutherglen, I'll always remember, off Bankhead Road, and he introduced me to this lady, Miss McGuigan, Mary McGuigan, Lord rest her. And it turned out she was a niece of old Nap McMenemy who was a famous Celtic player in his time. In fact he was a member of the team, I think they won five or six Leagues in a row.

Six in a row and four in a row.

Aye. Well, she was giving me a room of my own but I always remember the chairman going up, examining the bed, testing the springs, "Do you think this will be all right, Sean?" This is the chairman of Celtic Football Club and me just a young boy and him going up, seeing if the bed was all right. I was embarrassed actually, but that's the kind of a man he was, wanted to make sure everything was right. He wanted to make sure I'd no excuses. So I thanked him very much and, as it turned out, the digs were tremendous. Miss McGuigan was very, very good to me. In fact, all the players used to make it their home. It was a great place. It was great digs. Towards the end of that season I was selected to play for the club and the first game was against Clyde at Shawfield. The game was about half an hour under way – it was a terrible wet day – the ball came to me and I stuck out at it and right into my own net. What an embarrassment for a young man! And it didn't do his confidence any good but we got through it okay, two each. I always remember that game for Jimmy Hogan. He was coach at the time. In the dressing-room before we went out, he was going round the players, and I felt something wet on the back of my neck. I looked up, you know, but Jimmy had moved on. I looked at Tully and Tully looked back at me. "Don't worry", he said, "it's only holy water." Jimmy's holy water didn't do me any good that day, I can tell you!

Sean, you break into the Celtic team, on 25 September 1950, in the Glasgow Cup at Hampden, a 65,000 crowd on a Monday afternoon. Celtic 1, Partick Thistle 1 and you're up against one of those great Firhill wingers, Jimmy Walker.

Jimmy Walker, yeah. Canadian. Tremendous pace. You had to play him very tight. You had to be on the ball with him or before him or you were in trouble because if he got space he just stuck the ball by you and he was away. Jimmy would run off the park, outside the by-line, because he knew if he stayed on the pitch he was going to run into you. It was the sort of thing should never have been allowed.

Now, you're picked for Northern Ireland against England, to play on 7 October and you call off because there are elements in the Republic who are asking her sons not to play for the North and in the light of later events, it's one of these disastrous political attitudes which does nothing to alleviate an already fraught political situation.

It was a disaster because they selected me to play against the British Army before that, which I did. It was at Windsor Park. John Charles was playing against us, he was in the British

Army at that time. After that game I was asked and they sent me a letter confirming the conversation: If selected, would I play for Northern Ireland against England? I said, "Certainly." It meant I would be playing against Matthews. Because Matthews at that time was a fixture, Finney used to play on the left, Matthews on the right, and I gave them my word, certainly I would play. Then the politics started. Joe Cunningham and company in Dublin who ran Shamrock Rovers at that time, they got in touch with me. They sent me a letter and also 'phoned me, Under no circumstances was I to play for Northern Ireland. And I said, "I will, I'll be playing." And next thing, they started bringing my dad into it who at that time was in politics. He was a Fine Gael man. He was on the County Council and also on the Corporation and they could stir things up. This is true. I 'phoned my dad. "Politics should never come into football," he said, "you play! I can look after myself." My dad was ex-British Army. He'd been wounded in the '14-18 War at Gallipoli. He was also secretary and treasurer of the British Legion. He used to look after all the ex-servicemen, to get them parcels every Christmas for their wives. He used to look after all the pensioners so he was very involved, you know, locally. He was also senior alderman which shows you what the people of Sligo thought of him. He topped the poll every time there was an election. He said, "Don't worry about me. The people know how I stand here." But – I was worried. And I pulled out. Because the people in Northern Ireland had been very good to me and I feel that football and politics, I don't feel they come together. That was the split of the Associations because at that time boys born in the Republic played for Northern Ireland, Johnny Carey, Dave Walsh, Con Martin, they all played for Northern Ireland so I didn't think I was doing anything wrong. I probably would do the same thing today. I probably would play for them in the hope of bringing people together.

Now on 21 April 1951, at Hampden, before a crowd of 133,343, the Scottish Cup Final, Celtic 1, Motherwell 0. I was down near Southampton at the time but I cannot describe the elation when I got the final score.

Ah, that was a great result. We were so pleased. And one of the main reasons we were pleased was not for ourselves, but for the support, because they had followed that club in the bad times and we'd given them nothing and there we were, winners of the Scottish Cup. We spoke about that in the dressing room. The fans may be reluctant to accept that, but at that time – I don't know about now – we were delighted with the support we got. Now we could give them something in return.

And off to the USA with McPhail's Cup in a brown paper bag, brown paper bags being the technological wonder of 1951.

That was the tour there was a grouse we weren't getting enough pocket money. The main men that were on about it were Charlie and Big John, Big Hooky, we used to call him.

Tully and McPhail.

Correct. But it was Charlie that started it all, "We don't have enough money!" Charlie, of course, was looking for spare money, and actually, we didn't need a lot of money, because you found when you went there, people that lived there, Irish people, Scots people, they were so generous, it was embarrassing. They were taking you everywhere. They wouldn't let you spend anything. We used to talk about it. And I used to say to Bertie Peacock and Willie Fernie, "How, in the name of God, can we reciprocate?" They wouldn't allow you to. To do anything for them. The only way we could reciprocate was when they came here to Glasgow. But I will always remember that incident. We got together, we were looking for more money. So we're staying in the Hotel Paramount on 46th Street, and I'll always remember there was a balcony with a stairs up and there was a floor there with a table and sitting on one of the chairs was Bob Kelly. He was there to talk to the players, not collectively, but one by one, individually. And one of the first players up was Charlie. So Charlie went up and Charlie was one of the few people that called the chairman, Bob. So Charlie went up.

"Hello, Charlie."

"Hello, Bob."

"Have a seat, Charlie."

"Thank you, Bob."

Now the acoustics were such that the voices hit the ceiling of the balcony – and Charlie wasn't aware of this – and came right down to us. So we could hear Mr Kelly ask Charlie, "Right, well what's the problem?" Charlie said, "They're looking for more money, Bob. Actually I think they're getting too much as it is. I think they're getting far too much." "I thought there was a complaint," says Kelly. "Not as far as I'm concerned, Bob." We're all down below with our mouths agog. So Tully comes down the stairs for the next one to go up. He looks at us and we all look at him. "I bloody well told him!" he says. That was Charlie. He was one of the few players who could get away with it. A character. A great character.

Sean, you have a holiday in Ireland after the USA and you come back for the St Mungo Cup, Glasgow's football contribution to the Festival of Britain. And all of a sudden you are pushed in at centre-forward and score two goals against Aberdeen on August the first, both equalisers, before Jimmy Walsh gets the winner, 3-2.

Celtic kept me at centre and unfortunately, I hated the position. The reason they played me at centre was to take the weight of the other forwards who were on the light side bar Collins because Collins could look after himself. They were all on the light side and I was supposed to rumble them up – the opposing defences, that is, which you were allowed to do at that time because we played it physically but within the laws. But in the process, I happened to score goals.

Gil Heron comes into the side in the League Cup against Morton, on 18 August at Parkhead, and you go back to right-back. Why did Gil Heron not make the grade?

The Scottish weather. I remember one time it was a really cold day and the sleet was coming down against Third Lanark. And poor Gil, "Oh, this is not for me! I don't play in this weather"! Ah, he was hopeless that day. He'd also been a boxer too, represented some area in boxing, but I remember he and Jimmy Mallan fell out and had a fight behind the goals. Gil and Mallan fought over a tackle. I always remember Mallan invited him into the gym but Gil didn't want it, "Oh no, not for me." I don't know if I'd have gone either. Mallan was useful.

Now, on 17 October 1951, at Dalymount, Eire 3, future world champions, Germany 2. Fallon at right-back.

I think they put me up centre that day because I will always remember the German goalkeeper hitting me. I charged him but I'd taken on more than I thought because he hit me, he caught me under the heart. And if the ball had come near me for the next ten minutes, I wouldn't have been able to blow at it. I didn't want them to know. Never let on you're hurt – that was the attitude in that time anyway. You could be hurt but never let on. So I was very careful about charging him after that. We beat them 3-2 and it was a good German side.

And on 16 November 1952, packed crowd, 40,000, Sean Fallon centre-forward for Eire against France. Scored in 20 minutes. Went at the French defence like a battering-ram.

One each. The great Kopa was playing for them. And Fontaine played. Some great players.

They would make their names in the 1958 World Cup. Now, Sean, you had picked up a bone injury against Derry City on the Irish Tour of 1952 and now, five days before Christmas '52, you clash with old Celtic favourite Jimmy Delaney playing for Falkirk at Brockville. You come off worse with hairline fractures of the arm.

What happened was, I always remember Jimmy Delaney wrote to me after the accident, that he hoped and prayed I would recover quickly. He had had a lot of trouble himself with an arm injury. What happened, I went in to tackle him and my forearm caught between his hip bone and my hip bone which is the strongest part of your body. And my arm was broken in two places. See this bone? It should set like that one. But I broke it three times after that. And I was just after being selected as captain of the team. But I finished the game. I went in at half-time. And the doctor did that – I always remember – put my arm up to his ear, gave it a shake, passed me fit to resume action. I finished the game at full-back, left-back, and I always remember I was in agony playing out the time. And on the way back, Alex Dowdells was trainer at that time, I said to him, "Alex, it's very, very sore." He says, "Right, we'll get off the bus at the Royal." So we got off the bus and went in. I was X-rayed, the arm was diagnosed broken in two places, I was put in plaster. We were playing a Cup-tie. We were drawn against Stirling Albion on 7 February 1953, in the Scottish Cup, ice-bound surface. I'd just come back into the team. The doctor had come to see me and he says, "Ach, that plaster shouldn't be on you at all! Take that plaster off." So the plaster came off and I played in the Cup-tie. In the last few minutes of the game, I happened to get a kick on the forearm and I knew it was hurt, really hurt. But I finished the game and told Alex, "It's bad again, Alex." What had happened was, a callus had formed on the crack, but it hadn't become solidified. It was still soft and the kick had opened everything up again. So I went into the Royal again and it turned out it was the same doctor as had treated me after the Falkirk game. He says, "Your arm was broken only a few weeks ago! What were you playing for?" I said, "The doctor said it was only muscular." He said, "Not at all! I can still get the plates. You've woken the whole lot up again!" The callus hadn't become solidified. I was playing again far too soon. But what could I do? You're young and I wanted to play and you think people know better than you do. I missed a whole lot of games because of that.

Then you did it again in Dublin on 20 April.

I broke it in Dublin and couldn't get it sorted out until the following day. The boy caught me there with the boot. Celtic were playing an FAI select in Dublin, for An Tostal at Dalymount Park. I came back and this time I went up to Duke Street hospital. It's closed now, I think. There was a grand man there, I just can't remember his name, and he put me in plaster, and he said, "You've suffered all right with that." I'd never suffered so much in all my life. I couldn't sleep. Then we'd to get the train back from Dublin to Belfast, get the Glasgow boat that night and I was lying there with it. They gave me tablets but they were no good. So it was put back in plaster again for the third time – for the fourth time! Then we were playing against Hearts at Celtic Park, on 24 October 1953, Scottish League, and at that time we used the diagonal system of defence. We didn't play with a sweeper, the full-back became a sweeper depending on what side we were being attacked. If the attack was down the right, and I was playing left-back, I'd move in to cover the centre-half. Jock Stein was playing. Jock had the ball. And Davie Laing, the Hearts left-half, he finished up at Clyde, I think. Good player. He was injured so they moved him up to centre-forward. Sometimes they did that instead of putting them on the wing because, as you know, in those days there were no substitutes, you just played on or left the field. So anyway, I was there. Jock should have had the ball away but with Laing being semi-injured, he lingered. I'd moved out, thinking Jock was going to clear the ball but he lost it to Laing who was coming through. I was late in coming back in and he was just ready for a shot at goal so I threw my body to get between where I reckoned the ball would be and the goals. The ball hit me, travelling like a bullet, caught me here, stuck in here and broke my arm. Feel that arm.

I went out for the second-half at outside-left. Bobby Parker was playing right-back. "Sean, injured or not," he says, "I'm going for every ball!" "Oh," says I, "I know." "That's your fault," he says. Says I, "Don't worry." We had a bit of banter. But seriously, he says, "I'm going for every ball." But I remember I was in agony.

That was the day you said, "At least it's not a broken a leg!"

I went back to the same man to have it put in plaster. He told me the body could only give off so much calcium and: "As far as you are concerned, Mr Fallon, it's working overtime. Wait and I'll give you a letter to Celtic Park. They should send you home to Ireland and give you a real rest." And I'll always remember, he wrote the letter, that the arm had taken too much abuse, that I needed a rest in Ireland. That was good enough for them. They sent me home. It was the swimming season. The Henry Cup was being swum for, a long swim and I'd won it twice. The sponsors wanted me to swim in it. I said, "I can't, I'm in plaster up to here, I'd get the plaster wet." "Ach," they said, "you can swim maybe half a mile or so, you know." And I stupidly – typical Irish, brain full of stones – I went in for the swim and didn't the plaster get wet? "God," I thought, "if I go back to Glasgow and the plaster's all soft and wet, they're going to jump to one conclusion that I haven't been looking after myself." So, needless to say, I didn't win the swim! But my dad, God rest him, brought me up to the surgical hospital. He was friendly with the surgeon there, Charlie McCarthy. He was the orthopaedic surgeon in the hospital. He put a new plaster on. So that was me. And I went back, and eventually I got it off in Glasgow and I never had any more bother after that. But just pains, you know.

You have pains in it nowadays?

Oh aye, pains in it all the time. But that wasn't the last of my injuries because I broke my nose twice after that. A fractured rib. Then my knee got a bad twist. Unfortunately the first operation on it, he left a piece of cartilage, the surgeon at the Victoria. The second one, it had moved, it had moved back, and he thought he'd leave it for a couple of weeks and then he went back again and he got it the third time. Nowadays they have a different type of operation.

Keyhole?

Keyhole surgery. They did that on my left knee, no bother. But the right knee I finished up with about 27 stitches in. My right knee. And when I played, the knee would fill up with blood. And I went to Mr McDougall. He was the chief orthopaedic surgeon in the Royal. I used to go up and get blood drawn off my knee and a cortisone injection to play. After I went up the second time to have the blood drawn off, Mr McDougall said, "Take some advice, son, I'm not happy about giving you cortisone." You know cortisone nowadays, a lot of people, they don't use it at all. He warned me with cortisone I could even lose my leg. He said, "I'm not giving you any more cortisone." He said, "If you'll take some advice from me, you'll retire from the game," which I did.

Sean, some very progressive moves by Celtic around this time. You were taken down to Wembley for England versus Hungary, on 25 November 1953, England 3, Hungary 6. And the month before, you'd been down to see England versus the Rest of Europe, the 4-4 game. I mean, very progressive stuff, at that time, you know?

That was the chairman, you know. The chairman believed that you must learn if you're looking at the best. You can't help but try and emulate what you're watching. You can't but try to emulate if you're watching the top players in the world.

And have you a memory of the Hungarians?

Oh, the Hungarians were fabulous! There was Boszik, wing-half, Puskas did the hand-shaking but Boszik was the captain of the team. I always remember someone saying, Oh, he's quite slow. But he proved that speed of thought could always overcome speed of movement. To anyone looking at him, Oh, he's slow, he's slow, he's too slow for first-class football. But he was always on a jog, always on a jog, and the way he could pass a ball and his control was immediate. Control was immediate. And he could see things so quickly. That was the reason he didn't have to be fast because you get guys that can run like greyhounds, but you say, Can they play? It's a different thing altogether. Puskas was something too and Hidegkuti.

Now the Scottish Cup Final versus Aberdeen at Hampden, Aberdeen 1, Celtic 2. Fallon at centre gets the winner in 63 minutes, following a run from deep by Fernie.

Another of those great mazy runs. I'd have been in trouble had I missed it, the pass was so perfect.

And Jock Stein received the Cup although the club captain was in the side?

Jock had become – when I was appointed captain, you always had to nominate a deputy and my closest friend there, a great pal of mine was Bertie Peacock. But Bertie was younger than me, about six years younger than me, and I wanted a man of experience so I recommended Jock Stein. Jock became my deputy. He reciprocated then when he became manager which went to show he hadn't forgotten. He could have brought in his own man. We went off to Switzerland and he nearly drowned Bobby Collins at the Lido in Lucerne. He threw him in off the raft and didn't realise Bobby couldn't swim. Wee Bobby wasn't pleased one bit. I saved him from drowning. Poor Bobby. Puskas, he got injured in the 8-3 game against Germany in Switzerland and he was in plaster and I remember Bobby Collins going up to him and asking him for his autograph, you know. There was a few of us used to run around together, Collins, Fernie, Peacock and myself. We were standing there and Bobby walked up with his sheet of paper and his pencil. Puskas just looked at him, Och, away you go! And he walked away. You should have heard wee Bobby! Boy, he called him for everything! In fact, we were ready to protect Puskas because Bobby was very fiery. He was ready to put one on his chin. But Puskas was wrong. There was no reason why he shouldn't have given him his autograph. I'll always remember that incident.

And Peacock, Fernie and Collins would play in the 1958 World Cup in Sweden. Now here comes something, 21 August 1956, Celtic 3, Rangers 4 in the Glasgow Cup. Fallon uses a 100 per cent muscle charge on Sammy Baird, lays him out.

I broke his collarbone. The reason for that, it was his own fault, he came in square to me, stupidly. Three years before that, he was playing with Clyde. I was playing right-back. It was a very muddy night at Shawfield and I had fallen in the goalmouth. Next thing I got a kick in the back of the head. I looked up, I saw Sammy running away. Sammy used to run with his chest out. Big guy, Sammy. But the following week he was transferred to Preston. The manager at Preston at that time was Scot Symon. Three years after that particular incident at Shawfield, Rangers appointed Scot Symon manager and he brought Sammy back with him. And that was the first opportunity I'd had, for I always remembered the kick in the head, when he was wearing a Clyde jersey. Stupidly, he came in square, broke his collarbone and his shoulder and was carried off. Yet strangely enough, Baird was quite a nice guy off the field. I met him several times socially, a nice guy, but on the field, he'd that wee bit in him, you know.

Now into 1957 and 80,000 people for a three o'clock kick-off against Rangers at Ibrox on a Wednesday! Scottish Cup replay. Can you imagine!

They had Billy Simpson with them. Billy Simpson drove the ball at me in the first ten minutes and the referee, Jack Mowat, Jack sorted him out. Then he came up to me, "Now, Mister Fallon, don't retaliate, I know you're hurt but don't retaliate. I'll watch him." I always thought Mowat was a great referee.

I want to ask you about Sammy Wilson, the forgotten man of the 7-1 side? Snappy ground passes, positional intelligence, ace schemer, a revelation as one newspaper report said of him. How did you rate Slammin' Sammy?

Sammy Wilson? At that time, we were one of the first teams to introduce the four man forward line, the centre-forward and a player alongside him. We played Sammy Wilson up alongside Billy McPhail. Billy got everything that was going in the air, he could knock them down, and one thing Sammy could do, he was a great finisher. But he wasn't a worker. He was given that area to play in but that threw a lot of work on us. The old-style inside-forward came back and did a lot of work in midfield. With Sammy, it meant we were short a wee bit on the left side. And at that time on the left side you had Tully, Peacock, Fallon. That threw a lot of work on Peacock and myself. Because Charlie, you know, Charlie wasn't a great worker. Charlie wanted the ball to his feet. And if Charlie had been out the night before, he'd never get back in his own half of the field anyway. But Sammy was lost when Billy McPhail retired. He retired in '58, same as myself. A lot of the old players retired about then and they started producing young players around that time. After McPhail went, Wilson wasn't profitable without him. He wasn't the same player. McPhail could get up over a ball and head it down. Very few forwards can do that. They can get under a ball but McPhail could hang and get the ball down to people's feet. It's a lost art.

How was that 7-1 game for you?

Oh, it was tremendous for us. We expected a hard game. The usual Old Firm rivalry. No matter what people think, the spectators, we had a lot of respect for one another and that game, irrespective of how the game went, we shook hands, because we were professionals. We were the better team on the day. We accepted that. But that particular day, we always wanted to win, of course. We were playing the Rangers. That was a very important game for the Final of the League Cup. All games are important but a game like that against Rangers has extra importance in the eyes of the spectators. It still has, in fact. And always will have, I think. We went out and we were quite surprised ourselves how easy it was. You get games, you know, when everything goes right for you. You're finding your teammate with a pass, there's nothing going astray, you're playing well but the other team's struggling. I have to say, you're only as good as you're allowed to be. I think on that day, every player contributed. Every sector of the team was playing well which is unusual because the team might play well and yet you might point to a player and say, He wasn't so good.

And all this in spite of the Fight of the Century a few days before in the dressing room, Tully versus Evans? 17 October?

Ach, the things I've heard about that! I was there! They're supposed to have knocked the massage table over. The entire team couldn't have turned over that table! Bobby had taken offence about something in Charlie's newspaper column. Charlie was pretending he wanted to get at Bobby. Bobby really wanted to get at Charlie. Charlie was no fighter. Charlie's body wasn't built for fighting. We were holding on to Charlie, that was the easy part. The real problem was holding Bobby down. Bobby would have killed him. Charlie's column was ghost-written. He had probably no idea what was in it till Bobby lost his temper.

Sean, ten million thanks.

Eugene, thank you. It's always a pleasure talking to you.

Jim Sharkey
Forward
1954-1957

Tell me about the half-a-crown a head games, Jim.

When I got demobbed from the Forces, I discovered there was a game on at the local rec and they played for half-a-crown a man. I joined in. I looked forward to it every week, it was great stuff. The winners got the whole pot. You would go home with five bob in your pocket. The reason I gave it up, was a little juvenile club called League Hearts. I started playing with them.

How did you know that Celtic were interested in you?

I was playing for League Hearts and after the game an old man came up to me and he said to me, "How would you like to play for Celtic?" And I thought, "Here, I'd love to play for Celtic!" So, he took my name and address. So when I went home, I told my father. And my dad said, "Don't be so bloody silly!" So I said, "Well, he's coming to see us on Tuesday night." So when Tuesday night came, a knock came to the door and there was my old man again – Jimmy McStay! He took me and my father up to Celtic Park which was only a couple of hundred yards up the road and we got introduced to Jimmy McGrory. Celtic loaned me out to Rutherglen Glencairn juniors.

You've been playing this half-a-crown a head game, you're playing juvenile and now you're bounced into junior football, plunged into this much higher standard. What was that like for you?

Well, that was a nightmare, actually, because now I was Jim Sharkey, provisionally signed for Celtic and all that, and when you were playing in that junior league, when people knew that you were earmarked for a senior club, they gave you a bit of a rough time, you know, because they were out to prove they were better players.

Was this on the park or in the changing room?

Oh, on the park. I thought the tackling was a bit severe, you know. I was there for about six months.

Do you feel that you learned anything from the junior game?

No, I just learned it was a tough league we played in, that was all! Most of my time was spent looking after myself.

Now you played for the reserves in the Public Trial on 6 August 1955. You played inside-left in a team that comprised Dick Beattie; Vince Ryan and Frank Meechan; Ian Reid, John Jack

and John McPhail; Billy Craig and Matt McVittie; Jimmy Walsh; yourself and Neilly Mochan. Can you remember those fellows?

I can remember it just as though it's yesterday. There was another chap played – Jim Kennedy, full-back. That was one chap I noticed a lot when I was playing for Celtic. I thought Jim Kennedy had great potential and he did turn out a great player for Celtic. Of all the young lads coming up, I thought he was made of the right stuff.

And yet he was another late-developer, same as yourself.

He didn't make it till he was 28 or 29.

Who were your pals in that team?

Dick Beattie was a good pal of mine. So was John Jack. We always seemed to be together, us three. Remember the size of John Jack? I can remember wee Bobby Collins threatening to do big John if he didn't finish a card game!

And a few days later, you're playing inside-left again with Beattie, Ryan and Meechan; MacKay, Jack and Conroy; Billy Craig and McVittie; Frank Whyte; yourself and Bertie Auld.

Bertie Auld turned out to be a great midfield player. Celtic sold him to Birmingham and when he came back he played in the middle of the park and he was absolutely brilliant. I don't know who discovered midfield for him. I don't know if it was Jock Stein or not but Bertie was one of the mainstays of Celtic coming good in the sixties.

He knew how to look after himself, did he not?

Bertie was a handful, yes.

Now, Jim, there is a reserve match, on 30 August 1955, Rangers 2, Celtic 3. The forward line is Billy Craig and Jim Rowan; James Docherty; yourself and Bertie Auld. In 77 minutes, Jimmy Gribben orders Sharkey to outside-right, Craig inside-right, Rowan inside-left and Celtic score immediately!

I remember Jimmy Gribben ever so clearly. Lovely old man, he was. I think he had a soft spot for me, actually. He never got a lot of credit.

His name keeps coming up. Wasn't it him that brought Stein in?

Celtic had a centre-half problem with injuries and Jimmy Gribben recommended an old Albion Rovers pivot down at Llanelli. He was 29 years of age, Stein. Jock cleared the ball more with his knees than he did with his feet. Good talker. On the ground he used to keep everybody right. I thought that was fantastic. He was definite in what he wanted and he became a great manager after. He went to Dunfermline and made them into some team.

See, this is what amazes me, this business of Stein. You fellows on the field, you knew that there was something special here but did he stand out in the changing room?

Tully was the leader in the dressing room. He was always pulling little pranks. He was a character, a real character, Charlie Tully was.

Yeah, but Tully wasn't laying down tactics or was he, saying what we'll do or anything of that sort?

No, Charlie never went to that extent. Just little jokes and that.

Was Stein up to anything like that – talking tactics?

Jimmy McGrory was the man. He would give us a little lecture before we went out. He was the manager but when Stein got the job later on, later in life, he was a good talker, a very good talker.

Did you get on well with him?

I got on well with him, yeah, I think. We went to Seamill for the weekend after one of the games. I always remember, all the big boys, that was Charlie Tully, Jock Stein, Willie Fernie, people like that, they all seemed to hang about together, you know. And the one or two younger lads that came in, I don't know, I think Jock was captain and he might have made more of us. But he was good company. He was a good singer.

Now you make your big-team debut, on 1 October 1955, 2-0 against Raith Rovers at Parkhead and you score on your debut, you score the second goal. The team was Beattie; Boden and Fallon; Reid, Evans and Peacock; Collins and McVittie; Sharkey; Fernie and Tully. Now how did that feel playing with people like Bobby Collins, Willie Fernie and Charlie Tully? I mean, you've virtually just come in from the half-a-crown a head games?

Well it never worried me, playing with these chaps because sometimes I was doing things that they never did. I appreciated their talent but I never thought that I was inferior. I always felt I could hold my own. It never really worried me. I had an admiration for Willie Fernie. I felt Willie Fernie was special. We were over in Ireland about that time, at about two o'clock one morning, sitting out the hotel window, listening to the hens making noises and that in the dark and we're answering back, Cluck-cluck-cluck, Cock-a-doodle-doo! Willie said to me, he said, "Look Jim, I'm the best player in Scotland." The best player in Scotland! I'll never forget that. Then he said, "And you're the second best!" I 'phoned him up not long ago to remind him of that.

Now, on Christmas Eve, at Easter Road, a game of high excitement, you beat Hibs 3-2. Mochan gets number two with a rasping left foot. Sharkey gets number three and actually dribbles round Tommy Younger! Any memories of that one?

Well, actually, Eugene, the memories I have of Easter Road are not when I was playing for Celtic but when I was playing for Airdrie. The manager was Willie Steel. I was running across the middle of the field, I came down the touchline and Willie Steel says his directors were saying, "Look at this, this is ridiculous, what's this? Why did you buy him?" And as I ran along the by-line, I cut the ball back to Gibby Ormond and he banged it in the net. And Willie Steel says he turned to his directors and said, "That's why!" That's my memory of Easter Road.

Had you ever played at Hampden before Boxing Day 1955?

No, I think that was my first time. I maintain I got a hat-trick that day. I'd scored two and I got the fourth goal as well. You've probably seen it before, when a ball hits the underside of the crossbar, it bounces down on the line or over the line. As far as I could see it was over the line, it was my goal, but Bobby Collins chested it in and he gets it in the record books. I wasn't all that worried at the time but I got three against Rangers that day. It was a hat-trick and to score a hat-trick against the Rangers would have been something special.

But you would claim that goal, Jim?

Yeah, but it makes no difference now, I still didn't get it. It was put down to Collins. Collins got two, I got two and I think Fernie got one.

Now, this is the game that got you the reputation for stroking the ball with your shooting foot before you hit it. You had this business of teeing the ball up and then hammering it.

I seemed to make plenty time for myself when I was playing. I could see the situation and I made time. I kept my cool. I was not so much a goalscorer as a goalmaker. I liked to lay balls off to people. I was never really a goalscorer.

Maybe we should ask George Niven?

Maybe it was the golfer in me, teeing it up.

Well, it's in the papers. Now, I just want to remind you of the team with regard to what happens in April. It was Beattie; Haughney and Fallon; Evans, Stein and Peacock. Smith and Fernie; Sharkey; Collins and Mochan. How did you feel about playing centre-forward?

Well, I tell you something, Eugene, I never worried where I played. It didn't worry me one little bit. Actually, I think I preferred the right wing, to tell you the truth.

Snake Hips. Scotland's answer to Matthews.

They put me centre-forward, everybody was quite happy.

But with two inside men like Fernie and Collins, now that must have made your day!

That was special, yeah. They were the top men in the country at the time, great football players. Yeah, it was marvellous.

Now 1956, 4 February, on a mudheap at Cappielow, Morton nil, Celtic two. You took a ball in the face from goalkeeper Tommy Harvey, at point blank range, that nearly killed you, didn't it?

Yeah, I was off for six weeks. I was taking blackouts regular and when I got fit again, I got fit physically but I'd lost my confidence.

And a mouthful of teeth. Was he clearing the ball?

In those days, Eugene, you could charge the goalkeeper. He took the ball out of the air and I was about 15 yards away from him so I just hauled up for to try and harass him a bit, you know. And he hit the ball and that was the end of it. He nearly took my head off. Isabel, my wife, had no idea I was so badly injured and to this day I just cannot tell you how I came home.

The fact that you were just sent home and not kept in hospital for observation is an amazing thing. I mean, if you'd died, where would Celtic have been legally?

At the time, I think it was regarded as just one of those things. People are a lot more Health and Safety conscious nowadays.

Now, Jim, the semi-final of the Scottish Cup, on 24 March 1956, Celtic 2, Clyde 1 at Hampden. Sharkey Fishes Celtic From The Clyde. You put Celtic one up within two minutes.

That goal was so fast Isabel hadn't even taken her seat. I came home and I said, "What did you think of my goal today?" She says, "I didn't even see it. You were too fast."

Now, if you have tears, prepare to shed them now. In April 1956, up to the semi-final, Celtic have tried-out eight outside-rights, six inside-rights, six centre-forwards, six inside-lefts and four outside-lefts since the start of the season and the experimentation goes on – even against Hearts at Hampden.

We played Manchester United just five days before the Cup Final, me in opposition to one of the greatest young players of his generation or any generation, Duncan Edwards. Sharkey versus Edwards. And what happened was, I think Hugh Goldie took a throw-in in the middle of the park, right below the stand and I went to meet it. Duncan Edwards was at my back and I sold him a little dummy. I pretended I was going to hold it but I let it go past me. I wheeled to chase the ball and he was left standing there – a wonderful feeling. I remember Duncan Edwards because of his physique, the size of his legs and that, and he didn't wear shinguards. The heels of his football boots were nearly level with the ground, as if he was standing on them in fact. Brilliant! John Higgins played that night.

Dick Beattie got himself a dodgy arm which might explain his performance in the Final and Tully came off at half-time.

And so to Seamill. My father used to say to me, "I'll do the drinkin', you play the football!" I wasn't a drinker and I never have been but there was sherry and I think Tully got me tipsy. Whether he meant to or not is another matter. But it wasn't Tully that dropped me in it, it was one of the other senior players or so I think. He reported I was drunk or somebody said I was drunk and maybe as a result that's why I was not picked for the Scottish Cup Final. That was a big, big blow to me. I did not know until the last minute that I wasn't playing. They didn't announce the team until about an hour before the kick-off. And who was taking my place at inside-right but this right-back, Mike Haughney! He'd been playing full-back for years but because of the Hearts being so strong at the back, the other point of view was, he'd provide more punch than me to the Celtic forward line.

But he didn't, did he? And think of Billy Craig at outside-right. Five foot seven, just two first team games under his belt, thrown in before a crowd of 132,842! That team was a disgrace. No wonder the supporters were in such a murderous mood at the finish.

I think it was Haughney for Sharkey to provide more punch to the forward line.

You think that was really the reason?

That was really the reason. Even if somebody had said I was drunk, the reason I was dropped, there wasn't enough weight in the forward line.

But you'd just been playing against Duncan Edwards! I think you're being very charitable.

Yeah, well they don't think friendlies count all that much really. Hearts were a different team from Manchester United.

But on St Patrick's Day you'd come back from a serious injury and you'd been scoring goals. How many goals did you score to see Celtic to the 1956 Final?

I scored about six goals en route to the Cup. And to score a goal in the semi-final and to get all the headlines, Sharkey Fishes Celtic Out Of The Clyde, I thought that was special. I couldn't believe it. That was more the reason why I was upset. I sat the Final out in the stand. We went to Ferrari's after the game. I don't drink a lot but I was really upset for being dropped. That night I did have one or two too many so I thought I'd tell the manager what I thought about it. I wasn't very happy. I walked up to the top table and told Mr Kelly and Mr McGrory that I would have played for their team for nothing but that now they could stick it up their bum, Mr Kelly in particular. And I walked away. The following Tuesday evening they called me into the office and Mr Kelly told me he'd never been spoken to in such a manner. He'd only one good arm, you know, and his hand was wrapped round this piece of paper like a charge sheet held up to his face. I was in my training gear and I told him I was sorry and that, I didn't have a habit of drinking but I was upset because I got dropped and I felt I was responsible for getting them into the Final of the Cup. And they – they accepted that and they all gave me a clap. Then the next Tuesday, a week later, the manager had me in the office and told me there were one or two clubs after me so I felt that it was the end of the road up there.

Jim, you were in the team that went down to Elland Road on 3 December 1956, Leeds United 3, Celtic 4. Do you remember John Charles? He was inside-right for Leeds and you were inside-left for Celtic. You must have bumped into each other.

John Charles was, I would say, the best all-rounder I ever played against. He lives beside my brother in Wetherby, a little village called Cliftonville. Oh aye, I remember him all right. He used to do a lot of shouting. Oh, a brilliant player.

Did you do a lot of shouting on the park?

Ah, I think I was a bit shy. I felt that because everybody was older than me, I didn't think I should. I might have had a few words now and again. Sometimes it's good just to keep your mouth shut. One incident I remember was against Aberdeen at Pittodrie and I'd just walked round Fred Martin, the goalkeeper. I was just trying to roll the ball into the net. Neilly Mochan came running in very nearly on top of me, "Leave it! Leave it!" and we both missed it. I didn't know whether I was going to hit it or he was going to hit but we both missed it. I always remember that for a shout I could have done without.

Did you have any hopes at all of going on the USA tour of 1957?

Oh yes. We went and played Motherwell reserves on a Wednesday evening. They were a great team in the making, Ian St John and Pat Quinn and Andy Weir. I think we won 1-0. I was injured that night, my Achilles tendon went, and we were going to America on the Friday. I had my blazer and my injections and everything. Then the manager came up to me and said, "There's no use taking you, Jim, because you're going to be off for about six weeks." So they didn't take me.

That was a blow.

That was a blow, yeah. He came up to me at the back of the bus. That was a big blow to me, yeah. I went to my own doctor. Willie Johnstone, who was the trainer then, went off to America with the boys. I went to my own doctor and my own doctor had me fit in a fortnight. Which was amazing, you know. That was a big blow in my career. Alex Dowdells was special when you had an injury. Alex said to me one day I got injured," Now look, you can't lie down with these things, you've got to exaggerate the movement." That was his favourite saying, Exaggerate the movement. He was never a man for making you sit out. He'd make you do exercises. I thought he was good. He was Scotland's trainer so he must have been pretty good.

When Alex Dowdells trained a team, was he training them for physical fitness?

No, medical fitness.

Medical fitness? He used to wear a white coat. Even with Scotland.

That's right, yeah. Like a dentist. But I wouldn't have liked him to pull my teeth out. He was too nervous. He'd a nervous attitude. But he was a good man. You don't become trainer of Scotland if you're not any good. I don't think he was so much a trainer as a medical man but they called them trainers in those days. But at Celtic Park we had a doctor, Dr Fitzsimons, Johnny Fitzsimons. He was a left-winger in his day. You couldn't get a word in edgeways, you know. He told you what, he knew exactly what was up with you.

Now, on 21 September 1957, in the League, Rangers 2, Celtic 3, Celtic's first full points at Ibrox since 21 September 1935. The forward line is Sharkey and Collins; McPhail; Wilson and Tully.

I remember that game. I played against Eric Caldow. There was something about that game that suited me that day. Everything suited me. Caldow was a fair player. He was very quick, very fast. You'd get past him and he was back again, good powers of recovery. I think I had a fair game that night.

What was George Young like to play against?

George Young was a tower of strength in the middle of the park. I was never very fast but I used to take the ball up, through their legs and things like that. It gave you yards of space to work on, playing shimmies and little things like that, my way of playing football. In the main, I gave the centre-half a wide berth. So I never really saw a lot of him.

Now, Jim, you're getting near the end of your time at Parkhead when you play against Rangers reserves: Sharkey and Jackson; Conway; Divers and Byrne. Jim Conway has an outstanding night.

Did he score a hat-trick then?

No, it's 2-1 only, Conway and Ryan scored. Now there's another failed prospect, Jim Conway.

Conway should have made the grade. His heading ability was brilliant, he was strong as an ox, he could shoot. I just don't know why he didn't make it. He had every chance, he had a good chance because he was a natural centre-forward. Very few of the centre-forwards at Celtic in my time were genuine centre-forwards. Conway was a natural. He was never makeshift. I never thought to myself I could play centre-forward but it suited my style because I could fall deep. Because I couldn't run very fast I'd pick it up deep and spread it about. Centre-halves didn't like you to do that, they liked you up so they could tackle, hit you when they wanted to hit you. I used to fall back, I was more like the Don Revie type of centre-forward. When I used to get it, I'd make room for myself, push it through, because I enjoyed playing it that way, you know. But Jim Conway, he'd all the ability to go the full distance. I don't know what happened to his career. I remember him very, very clearly, short blond hair, well-built, quick, good in the air. I don't know what he lacked. He must have lacked something.

One of the big disappointments, Jim Conway's failure to develop. Now on 19 October 1957, the League Cup final versus Rangers, the 7-1 game. You weren't on the park. Were you at the match?

No, I never saw that game. I don't know why I never saw it.

Were you surprised when you heard the result?

Do you know something, I can't even remember hearing the result! I can't remember the game. It was only just recently when I read about Billy McPhail that I knew he played that day. To this day, I can't remember anything about Celtic beating Rangers 7-1. But they all talk about it. Whenever I go home to Scotland, I always go up to Celtic Park and have a bit of lunch and the 7-1 team, their photograph's up there, and I often think I wish it had been me up there with them. That was my era anyway.

On 8 November 1957, you go to Airdrie. Why Airdrie?

Well, I chose Airdrie because I thought their little stadium would suit me and it was nice and everything was so neat. The chap who came to see me was the manager, Willie Steel. He was a man's man. He spoke how he felt, you know, he wasn't fly, he knew what he wanted. He told me I could do a job for him, I'd suit his team. I said, "Well…" He gave me a lot of money, he gave me £750 in 1957. I bought a house for £600. I didn't hesitate in going to Airdrie and I was there along with Lawrie Leslie who was Scotland's goalkeeper, Dougie Baillie, Gibby Ormond, all these great players. I was the star man of the team. At the end of the season I was nominated the supporters' Player of the Year. And what I enjoyed about it, Eugene, was when I played against Rangers or Celtic, I used to take the ball out to the wing and the centre-half would never come with me, I used to wave to whoever it was, "Come over here, the ball's over here!" And the crowd loved it. You know, Broomfield was so compact. I had some great games against Celtic and Rangers. I played with a chap called John McGill. He was on one side of me and Jim Storrie that went to Leeds United, he was on the other. I would pick the ball up, away deep in my own half, then it was me and John McGill, up the park, me to you, you to me, we left the Rangers players standing. I always remember that, I don't know why, I had a special day that day.

What was it like playing against Bobby Evans?

Lovely. I loved it. Bobby didn't like you dribbling and that. He always wanted a chance to get his tackle in. But he was a great, great player, Bobby Evans, a great wing-half and then a great centre-back.

He was. Now, Jim, you were known as the Tully of Broomfield. Right? I mean, why the difference between the character you were at Parkhead and the one you developed into?

I felt at Airdrie I was a better player than everybody else. I'd come from Celtic. I'd come down the ladder a wee bit but we were still a First Division team. I'd played not with better blokes but with better players. I just felt ten foot tall. I used to go out there, I wanted the ball all the time, you know. I always remember playing the ball into the back of the net and I went over on my wrist, my thumb jumped, jumped up out of place, like away out here. I ran round the park, shouting for the trainer, "Bobby, Bobby, look!" Bobby Reid was the trainer. He got a hold of it, jerked it back into place – "…aaaggghhh!" Crowd going crazy. I remember that, yeah. I was well thought-of at Airdrie. I thought it was a Rangers supporters' area – if you didn't support Airdrie you supported Rangers. Rangers had a big support there. Airdrie used to play to 4-5,000 people. I was used to playing to 30,000 people. So that was little bit of a comedown.

You left Airdrie under a cloud, in fact it was a calumny, and you've repudiated this before, but on the first of April 1961, Airdrie met Celtic at Hampden in the semi-final of the Scottish Cup. You were accused of not trying against your old mates.

I'll tell you something, I've still got a letter from The Bhoys – that's how it's signed – The Bhoys, and it says, Don't forget you're one of us, if you get up to any of your old tricks, we'll be looking for you. I never thought for one minute I wasn't going to try. I wouldn't say I didn't try. They beat us 4-0. I was playing against Billy McNeill. So I got this letter, postcard it was. I don't think I ever told anyone about the threat but I didn't have a good game. And the way it was with the press, I built it up during the week. I told the press that I was going to get my brolly and stick it over at the corner flag with my bowler hat on it and Billy McNeill could stand there all day. But it didn't work out with Billy McNeill. He ran all over the top of me. A brilliant centre-half. Every department.

So now, Jim, you move off to Bert Herdman at Raith Rovers. Up into Fife. That was a long way to go, was it not?

I've got to tell you a story about this. The story is, I'm playing for Airdrie. Bert Herdman contacted Airdrie. He said he was looking for a centre-forward. They had a discussion and Willie Steel asked me what I thought, so I said, "I don't mind if there's something in it for me." So we met Bert Herdman in Edinburgh, me and Willie Steel, in this hotel, and the effect Bert had on me, I've never laughed so much in all my life! In himself, he was one of the funniest men I have ever met. I signed for Raith. The conditions were all right, they suited me fine, I was very happy. And then Bert put his hand round my shoulder and he said, "Ohh, ohhhh, I like you, I like you!" – he'd a very bad stutter, Bert – "I like you because you laugh at my jokes!" What he didn't realise, I was laughing at him, poor Bert. What I'm going to tell you now, you'll crack up. We were playing Dunfermline for the local derby. Well. He came in there and he said, "Now then, lads, just – just you go out today," he says, "and do the business," he says. "Make me happy." So we went out, playing Dunfermline, and we're winning two-nothing at half-time. He came in and he said, "Ohhhh," he said, "this is – this is great!" he said. "When you go out for the second half, listen, keep the ball up in the air. If you keep the ball in the air, they can't score goals up there." So the outcome is, we get beat 3-2. We come off at the finish and Bert comes into the dressing-room, hands held out like Jesus on the cross. "Boys," he said, "whoever's got the nails, I'm ready. Pu' – pu' – pu' them in!" We were doubled up, I'm telling you. That was the Shankly-Herdman era of football. Talk about characters.

You broke your ankle with Raith Rovers.

I broke my ankle, that's right, against St Mirren. There was nobody near me. It was a wet day. I've got the ball on the centre line, I was just going to put it inside the full-back, he was a trialist, I think. Anyway, as I went to kick the ball, this other foot went from under me, I fell back on it. Well, that was a serious thing. That put me out of the game.

That was the end of your Scottish career.

Yeah. I was happy when the manager of Cambridge United came to see me. It was Bertie Auld gave me a lot of good advice about the money to be had down here. He said non-League clubs have got plenty money, so that was my next move and here I am today.

Jim, thank you very much.

Eugene. No problem. Any time.

Iain Gillies
Centre-half
1954-1955

Iain, New Zealand is a long way from Parkhead but I think you still have some strong feelings for Celtic.

The Celtic experience for me was great. It still influences my life and always will. I didn't have long there and I didn't make the break-through to the first team but what was important is that I got there, rubbed shoulders with my heroes, Bertie Peacock, Sir Charles Patrick Tully, Prince of Ireland, Bobby Evans, Willie Fernie, Neilly Mochan and John McNeverPhail. And all the others of the 1954-55 season. I even got to play with them. Manager Jimmy McGrory asked me to go on full-time training during the University holidays when I was a student at Edinburgh. Believe me, those holidays even began to appear in mid-term. But those full-time days were really Paradise for me.

Did you find that an enormous step-up, training with players who had just won the Double?

There was certainly an ability gap between us and the first-teamers. Here's a quote from my 1954-55 diary: 'The Boss is not too happy with my extended holiday. Feels it'll affect my studies too much. But Billy Gillies' mum says I can stay with them as long as I want. Been there three weeks now. Great people. Billy took me up to stay for the weekend and Mrs G. said I could stay on. Charlie put one over me at training today. I was coming out of defence with the ball and looked up to pass it. Green and white hoops everywhere I looked. And every time I shaped up to pass, Bertie, Bobby or Willie would be like shadows moving in to pick it off. I panicked a bit and decided to push forward myself with the ball. Surged forward, but got my head down too much and heard the shout, "Shoot! Shoot! The 'keeper's out!" After three seasons as a forward with Nairn County in the Highland League, I fancied myself as a goalscorer so I let fly. I hit the ball well and it flew from my right foot. But when I looked up, Johnny Bonnar was on his line and the ball bouncing gently into his arms. And there was Charlie just ten yards away from me with a big grin on his face: "Gotta keep the head up, son!" There were a few grins around but it was a valuable lesson.' The training was hard but George Paterson's Tuesday and Thursday night sessions for the reserve team were the toughest I ever experienced. I thought I was pretty fit. I didn't drink, I didn't smoke, and I trained nearly every day to build up strength in my suspect right knee. Mr Paterson was *The Man*. He'd been to where we all wanted to go – the top. He could be tough but he also had a kind streak in him. He was an understanding person. Jimmy Gribben was gruff with a quirky sense of humour. He had a great love of the game and of Celtic and a quiet presence we all respected. He was the other half of the reserve team hierarchy in those days. I say it was tough but not as tough as it would have been if I had not been fortunate enough to get picked up by Nairn County when I was playing centre-forward for Mallaig Stars at 15.

The Stars were just a team of mates who fancied themselves as would-be greats. We won the local league and I was asked to go for a trial with Morton. I played in their public trial for the Reserves against the First Team. Their centre-half, Gordon Thom, never gave me a sniff of the ball during the first 30 minutes and I think he began to feel sorry for me. He started telling me what to do: "Don't wait for the ball to come to you, son. Go and meet it or I'll win it every time. Move about more! Drag us out of position! Call for the ball!" The ground was heavy but the weather was fine. Johnny Hannigan was having a great game for us on the right wing and he cut one back which I belted in with a left-foot volley. I scored another with a header from his cross in the second half and felt really pleased with myself when I slipped a third quietly into the net past Jimmy Cowan, one of Scotland's greatest ever goalies. The ref ruled that one offside so I missed out on the hat-trick. Coming off the field, Cowan patted me on the head and said, "Well done, lad!" I felt 100ft tall. Actually, I was then six feet two inches and built like a stick, all arms and legs. It was a great introduction to the professional game but it wasn't enough to persuade me to take my shorts and underpants off and get into the big communal bath with the rest of the players. I washed my hands and face and got my clothes on while nobody was looking. It was mind-boggling to meet Cowan, Thom and Tommy Orr. The following Saturday I played in a trial game for Nairn against Forres in the North of Scotland Cup and they signed me after I scored a flukey goal with a miskick. I was at school in Fort William then and travelling from Fort William to Nairn every weekend wasn't easy but again it was a great experience and I loved my time at Nairn under Johnny Mathers, a former St Johnstone player. I started University in Edinburgh and got a letter from Hearts' manager, Tommy Walker, inviting me to play a trial. It's the beginning of the 1954-55 season. Fort William are playing Port Glasgow Hibs in the Scottish Amateur Cup and I'm marking a guy with wings on his feet. He's giving us hell and as I say, I'm supposed to be marking him. He's chunky, big in the shoulders and one of those centre-forwards who doesn't hold the ball. He just darts back to meet it, knocks it back and then takes off on a shallow run, making sure he's never offside. I'm worried because our full-backs don't swivel. They like to go forward and they leave me as the last man all the time. The Port Glasgow ground is hard and the ball is bouncing high, making it awkward to judge. It's only about 30 minutes into the game and the scores are level when the ball comes swirling high upfield. My man scoots back to meet it and I go with him. But just after we've crossed half-way and he's obscuring the ball from me, suddenly he turns and darts back past me. I realise it's bouncing high and it's going to go over my head – and I'm the last man. I leap high. It's a great catch and the beauty of it is, there's no yellow or red cards in those days.

You'd have been sent off nowadays.

He called me a big skinny bastard but my team mates were full of congratulations: Great stuff, Rodgie!

Rodgie?

My dad was nicknamed Rodgie and in the village I was Wee Rodgie. We were expected to do almost anything to save a goal in those days. But anyway, I was just hoping that nobody from Hearts was watching. I gave myself a good shake-up and decide I'm going to get really stuck-in to this centre-forward because, in my own mind, I'm still playing too tentatively. It's three months since I had an operation at Raigmore Hospital and in that time my whole focus has been on building-up my quads, the thigh muscles that had become a bit wasted after the leg had been three or four weeks in plaster. My striker took off on another angular run out to the wing and I tried to go with him. He got to the ball first and I had to launch a sliding tackle from away downtown to get a block on him. This worried me. Obviously I needed to sharpen up. I'd been preparing for two weeks at Tynecastle for my trial and felt I wasn't doing too badly. But this game against Port Glasgow Hibs was telling me different. Now the unbelievable happens. In the dressing-room, a man in a raincoat congratulates us. No one pays much attention to him. He doesn't mind. He chats and laughs. This middle-aged man is a club scout but he isn't letting on which club.

He turns to me, "Good game. son, but you're playing too deep. You're covering both full-backs. One of them should always be covering you. Then you wouldn't have to play goalie on the halfway line." When I'm dressed he catches up with me outside. He reveals his identity: Teddy Swift, ex-centre-half himself, Celtic scout. He wants me to go through to Celtic Park on Tuesday at 5.30 pm to talk to the manager, Jimmy McGrory. Could I do that? Oh, yes, no trouble. I was trying to sound normal but my voice must have sounded as squeaky as a mouse under Wild Young Tusky's foot. Meet Jimmy McGrory! Inwardly, I'm screaming. I'd go to the bloody moon to meet Jimmy McGrory!

So I walked awe-struck through the Parkhead doors on the Tuesday night. I'd got a taxi from Queen Street station to Parkhead and the driver must have realised the condition I was in. "In ye go, son," he said. "They'll no' eat ye! No' until after they've seen ye play onyway!" Inside, the first thing to strike me was the emptiness. There seemed to be nobody around. I waited and listened. I was standing there in total awe when someone spoke at my shoulder, a friendly voice, "Can I help you?" I jumped. I said, "Yes please, I have an appointment with Mr McGrory." I was Iain Gillies from Mallaig and I'd just come through from Edinburgh University. He was a tall man in a white shirt and dark suit. "I'm Desmond White, club secretary." He told me to follow him. We stopped at a door and he knocked. He ushered me in and away he went. I was alone with Jimmy McGrory. Jimmy McGrory stood up and shook hands with me. There was an air of gentle benevolence about him that set me totally at my ease. He wanted to sign me straightaway on a provisional form. He'd probably farm me out to a Glasgow junior club to let me mature as a defender. I'd be on £2 a week and I'd need to travel through from Edinburgh every Tuesday and Thursday for training with the part-timers. Was that okay? I couldn't believe what was happening to me and I think he took my bewilderment for uncertainty. He asked me was I not happy with that? I said it was fine but what about Hearts? He said, "Are you a Celtic supporter?" "Hell, yes," I said. He shrugged his shoulders. There was no problem if I wanted to sign for Celtic. Hearts had had nearly three weeks to have a look at me and to do something. They hadn't done anything yet. I signed the form he placed in front of me. I was to come through on Thursday and bring my boots. Celtic were experimenting with a new stud formation and they'd re-stud them for me, one stud in front of the front two. It cut down on the strain on the knee muscles when you had to turn quickly. I reported back to Parkhead on the Thursday. I was introduced to John McPhail, Neil Mochan and the great Alec Boden of Evans, Boden and Baillie in the 1951 Cup-winning side. I wondered if anyone at home would believe it if I told them. I was in the players' recreation room. There was a game of snooker going on and a lot of banter. I noticed nobody was smoking. That first game I played for the reserves on the Saturday, George Paterson and Jimmy Gribben were in charge and they looked as if they'd stand no nonsense. The Aberdeen reserves were at Parkhead. We were in the home dressing room. I counted 18 players. The famous green and white hoops were hanging from the wall but who would be wearing them? Then George Paterson read out the team. The goalkeeper was Eamon McMahon from Lurgan. I caught some of the other names: Frank Meechan, Vince Ryan, Mike Conroy, Iain Gillies. I couldn't believe it! Had he confused me with Billy Gillies? No. George Paterson told me I was centre-half. I was going to have to pull a game and a half out of the bag. My season in Paradise was about to begin. Jimmy Gribben handed me my boots. The studs were extra long and I liked that. They'd put the new ones in as promised. But I just sat there. I was in a real daze. George Paterson had to tell me to make a move. I was numb. I just nodded. It was ridiculous. We had John McPhail and Neilly Mochan in the side. What right did I have even to be in the same changing room as them? I began to strip off and felt puny in comparison with the guys around me. I was like a string bean. The other fellows were built like professional boxers. I didn't linger long without a shirt on. I pulled the Celtic jersey over my head for the first time and the green and white made a complete and utter wreck of me. I wasn't numb any more. I was like a wrecked ship, crushed by the Arctic ice. I just could not credit that my legs were mine. They seemed determined to go in opposite directions. I think George Paterson told me to get on the bench and get my legs rubbed. Jimmy Gribben began to slap on the linament. My muscles were being stretched like chewing gum. He began to trace the scars on my right knee where I'd had the operation. He began to poke them and prod them. Each time he'd stare into my face and say, "Can you feel that?" I said no and it wasn't a lie. I was so numb, I could feel nothing anywhere. I got off the bench and pulled my socks up. All I had to do now was walk down the tunnel. I just did not know what was the matter with me. The dressing room by now was a welter of noise and I had to find some calm. Out of this panic I had to find confidence. I wanted to give of my best but how? If I didn't, I would be scarred for life. This was my big chance. I might fail but I wanted to fail having done my best. I went to the toilet and I went down on my knees. I called on God not to let me make a fool of myself, not to let Iain Gillies let the Celtic down badly. I prayed the Morning Offering and I felt the peace coming over me like a sea mist, rolling and slow. The nervousness was gone and I felt strong, mentally and physically. I would give the game everything I had on offer and if it wasn't enough, I'd have no regrets. Then we began to file down the long darkness of the players' tunnel into the daylight and the roar from 10,000 fans. I was entering a new world. We kicked in as usual and then the whistle sounded for kick-off. Now I could see the man I had to mark. His name was Jackie Dunbar and he looked big, at least six-foot three. The ground was covered by a layer of slush but underneath it was frozen hard. My long studs were gripping well and my footing felt sure enough. All around me, the players are talking, encouraging, snapping, calling for the ball. I watched Dunbar moving around like a prowler on a dark night. The ball was bobbing about in their half and I moved closer to him. "What's your name?" he asked. I was just about to blurt out, Iain Gillies, when it struck me that if he thought I was one of the Celtic regulars he might treat me with more respect. So I said nothing. "Are you John Jack?" he said. I nodded, just enough so as to keep him worried. I was still feeling smug when the ball came fast to Dunbar. Before I could get in a tackle, he let fly. It had goal written all over it. He was prancing up in the air and his mates were swamping him with congratulations. I had got so wrapped in my psychological Highland cunning that I hadn't been concentrating enough on the game. I could see the grin on his face as we lined up for the restart. He hadn't said anything but I could read the message: "John Jack, eh?" That'd be the day. I was another mug trialist. John Jack would have had him half way over the stand with his tackle. Those Aberdonians were piling on the pressure now. It was as if they knew they'd got us on the run. And they had. The ball was moving from man to man faster than I'd ever known it before. I kept arriving just too late to get the tackle in. A wave of red shirts kept racing through. They were all around me like swarms of wasps. Sweat got in my eyes and I rubbed it away. There was mud all over the sleeve of my shirt. Now it was all over my face. But I couldn't even remember being on the ground! Then the ball was loose on the left. My mind was screaming at me to make it, make it! If I slid in, I'd get him. But oh hell no, he'd cut it back inside, and I was swishing past him like a runaway sledge on a snow-slope. I looked round in alarm. I had a worm's eye view as a Pittodrie boot blasted in goal number two. And the crowd? The Faithful? The People? As we came out of the tunnel, we were their babies. Now the Jungle told us exactly what we were: "Yerrapackabloodymugs!" And a few minutes later when the ball broke to a red raider in our surging, seething mud-bound penalty area and ended in a swirling bulge at the back of our net for number three, you can imagine Glasgow anger at its peak. Blood wasn't enough. They wanted scalps, instant burial, anything. The faces behind our goal leaped into a snarling, cursing focus. I stood there gasping and I could hear them shouting at me, "Come oan, Jessie! Getyerhairootayereyes!" Goalkeeper Eamon McMahon was glaring at the bedraggled world around him and the players were glaring back at him. This wasn't a place to hang around. I was just glad it wasn't Dunbar who had hit that one in. My mates weren't happy about the situation. Vince Ryan was looking grim. Nobody could call Neilly Mochan Smiler now. He looked ready to make mincemeat of all of us back there. This was poison to him. He needed a good game to get back into the first team where he belonged. This was a Celtic defence with more holes in it than a machine-gunned bucket. We were three down in 20 minutes but there was a long way still to go.

You must have felt bad!

But I was determined if they got another it wouldn't be my fault. It was desperation defending now. Even wee Eric Smith, our pocket dynamo on the left-wing was back in the penalty area tackling. Then the ball went to Dunbar and I flung myself into the fray. I couldn't believe it, but I won it. I had fathomed the thing out. Don't wait for it to happen. Anticipate. Move in quicker. Look for it to bounce about a yard away from him if it's coming at him fast. I slipped it to McPhail who set an attack in motion but moments later the Dons were back. I could read the next move. It had to be to Dunbar. Joe O'Neil gave it hard and low but I could see it all the way and again I got in fast enough to win it. But back came the Dons and this one was a bullet. If I don't get it, it's in. I put everything into my jump, I made clean contact and managed to head it out from just under the crossbar. Then Mochan got a goal and half-time came in a blur.

What did George Paterson have to say?

A flow of words! Some hot, some encouraging. All I know is we went out a much more confident team for the second half. Mochan banged in another glorious goal and we were right on top. I remember wondering what had made me think professional football was tough at this level! The ball came soaring into our penalty area. I trapped it really clean and pushed it forward. Dunbar came rushing in to challenge. I pretended to blast it clear but twisted at the last second and trailed it away sideways. Really classy. I slipped it upfield and the crowd cheered. Two minutes later, the same thing all over. But Dunbar had anticipated the sidestep this time and instead of buying the dummy, he leaped straight into my path, robbed me of the ball and went right through. McMahon came racing out and I knew my future hung suspended on the next fraction of a second. If I give a goal away it's curtains. They'll never forgive me and serves me right for being so damn smart. But trust Eamon. He made a miraculous save at Dunbar's feet. I lived again. Meanwhile the pain was back in my knee. It came like a sharp burn and the joint seemed loose and week. It frightened me. It wasn't going to happen all over again, surely? I'd already had the one operation up in Raigmore Hospital in Inverness. I'd been one whole summer when I couldn't even climb the stairs at home. It had been so good lately. But it was just as if it was refusing to do any more work. Mike Conroy had spotted it. He asked me, Is there anything wrong?

He would have known. Poor fellow was hardly free from injury in about seven years at Celtic.

I said I was okay and I followed him up the field. That was when the whistle sounded and it was all over. Had I done enough? Was it the end or the beginning? I looked around me to savour the moment. A grey, drab Glasgow afternoon had closed in on the stadium. The crowd was drifting quietly away, a legion of disappointed faces under cloth caps, hunched backs swaying towards the exits. I trudged off the field on my own. My legs were like lead now. They were so tired it was painful. It must have been the nervous energy, the sheer magic of the occasion that had kept me moving. The others were all ahead of me and the tunnel was dark and cool. I thought of all the great players who had walked this way down the years. I was not far behind big John McPhail as I reached the changing room door. Nobody had said anything to me so I couldn't have done very much out there. But I knew deep down inside that I'd done my very best. There could be no regrets really if they didn't sign me as a professional. Big John turned in the doorway as I came up and held out his hand. His face was sober: "Well played, son. Have they signed you yet?" He seemed to sense the mixture of awe and humility I felt as he shook my hand because his face relaxed into a smile: "Well, don't worry, they will." Then Neilly Mochan, Alec Boden and the others came forward to shake my hand. I had to fight back the tears. I had never felt so happy. These players felt that I had done my job well out there today. That was more than I ever expected. I was a long time just sitting there in the room amid the mud-stained, sweat-soaked green and white jerseys. Somehow I wanted this moment to drag on and on. I felt I'd been welcomed into Heaven by Saint Peter and the Disciples. But Jimmy Gribben ushered me towards the big communal bath in which the others were laughing and joking. It hadn't been such a bad day for them either. They'd fought back hard and been unlucky not to get a draw. Afterwards, as a team, we had dinner in Ferrari's restaurant.

222, Buchanan Street.

Was it? I had to try very hard to disguise the fact that my right knee felt like a furnace. I must have made a good job of it. I was told I wouldn't be farmed out to a junior team after all. They reckoned I was ready to sign as a full professional, not as a provisional. I was as proud as any man could ever be when I signed for Celtic on the dotted line.

This was at Ferrari's?

No, this was the following Tuesday, Mr McGrory's office. But my proudest moment was still to come when I went home to the Highlands the following weekend and told my father and mother that I'd signed for Celtic. I was the first Mallaig kid to make it! I handed over my £20 signing-on fee and told him I'd be getting £9 a week and would send them on what I could. Billy Gillies asked me how much I'd got as a signing-on fee so I said, "Oh, the usual…£20." He raised his eyes skywards and said, "You're a mug, Iain. If you'd have asked for the grandstand they'd have given it to you. The players reckoned they'd never seen anyone play a better trial." "Fair enough, Billy," I said to him, "but I can only pray that hard once every ten years." I think I said the *Memorare* every time the ball came near me. He didn't seem to know what the *Memorare* was. It's the famous prayer to Our Blessed Lady. I began to say it for him but I was halfway through when he stopped me. "Okay, okay, I get the message. On second thoughts, the way you played, I think she must have got it too!" I was full of confidence and perhaps too full. I remember going into the dressing room on a Saturday and sitting down under peg number five. Before the team was announced and without thinking, I began to take my jacket off. Billy was standing next to me and said very quietly, "Hell, I wish I had your neck." As the season progressed I enjoyed a number of games at wing-half including a win in extra time in a replay at Parkhead in the Reserve Cup. After the game, the club medico, Dr Fitzsimons came up to me and said, "Great game today, son. You reminded me very much of a young Doug Cowie. Keep it up." I was chuffed because Cowie was the Scottish international wing-half and I'd played at centre-half on Saturday before being switched to wing-half for the replay.

It's a big change.

It's a big change because the wing-half has to do far more running and we had gone to extra time. Towards the end of the season I was given a few games at outside-right. I could never understand why.

Celtic tradition. Celtic players play anywhere.

Yes, but although I was comfortable playing up front, Jimmy Rowan was a far better winger than I would ever make. The trouble was, we had also such fine half-backs in Eric Smith, Dave Duffy, Mike Conroy, Ian Reid, Vince Ryan and for much of the time, John McPhail as he worked his way back to fitness. Out there on the right wing, I probably did the club a grave disservice in my last game for them. There was great disappointment when the first team drew with Clyde in the Cup Final on the Saturday. On Monday the 25th, the reserves were playing Hearts at Tynecastle. I was stuck out on the right like a limp, elongated dandelion. The ball came out to me where I j was enjoying my status as the player just in front of a packed grandstand. I stuck out my left foot as the ball was coming to me at shin-high height. I flicked it with all the delicate aplomb of a Highland League winger so that it dropped nicely in front of me. Then I booted it hopefully towards the distant burliness of our lone star striker, converted full-back and master of all trades, Sean Fallon. Sean would break anybody's boots in for them no matter what size they were and in his bare feet too. He took just one glance at my inch-perfect pass and blasted the ball into the net to earn us a 1-1 draw and himself a place at centre-forward in the Scottish Cup final replay just two nights later which Celtic lost 1-0. I always wondered whether they would have played Sean up front if he hadn't scored that goal at Tynecastle. He was far better at full-back and would probably have creamed Tommy Ring before he scored that winning goal for Clyde. And big John McPhail could have led the attack in the replay. Och well, great days. They didn't last long enough for my liking but they gave me that Celtic experience to take with me for the rest of my life. After Celtic, I knew that team spirit is not something that binds us together on a football field only but in the workplace, in the home and on the streets. I never saw anyone at Parkhead who wasn't a Celtic supporter and I never met a second teamer that had a bad word to say about the seniors.

And you got a free transfer? Rejected after one season?

I never thought of it as a rejection, just that I had to move aside for better players. After all, we all play to different levels and there are always teams out there looking for ex-Celtic players.

So you weren't hurt?

Hurt? Of course I was hurt. There's a little bit of you that bleeds forever. But I'll always be grateful to coach George Paterson. Just by chance he came into my compartment on the Glasgow-Edinburgh train on my last day at Parkhead. He said, "Iain, I just want you to know you didn't get a free on my recommendation. I told them you played well for me and you deserved another season. But there's a crop of new players coming in and some of you have been a bit unlucky." Those words helped. The shock had been all the sharper because my three Irish mates, Vince Ryan, Eamon McMahon and Eddie Mulvey had told me that they had overheard the chairman Bob Kelly talking to the Boss: "Have you signed Iain Gillies on for next season yet?" Mr McGrory had answered, "No, not yet. I'm going to get him when he comes through for training on Tuesday night." This was outside Mr McGrory's office. That's what they said there and then they went in. I don't know but after what the boys told me I was happily confident that I would be retained for 1955-56. Then on the Sunday I read my name in the list of free transfers. I was all on my own at the time in Aquinas House, my University digs. I was absolutely stunned. I had no dough and my final exams for the year were still some time away. I went out for a walk, sorted things out in my mind and decided the best thing was to be grateful for the chances I'd been lucky enough to get. I'd go through and thank my mates for all their encouragement, clear up my stuff in Edinburgh and hitch-hike home to Mallaig. And that's what I did. At home I had a couple of months in which to prepare myself for the next stage in my life. I cut the hay on my auntie's craft at Bracara on the banks of Loch Morar and decided to get my two years compulsory National Service out of the way. But every step of the road, the Celtic experience has been my constant inner strength.

Iain, thank you very much.

Thank you.

Joe Logan
Kelly Kid
1956-1959

(Questions asked by Charlie Gallagher are in italics)

I've got a record of you, Joe, in a game against Dumbarton at Boghead for Jim McLean's dependants. That must have been a Sons' player that died. This was 12 March 1958.

No wonder they call it Boghead. It was a right muddy hole that night.

The team was Beattie; Meechan and Kennedy; Crerand, McNeill and Ian White; Gallagher and Roy Paton; Joe Logan; John Colrain and John Colquhoun senior. Now you were an ex-Maryhill Harp player?

I was provisionally signed by Celtic. In those days you couldn't sign full professional until you were 17. I was at Celtic Park from when I was 14 years of age with Charlie here. That was Easter 1956. They farmed us out in those days to Maryhill Harp. I was a big lad and big Stein maintained it was to fatten you up et cetera. It was to toughen you up they put us in the juniors. They put you in the juniors right away. Dunky MacKay was there, John Burns who signed for Celtic was there, John Colquhoun, Ian Burns and the big left-back who was with Celtic a couple of years, Hughie Thomlinson. He came from Possil. He was there a few years. Bertie Auld was outside-left.

I had no idea you played for the Harp as early as that. You must have been very young when you played junior then.

I was. I played junior when I was 14 years of age. I played against Maryhill for Maryhill Harp and that was the local derby. There were about 3,000 at that game. That was at Lochburn.

But you were a big fellow at 14, though, Joe.

I was inside-right in the hustle and bustle of the junior game in those days and we beat Maryhill that particular night. It was just like a dream come true because you're at school and you're invited to play. Do you want to hear the wee story how I got freed by Celtic? I was a wee bit unfortunate and I'll tell you why. I was serving my time as a heating engineer from 15. When I wasn't playing I wanted to do my trade. So I asked Howden's, a big engineering firm in the Garscube Road next door to me where I came from, I asked Howden's if they'd take me on, and I happened to get in there at 15. I was working away from home but I was back home every weekend. I didn't work away at weekends and there was one time we were on a job at Dumfries and I was home every weekend to play football. I was training with Queen of the South and they wanted to sign me because I showed up not bad. Then one Tuesday night at Parkhead – I'll never forget it – I said to big Jock, "Jock,

I'm going to Dumfries tomorrow, but I'm home on Friday night, I don't work the weekends, I'm home every Friday to play. I'm all right to play on Saturday, we've got the Junior Cup." He said, "Oh, this is not good enough. You better go and see the Boss." The Boss was Jimmy McGrory but it wasn't Jimmy McGrory he meant, it was Mr Kelly. The Boss had nothing to do with anything, he just gave out the wages. So Mr Kelly came, and we talked and he offered me two choices. He said, "We'll need to get you away from this pipe-fitting game, we'll need you get you based in Glasgow, Joe." I said, "Well, have you no contacts in the heating will keep me in Glasgow or round about?" He said, "No. Do you fancy being a joiner?" Now, there was no way I could put two bits of wood together and make them hold. That wasn't my game. And I wasn't a mechanic. But can you imagine having to make that decision there and then in an evening? So I said to big Jock – I was humming and hawing, you know – I said, "Well I don't know" – trying to see a way out. He said, "Are you refusing?" I said, "No, but I like what I'm doing. Could you not accommodate me?" He said, "Leave it with us." So I had said no obviously. I came back six weeks later and that was it, they'd freed me.

It's strange you saying that about them giving you a choice of jobs you didn't want. They asked me to go full-time right away and never gave me a chance one way or the other. They didn't want me to take a trade.

Well, they wanted me, but I was 15.

Ah, you were younger. I was still at school till 17.

I left school at 15, Charlie. I was training with Queen of the South. Queen of the South made all the arrangements for me to train at Palmerston. They were in the old First Division then and they had a good team. Some of them used to train at Parkhead. Billy Houliston was there. They wanted me to sign but I said, "I'm not going to leave Celtic." So I was only 18 when I got my free from Celtic. This is the letter there from Jimmy McGrory. "29 April 1959. J. Logan, Esq., 6, Pitmilly Road, Drumchapel, Glasgow. Dear Joe. We very much regret that we have had to reduce our playing staff and in consequence we are giving you a free transfer at the close of the present season. The Board and Management wish to thank you for your services in the past and wish you every success in the future. Yours sincerely, signed J. McGrory, Manager." I was only 18 when I got a free transfer in '59.

That was young. That was young to get a free transfer. It took the stuffing out of me. Six weeks. Yet later on, big Jock and I were the best of friends when I was working at the sport on television – I went into television at 25.

Did Jock remember you?

Of course. Oh aye! I used to see them all coming in, the Celtic players, when I was on the outside broadcasts. What I meant to say was, I was playing left-half for the wee Celtic before John Clark. John came up from Birmingham.

You were the same type of player as Billy Price. Do you remember Billy Price? But you were more direct than Billy Price. Joe here would play an attacking sort of game whereas Billy would spray the ball about, but the same kind of tackling and hard graft.

I used to stand there with Big Billy and mop up the attacks.

McNeill?

Aye. But I was a wee bit versatile, remember? I played against Big Billy when we were both in junior football when Big Billy was with Blantyre Vics and we were with the Harp. I scored a hat-trick against him that day and oh, he did not like it! On Tuesday at the training big Stein said, "Oh, Joe gave it to Big Billy, didn't he!" And Billy was in a bit of a huff as well.

Did you play pre-season public trials, Joe?

Yeah, I played pre-season trials. I played inside-left to Bertie at outside-left.

Did you play in the shamrock strip? I call it Celtic's political strip.

I played in that.

Everybody played in that, Bobby Evans and all. Bertie Peacock, Sean Fallon, Charlie Tully, all the big first-teamers. I never got a chance to play a game with Charlie Tully but I knew him to talk to. I was never in the same team as him. It was too late. I played my first game in August 1959. Charlie played a few games in the reserve team but I never played in any games that Charlie was in.

Did you play with Charlie, Joe?

I played with Charlie once. I was inside-left to Charlie in a close season friendly. That was the only time I played with him and then as I say, big Stein, big Jock, pulled me back to left-half. I wasn't mobile enough.

You weren't the same speed as me, Joe.

Aye! Aye!

Jock used to say to me, "If you go up there, if you try to cross the halfway line, you'll never get back."

That was his way.

And then he would say to you, "What were you not up there, trying to score a goal for?"

Aye, some man.

So your knees went, Joe?

Oh, my knees, aye. I've actually got knee replacements now. Aye. I've had knee replacements for the last four years. And they're magic! Full knee replacements. Two. I had my first knee operation at 16 and that was at Maryhill Harp. They had a look at me at Parkhead. They didn't think it was cartilage. In those days what happened, they were going to send me for an X-ray but when Sir Robert Kelly saw me on the treatment table, he said, "Look at the legs he's got! It cannot be cartilage!" So what used to happen then, they had me on the park, and Doc Fitzsimons kicked the ball and I'm turning and twisting and my knee used to come out but I could push it in again myself. It was excruciating pain but I'd say, I'm all right because the thing was, you'd have run through a brick wall to play for Celtic. I used to just push it back in myself. And when I used to maybe go for a bus, run for a bus, oh-ya! Block. Push. You know? Terrible pain. Agony.

Talking with Celtic

Who was it? Was it Willie Johnstone and Jimmy Gribben?
Willie Johnstone.

They were the trainers in charge of fitness in those days.
Aye, but I went to – all the Celtic players went to a boxing trainer in those days, a guy from Maryhill, he took all the boxers, name of Dick Delaney. He did all the business in his own house. He was magic. I went to him once – I knew him from Maryhill Harp – I wasn't going to him a week before he said, "Joe, it's cartilage. Get right down to the Western and get an x-ray. See where I'm touching? If you'd touched that spot then where I'm touching now, I'd have hit that roof. And yet I wasn't feeling it to the same extent at all when I was pushing the knee back in.

Celtic were always famous for this right up to Brian Scott, the present day guy who came. Before Scotty they did not have a qualified man in that field. It was always maybe this or maybe that. They never knew a thing. It always ended up with sending us to Bon Secours. Nobody was capable.
This Dick Delaney used to look after all the boxers and all the footballers. Even the Rangers players used to go him. Bertie Auld, John Colrain, Dunky MacKay, they all went. That reminds me, I was at Parkhead the night Paddy Crerand signed. We were playing the Clyde that night and Paddy couldn't contain himself that he was finally signed. As you know, he gave up his job.

What was Paddy? I can't remember what Paddy was.
He was in the shipyards, apprentice shipwright or something.

How could you remember that? Yet I used to go about his house.
I knew Paddy well. He married this girl –

Noreen? Noreen Boyle?
I knew her. She used to get the bus – she stayed along the road from me in Drumchapel where that free transfer letter came to. To get from Drumchapel to Garscube Road, you'd get the 56.

They were originally from Gorbals Cross, Norfolk Street, I think.
There was another boy from the Gorbals that I used to pal around with, great big fellow – Kurila. I went on holidays with him.

John Kurila! Do you remember the amount of cannon fodder that passed through there?
At one time, there was that many, you had to go into the gym to get dressed.

To get dressed! I remember that!
There must have been about 40 or 50 boys. They were more or less just schoolboys.

The one who took me up was John Murphy, the Head of PE at Holyrood. He had a badly burned face. He had one of these fine voices and he used to do the pre-match

announcements at Parkhead. He had a good way with the rest of the Glasgow Catholic schools or with the PE teachers and he used to get the best of them and they all played against one another, the schools. And I think this was how the Kelly Kids originated actually, through John Murphy to Bob Kelly, through John Murphy from the various schools.

Mr McGowan, Alistair McGowan, was the man that took me from St Columba's because, Charlie, you and I played right through, starting with the under-11s for the Glasgow Schoolboys. Big John Colrain signed about the same time as Paddy. He used to come in here a lot when he was down at St Mary's School working.

He used to go down drinking in Quin's, down there in Bishopbriggs. In those days – you were away from Celtic Park by that time, Joe, but you obviously still knew what was happening – there was a crowd of them at that time and great potential. But they started drinking and I remember up at the George Hotel opposite Ferrari's where we used to go for a meal – the George Hotel was right across the road and they would end up in there with a lot of the Rangers players. Everybody would say, Oh, it's great, they're mixing but not all afternoon, after training. I think big John was one of the ones that stayed on in the George. He was a very skilful player. But I think he was slower than you or I, Joe? Very, very slow.

But didn't that show up in the juniors?

You could see it but you could also see a classy player. He was in a class of his own, he was oozing class as a junior, same as Paddy Crerand. He played in the same team as Paddy, Duntocher Hibs. That was a good team then, Crerand right-half, Colrain inside-right. He scored a lot of goals. He could hit a ball from 30, 40 yards, long distance. He always knew where the target was.

I think nowadays he'd be a midfield man, stroking the ball about.

If big John had got the by-pass, he'd be alive today. He developed heart trouble. For such a big sort of hard man, he was afraid to get the by-pass done. I used to say to him, "John, you'll need to get it done." He didn't have any weight problems but he wouldn't get it done. Bertie told me he used to say to him, "John, go and get it done," and John would say, "I can't, I can't!" And that was that.

Poor fellow. Did you know Jim Conway at Parkhead, Joe?

I did. I knew Jim very well. Actually, when I went to Norwich, Jim was at Norwich at that time. A wee man that should have gone to Celtic, wee Tommy Bryceland, was there at Norwich City too. He went from St Mirren.

Tommy Bryceland! He and I used to fight one another on the park – we hated one another's guts! Maybe he was jealous of me because I was playing for Celtic and he was still with St Mirren? And of course, we were the same position, inside-right. Tommy Bryceland, swearing! Spouting at you. I don't know if he was like that at Norwich in his later years –

He was like that at Norwich. Charlie, you didn't go junior until you were about 18?

Seventeen. I went to Yoker but I was a very fortunate guy when I went to Yoker Athletic. There was this wee guy played with Yoker and he was well known in junior football, he changed clubs every year, a guy called Willie Davidson. Willie would probably accept it as a compliment if I described him as the dirtiest player in the world! If he didn't get sent-off ten times in the one year, he was having a bad season! 5ft 4ins, 5ft 5in...

Bobby Murdoch was my minder at Celtic Park. Wee Willie was my minder at Yoker. It was the same at every club he went to, he was somebody's minder. But you were definitely too young to be playing junior, Joe.

That happened to me at St Roch's when we played against St Roch's. There were two brothers, Flynn, Tommy Flynn and Peter Flynn. And I happened to be playing well that night at Garngad. I happened to be playing well, I got through a few times, I was having a good game. Then the Peter fellow came to me, "If you go by me once more, I'm going to break your leg." So I was quite a big boy and I said to him, "Away you go," or certain other words to that effect, "...mind I don't break yours first." But from that minute on, I had it on my mind. So I fell for it. But that was it because after the game we were all pals. But I was never afraid. If somebody said they were going to hit me, so hit me then. It was all this, "I'll get you, I'll get you!"

My first game for Celtic against Rangers I was outside-right...

Bob Kelly exploiting your speed!

Aye probably, but I was standing on the centre line, the halfway line and Bobby Shearer came all the way up and said, "If you go by me, I'm going to break your leg." I said, "You'll need to catch me, Bobby." And I was the best of pals with Bobby Shearer! As you know yourself, Joe, off the park Bobby Shearer was one of the nicest guys you could meet. On the park, he was an animal, a man-eater, an utter animal. But that was him because Bobby Shearer was slow and he could only intimidate people. See when wee Jinky played – I don't think wee Jinky ever played against him – Jinky was too young – but he'd have torn him to shreds.

He'd have torn him apart.

Wee Jinky did it to everybody, you know.

There's that tape of him going round Provan, then coming back and going round him again and round again.

I've got all the Celtic tapes upstairs. I take the Celtic tapes over to Spain with me.

Have you got the '65 one with me in it?

Oh aye! Charlie, I've got them all! I was at that game, the Scottish Cup Final in '65.

Joe, if you and Charlie were the first two Kelly Kids, do you remember Roy Paton, number three?

Roy Paton, St Mungo's Academy. He played with us right through for the Catholic schools from the under-11s. He was at St Mungo's, Charlie was at Holyrood and I was at St Columba's. He played right through. But the odd thing about Roy is, he broke his leg as a boy. I think he was only 12 when it happened.

I don't know if you know how he finished but from what I heard, he went to Ireland. From what I've heard, he was a wee bit to the Republican movement.

Yeah. He disappeared. We never heard another thing about him. Nobody knows what happened the guy. I knew people that knew him but nobody knows what happened to him.

A Will o' the Wisp type player. A John White type player on the ball.

A smashing player. A good player. And he could score goals. And he had the heart of a lion. I think he played just once for the Celtic big team, in a Cup-tie against Clyde. I think the score was 1-0 for Celtic. It was round about 1959 but Roy only played the once.

I think when he played, he was inside-right and he had to be moved out onto the wing. I think the occasion was too much for him. I think Bertie Peacock moved him.

Yeah?

I think that was the way it was reported in the Sunday papers, the *Mail*, I think.

I don't think Bertie would move him. I don't know who would move him. You had your position and you kept it.

Well, Bertie was the skipper.

Bertie would be looking after himself on the park. In those days there was no you do this or you do that.

That wasn't until big Jock came.

It wasn't until big Jock came. There was no tactics talk when Jimmy McGrory was boss. We weren't too bad in the reserve team. We had Jock and Sean Fallon. They would try and tell you what to do but if you were playing for the first team, Jimmy McGrory would come in five minutes before the start of the game and say, "You're playing so and so today, you wingers be sure and cross the ball." That was our tactics talk. By the way, I met Joe last year and he said to me, "Do you realise this is the 42nd anniversary of the time we started at Parkhead?" It'll be 43 years this Easter, 2000. Actually, I'm scared to mention money here, Joe, in case I was getting more than you or you more than me. A fiver a month?

Correct. That was all we got, a fiver a month.

It was quite a lot of money in those days. We're talking 1955, 1956.

They used to send it to you during the close season as well, so they did.

I used to give it to my mother and do you know what my mother did right up until the day I got married? She kept it and gave it back to me on my wedding day. What was I going to do with it? I remember Paddy and I used to travel to Celtic Park. He lived in Thistle Street and I lived in Cumberland Street. The two of us used to walk down to the corner of Ballater Street – no, we walked to Glasgow Cross and under the railway bridge we'd get the number nine tram, that was only a penny or something.

It cost us a penny.

Tell me about Dunky MacKay.

Dunky was full of confidence. He was the most confident player I ever met. He was the best player in the world.

Yet he never really hit it off at right-half. They had to pull him back to right-back. He was a

Maryhill Harp player as well, you mind I told you?
He was a great player on the ball but off the ball he couldn't tackle a fish supper. He had to have the ball at his feet. You remember the guy that played right-back for Dundee, he died not long ago? Hamilton?

Alec Hamilton.

Alec Hamilton. He and Dunky were vying for the position of right-back in the Scotland team. Both of them thought, I'm a better right-back than him. That was their attitude. They were both the same type. I remember playing a game against Dundee one year and Dunky MacKay wanted the ball all the time to go up – we're talking about a right-back and Alex Hamilton was on the other side of the park – to take it up to Hamilton and stick it through his legs – nutmeg him! And Hamilton was the same, wanted to do it to Dunky! Dunky could have been at Lisbon.

He was ages with Bertie.

Dunky succeeded John Donnelly at right-back and Ian Young took over from Dunky but Dunky was something special. He should have been in the Celtic team for ever. Dunky was the forerunner of the attacking full-back.

To get back to you, Joe, who signed you? What were the circumstances of your being signed for Celtic?

It was because a few other clubs started milling around. Aberdeen made me one of the best offers and it was a good offer at that time, full time on £20 a week. I went over to the training at Parkhead and all of a sudden McGrory says to me after training, "Don't go away, Joe, I want to see you." The forms were all ready and I just went in and signed them.

How much did you get?

£20.

I got nothing. If I got £20, I cannot remember it.

Clyde had a good team in those days and they wanted to sign me as well, Harry Haddock and Basie Keogh. They had a good team then. Actually, Basie's married to my wife's cousin and Basie was trying to talk me into it. "Keep away from Celtic, Joe! Come to Clyde! You'll get taken here! You're guaranteed it. You know," he said, "You're just one of the many up there. You might never get your chance." But he knew I had to please myself. It was up to me. There was a chap that played for St Johnstone, Robert Reilly, a relative of my wife. He signed for Maryhill Harp, he was Celtic daft and he ran the Celtic Supporters' Club in Garscube Road for about 50 years. I told him what Basie had said and he said, "Och, no way, you go to Celtic." So I went to Celtic and then I got the injury. Do you know in the long run, it got so bad, I wakened up one morning – I was 50 – it was St Patrick's Day. I was going out to work at STV and I said to Jean, "I just cannot do it, I just can't go out, I cannot get out of this bed." And within a month I'd made a decision I was quitting. With these knees, I just couldn't go to work. I'd made the decision I was finished. And that was me, 25 years with STV and within the month I'd made the decision, I was finished. I'd been under this same man, Mr Remaschevski, for 20 years. He'd done everything. He'd broken my legs and relined them. I'd had 12 operations on my legs. My knees were completely gone.

This is because of playing so young?

Of playing so young. The standard was too much. It was hard.

You know, Joe, there was a television programme recently, I had it done to me – did you have such a thing as a cortisone injection? I had cortisone injections.

I had cortisone injections. I had them done as well. I only had two and I didn't take any more.

You took those two and you thought you were fit and you went out and you played, you played well.

In those days, I mean, the first knee operation I had, they had me back playing within six weeks. Yet cartilage in those days was a big thing. Within six weeks I was back playing. "Oh, you're fit enough, you're a big boy." My right knee, my right leg, was never the same. I was lucky I was two-footed. As I say, that's one of the reasons big Stein put me back to left-half. After the operation, I would hit it with all my might and it couldn't go from here to there – it couldn't go 20 yards. Then they took me in for an another exploratory operation because they said there's something in there. They found seven foreign bodies in my knee. I'm talking about 1956 or '57, Killearn Hospital. It was still a war zone.

That's where they used to send you with TB.

TB. So I got sent there. It was the Celtic doctor that sent me there. Maybe they were trying to tell me something! I was never right – my knees were never right after that. And then it developed in my left. I got the first cartilage out of there and as I say, 12 operations all found and this is the best I've been. In '94 I had two knee replacements.

I remember the first time I had a cartilage and as soon as it happened on the park, I knew it, I said, "That's my cartilage away." Bob Rooney said, "How do you know that? That's rubbish! Get up and run about!" But with a cartilage, you can't run about, you can't even walk. So what must it have been like with you, Joe?

I kept breaking it all the time. As I say, I was pushing it back in myself.

But look at the damage you were causing yourself.

That's right, you don't realise the harm you're doing. You just want to play. And football got me into STV. I was a scenemaster, for 20 years the best job in the world. One day near when I was starting on the job I was on this outside broadcast and Arthur Mountford was doing interviews before the game. Suddenly we see big Stein coming along and big Arthur thinks it's him but Stein throws his arms round me. "How's it going big man?" You could see the look on Arthur's face. "Who's he?" I didn't say, you know, not at that time. I worked with Mark McManus on the first *Taggarts* when they first came on the scene. He was Celtic daft. He threw in the towel after Marion took cancer. She was a gem of a woman. When I first knew Mark he had no money, skint, always skint. He took some drink. He was on whisky and then he gave up whisky and he'd drink vodka. He'd come to work plastered.

He enjoyed it?

No, he didn't really enjoy it. And he just gave up when Marion died.

Did you ever do any coaching, Joe?

I did but my knees wouldn't take it. I even got offered to play for the Old Crocks!

I played for the Old Crocks along with big John Colrain, Mike Jackson, Bobby Shearer, Eric Caldow, Jacky McInally, Bertie Black. This was us doing charity work on a Sunday. We were travelling all over Ayrshire and playing police sides and that and because of who they were playing, you should have seen the amount of fights that used to break out. On the pitch, I mean. Willie Lamont was the goalkeeper, ex-Hamilton Accies and Willie was a hard man. And he stuck it on this big police sergeant one night. He just went up to him. "I've warned you before, pal." Bang! Hit him. Bobby Shearer said, "I'll have you too, pal."

Do you still get to see the Celtic, Joe?

I've got two season tickets. I've got three boys so I buy two to give them each their chance. I still go to the old stand, I prefer the old stand. Billy McNeill sits just about two rows up from me. That's something I can never understand about Celtic. I know they can't give everybody a position over by the directors but surely a man like Billy – manager twice and captain of the 1967 side! He's paying his ticket for him and his daughter.

I heard a rumour Tommy Burns is back.

It was on the wireless. First-team coach till the end of the season. He deserves another chance. Van Hooijdonork was a moaner but Celtic should never have let him or Di Canio go. Cadete, I don't know. Wee Fergus must have been taking money off him to give him a game!

Do you know where he was staying? It shows you the advice they get. Glasgow Cross! A flat in Glasgow Cross! How could he get a wink's sleep on a Friday night or a Saturday night, the singing and dancing that goes on there!

No wonder the wife wanted out of Glasgow then.

When she goes out, all she sees is alkies.

Glasgow Cross. He'd be saving on his bus fare.

Joe, Charlie, thank you very much.

I think I've talked too much.

Charlie, whenever?

Mike Jackson
Inside-forward
1957-1963

I signed for Benburb from Holy Cross Boys' Guild on an amateur form in November 1956. I played two games for them when the Guild did not have a game before signing a provisional form for Celtic. Celtic gave me £20 for signing which was about March 1957 and called me up after about four games for the start of season 1957. I played a total of six games for Benburb.

Who fostered your career around that period?

Mr John Murphy was instrumental in most of the boys at Holyrood School in those days going to Celtic, like me, Crerand, Kurila, Gallagher. I think he probably acted as an unpaid scout. And for years he did all the public address work at Parkhead. There's a story to that if you want to hear it. It's about team selection. It happened to me this once but it happened to other players of my time. It was a Wednesday night League game at Celtic Park during the time of the Home Internationals. Paddy Crerand was with the Scottish squad so I half-expected to be playing at right-half. So I arrived at Celtic Park just after 6 p.m. and was met by Mr Murphy and he had just received the team to announce for the game. I was down at right-half. At 6.45, Bob Rooney came into the snooker room to read out the team and get them into the dressing room. According to Bob, I was now at inside-right but at least I was playing and I went in to get ready for the game. I did my usual preparations, had my rub-down with the oil and linament and was knocking a ball about in the shower area when Bob Rooney reappeared. He told me to go and have a bath. I wasn't playing now. So at 6.30 I was right-half, at 6.45 I was inside-right and at 7.15 I was out of the team altogether. That's a true story and all too commonplace during the time I was with Celtic.

Are there any outstanding memories from your first days at Parkhead?

There was the strange feeling walking down the tunnel with players like Billy McPhail and Mochan who only weeks earlier you were watching from the terracing. John Higgins always looked very frail and I never saw him play without his knee heavily strapped up. He was very unlucky.

A newspaper report spoke of 'Colrain, Jackson and Conway' as having a great season ahead 'if they mature quickly'. What did maturing quickly mean to you in 1957?

'Maturing quickly' means adjusting to the huge step-up as I was still playing Boys' Guild football weeks before going to Celtic. Also, the physical gap was tremendous. I wasn't 18 until 25 August 1957 and only about ten stone in weight. Today you would be on the Y.T.S. and playing in the under-18 Youth Team. I found junior football hard at first, the step-up in pace and the physical contact were immense compared to playing with the Boys' Guild. But also, as a senior, there were the expectations and the pressure from outside Celtic Park. You quickly realised that people had started to recognise who you were and suddenly you felt everybody was looking at you.

Nowadays, people might lick their lips at the amount of young talent at Parkhead in 1957. Yet there was a stark time approaching for Celtic. Why? What was wrong?

Now as an older man and having been involved in football for over 40 years as a player, coach, manager and at present, scout for Leeds United, the place was a joke. The training gear was disgraceful. We were made to wear rough, hairy jerseys next to our skin and the footwear was worse, old sandshoes that your mother would have thrown out years ago no matter how poor you were. I had a pair of Adidas boots at Benburb but when I went to Celtic, all the recruits of '57 were made to wear these old Manfield Hotspurs that must have been in a cupboard for about 20 years. We had blistered feet for weeks. Only the first team players got a cotton strip to wear next to their skin when training and to wear the decent boots. It was very much second class unless you were in the big team. Team selection was so inconsistent and you hardly ever saw a ball at training. I eventually bought my own football boots to play in. Can you imagine the players of today buying their own boots?

You broke into the 7-1 team against Dundee on 7 December 1957 in place of Charlie Tully and saving your reverence, Mike, it seems as if you were a victim of Celtic tradition on your debut, i.e. Celtic players could play anywhere therefore Jackson could play outside-right. You were surely out of place?

I had never played outside-right in my life and it was one position I would never have played in but I was excited about getting into the first team after such a short time as a senior. I would never have made a winger if I lived to be 100 but that was typical of Celtic during my time there. There were much stranger decisions than me playing outside-right. In fact, in my 17-year playing career, it was the only time I ever played there.

You went back to the reserves after your debut under Jock Stein's command.

Playing under Jock Stein for the three years he was in charge was the most influential of my early years in senior football. We beat Rangers reserves in the 1957-58 season by an aggregate score of 8-2. There were so many natural young footballers there in the late Fifties: Crerand, MacKay, Auld, Divers, McNeill, Colrain, McVittie, Chalmers, Clark. Jock's greatest gift was knowing where to play you to get the best of your ability to flourish. He never would ask you to do something on the park that you couldn't do. I just regret that he was not made manager in 1960 instead of going to Dunfermline. A lot of our lives would have changed dramatically and I am positive I would have had a handful of medals if only Jock had stayed. If you think about it, everybody talks about the lean spell from 1957 to 1965. I was there from 1957 to 1963 and every Lisbon Lion except Wallace and Simpson I played with. To me, that proves that the problem lay at the top of the house i.e. with the Board. Mr McGrory did not pick the team. Had Jock Stein been made manager instead of going to Dunfermline, the good years would have started five years earlier.

Do you remember the Irish tour of 1958?

Do I remember it! I will never forget the excitement of seeing my name on the list in the dressing room. I was going 'abroad' with Celtic, ha-ha! I remember going home and telling my parents and my mother saying I would need a new suit and shoes. I was getting £7 a week from Celtic and was serving my time as a stereotyper in Pollokshields. I had to take two weeks unpaid holiday to go on tour. My mother took me down to the Co-op in Bridge Street and bought me a suit which was too big but my mother said I was still growing and I would need it a bit bigger and using her Co-op dividend number when paying for it, 40384. We went on the night boat to Dublin and most of us were sick. It was a very rough crossing. We got our picture taken on the boat before we sailed and they stuck the few who had Celtic blazers on, like Meechan, Smith and MacKay, to the front. They never gave the young players the club uniform which is changed days indeed. We played three games in Dublin, Belfast and Derry and all the young lads like me were skint. Eric Smith headed a deputation to Mr Kelly, the chairman, asking for some pocket money. Mr Kelly decided to share £45 among the 15 players for two weeks which was £3 per player. We all decided that if that was all Celtic could do, they could keep it, which they did. However, it was a great learning experience footballwise and I know I benefited greatly from it.

Mike, to quote, 'The performance of the youngsters on this tour engendered a misplaced optimism.' What would you say?

Everybody was excited about our 7-0 performance against Derry because they had a lot of experienced pros in their team and to murder them like that was great. I was in Dublin two years ago to see Celtic play St Patrick's and they struggled to beat them with all their high-paid superstars after only drawing 0-0 at Celtic Park in a European tie. There is no way League of Ireland football or Irish League football has improved like that since I played. I firmly believe that if we had had the guidance of Jock Stein for another few years, say from 1960, a lot of our careers would have had to be rewritten.

You became a great pal of Billy McNeill.

Billy McNeill and me became firm friends from our very first meeting and still are. In fact, my children and his are more like brothers and sisters than just friends. There were a few of us who went around together for years and are still very close, Pat Crerand, Bertie Auld, John Divers, Billy, myself, and tragically, as we used to call him, the Leader of the Pack, John Colrain, who died at the early age of 47. We used to kid Big Billy on as to how Big Bob, Mr Kelly, kept him on yet he got rid of the likes of myself, Paddy, wee Bertie and Big Coley prematurely, thinking we were bad boys.

The new season 1958-59 got started with you playing centre against Cowdenbeath in the League Cup on 10 September.

I remember the match against Cowdenbeath well because I had not long arrived at the park for the game still in my working clothes as I was part-time. Willie Johnstone the trainer came into the snooker room and told me I was playing in place of Billy McPhail. I had never played at centre in my life before but it was just great to be playing with people like Tully and Collins who were idols to me a year earlier.

This was the Wee Barra's last game for Celtic. Did you have any idea at the time what a serious loss his transfer was to Celtic?

At the time Bobby Collins left I was still too young to realise the consequences. Bobby was great to all the young players at the club. However it was very bad for the careers of the young players to try and follow in the footsteps of seasoned internationals the like of Collins, Tully, Billy McPhail, Fallon, Evans, Peacock, Fernie, Mochan and even someone like Eric Smith, who was to leave for Leeds. How were we to maintain their standards? In the late Fifties, instead of young players like myself at that time benefiting from playing with them and listening and learning from them in training, we were flung in at the age of 17, 18, 19 without having served any apprenticeship and gaining the experience and know-how that can only come from working with journeymen. As an older man now but still involved in the game, I think the lack of forward planning and direction by the people in charge of Celtic F.C. was unbelievable.

Although the seven lean years were now beginning, John McPhail was eulogising Celtic's youth policy: 'Celtic fans…you lucky people!' Could anyone have been aware that the prodigies of talent in the late Fifties at Parkhead would reap no short-term rewards but cause a lot of frustration for the support?

John McPhail's opinion at the time was proved to be right but it took a decision which most of my colleagues and me at Celtic never thought would happen. Bob Kelly stopped running the football side of the club and handed the reins to Jock Stein in 1965. I think of the players who grew up with me as teammates without winning anything – Craig, Gemmell, Murdoch, McNeill, Clark, Johnstone, Chalmers, Lennox and Auld. Yet all of them became Celtic immortals along with Simpson and Wallace. Add in Fallon, Hughes, O'Neill, Gallagher and that's Lisbon 1967. But would it be presumptious to include MacKay, Crerand, Divers, Colrain and Jackson? I can't help thinking what might have been. For Celtic to have failed for so many years with so much raw talent proves to me where the blame for failure really lay all those years ago.

You played your second game for the League side at Broomfield on 18 October 1958, 4-1 for Celtic. You were described as 'a cultured forward in the Joe Cassidy mould' which was high praise indeed as your father would probably have told you.

This was my second season at Celtic and as you say, the game at Airdrie was my second League game and my third first team game. We talked about how I played outside-right against Dundee and centre versus Cowdenbeath. I got 22 first team games in that season, 1958-59, and I scored four goals which I felt was good progress. I had just turned 19 at the time.

John Higgins was striving to revive his career as your winger. How conscious were you of John's dicky knee?

It was a great pity that John Higgins had so many problems with his knee. He was a frail-built player but had a wonderful football brain and was what I would term a players' player as opposed to a crowd player. He was never particularly flamboyant but was a great lad to play with. John always gave you the ball at the right time and was always available to take the ball from you when you were in trouble. He was a really nice man and always ready to give advice and help when required.

Your other wing partner was Matt McVittie. How did you rate Matt?

Matt McVittie was a great character. He innocently used to call Mr Kelly 'Bob' and eventually he got pulled up for it. He was a tricky winger and like most wide players could take on full-backs and get past them which is a dying trait nowadays. Like a lot of us at that time, he probably underachieved considering the natural ability he had.

On 15 November 1958, you swapped positions with Willie Fernie, he to inside-right, you to right-half. Did right-half do anything for your game? I mean, it made internationals of inside forwards like Bobby Evans and Billy Wright.

This was the first time I was played in what I thought was my best position and I'm sure that if I had played there more often, I would have made a much better player. When I was at Holyrood School, I was right-half and my pal Pat Crerand was inside-left in what was a very successful school team.

You were back to inside-right the following week, losing 2-0 at Firhill. How do you understand a statement which says of this game: 'If these Celtic kids need anything, it's someone with experience up front'? The forwards on this day were McVittie and Jackson; Conway; Colrain and Auld.

Well, it's as I've been saying, we boys certainly needed the guidance of some senior players because history has proved that a team of youngsters has never won anything. Celtic should have appointed Jock Stein as first team coach or manager. Without being disrespectful to Mr McGrory, he was a lovely man, but he had little or no say in picking the team and the only time you saw him apart from match days was when he handed you your wages on a Tuesday. He was never on the training pitch.

Okay, Mike, experienced forward wanted yet Celtic let Fernie go on 1 December. Did you regret Fernie's transfer?

I think most of us at the time regretted players such as Fernie and Collins leaving because we held them in such high esteem.

John McPhail said 'Jackson, Colrain and Divers were three wonder boys' after the 1-1 draw at Tynecastle on 20 December 1958. Did you feel you were a wonder boy?

It's funny that people referred to us as wonder boys because we certainly never thought of ourselves like that. But, in fact, in those days, with hindsight, we sold ourselves short. We never had the brashness or confidence of today's young players because of the massive media coverage the game now gets. All young players nowadays have agents which might give them the impression that they're better players than they are.

Now, Mike, Thursday Ne'erday 1959 saw Rangers beat Celtic 2-1, a game played in gale and freezing downpour. Dick Beattie appealed to referee Mowat to abandon the match in the 75th minute. The sheeting rain was obscuring his vision. Thousands of fans abandoned the terracing.

It was the worst weather I have ever played in, gales, rain, snow, sleet, the pitch a quagmire with all the lines totally obliterated. Yet we played so well. We were 2-1 down with five minutes to go when Rangers' left-half Billy Stevenson pulled me down in the box and we got a penalty. The referee had to pace out the distance. The spot had disappeared. Wee Bertie took it, hit the bar and we lost. Matt McVittie suffered so badly he had to be treated by the doc at the end of the game.

It was at this time Jack Harkness was backing Bob Kelly's youth policy: 'By New Year's Day 1961, Celtic will have the finest team they've had in many years and one that will rank with the best in Britain.' And I would presume that meant with Mike Jackson at inside-right!

Jack Harkness should have been proved right but history says otherwise. The Celtic board must take a lot of responsibility for this. Not long after this display the half-back line of Smith, Evans and Peacock had gone, Higgins had retired through injury, Colrain was sold to Clyde, Auld was sold to Birmingham and Beattie went to Portsmouth. That left only four from a team that Jack Harkness would have ranked potentially with the best in Britain. Again, the board were the guilty men. Talk about building a team! They had no idea what they were doing.

In the Scottish Cup versus Albion Rovers on 31 January 1959, Tully was your wing partner for 50 minutes. How was it playing with the great patter merchant?

It was an honour to play with Charlie Tully, one of the all-time Celtic greats. He had fantastic skill especially in beating opponents in a one-to-one situation. But he was coming to the end of his career and his fitness was poor. All the same, Charlie didn't half make you fit. You had to do all his running. But he was a wonderful character.

Mike, from one extreme to the other: your wing partner on 21 February 1959 was the dourish Sammy Wilson. Any memories of Slammin' Sammy?

We used to call him the Ghost. What a season he had in 1957-58 when he was playing through the middle with Billy McPhail. They struck up a telepathic partnership which resulted in Sammy getting 32 goals that year, a lot of them so simple, like a long kick from Beattie, a head flick from Billy McPhail and the Ghost gliding in to score. Sammy was a character who we as younger players never seemed to get to know but I've got to admit I liked him.

You had a great, great victory, 2-1 over Rangers in the Cup at Parkhead on 28 February 1959. That was the day Frank Haffey came of age as Celtic's goalie.

I can't remember a lot about the game apart from the goals and a superb save by Frank Haffey late on. My good friend John Divers scored with a header and Matt McVittie just beat me to the ball to knock in the second. Again, that was a day when Celtic came up with one of their strange team selections, playing John Divers at outside-left. It boggles the mind. Imagine someone running Celtic F.C. thinking he could play men the likes of John and me as wingers and expect to get the best out of us!

Mike, in the Scottish Cup semi-final at Hampden on 4 April 1959, Celtic were annihilated 4-0 by St Mirren, a result of which no one could make any sense.

I don't think I went out socially for about a week. Could you imagine walking about the south side of Glasgow with the massive Celtic support in that part of the city? I was broken-hearted and embarrassed. We were all so confident of getting to our first final and to be beaten by such a score was devastating. One of the things I remember about that game was Bobby Evans continually trying to play offside in an attempt to counteract Gerry Baker. His pace was electric and Bobby's reliance on offside turned out to be a disaster. But having said that, when a team gets beaten 4-0, there is no one person to blame. Everybody has to take responsibility.

You now began to score goals on a fairly regular basis including one against Rangers at Ibrox on 5 September 1959. What sort of a feeling was that?

Scoring at Ibrox was a dream come true for me. I'll never forget the feeling when the ball hit the net. I felt 1959-60 was not too bad a season for me but I was disappointed I did not get more first team games. I had a few injury problems that season. I played 16 games and scored 10 goals which by today's standards would be a very good ratio in terms of games played.

You seem to have been injured at Partick Thistle on 28 November 1959 and I don't find you again until 23 March 1960 against Rangers reserves in a forward line of Carroll and Jackson; Lochhead; Gallagher and Chalmers. You go in against Rangers in the Scottish Cup semi-final replay at inside-left to Johnny Divers on 6 April 1960. Rangers win 4-1 and you disappear again. How was this?

This was another of Celtic's mystery selections. As you say, I had not played in the first team for months. The night before the semi-final replay I trained for two hours, all of it hard running round the heavy track at Celtic Park yet they must have had me in their thoughts for the semi-final the next afternoon. No intelligent person in football would ask a player to do two hours hard running the night before a game. I'll never forget the lead-up to the actual game at Hampden either. It had a 4pm kick-off as there were no floodlights at Hampden at that time. I was standing at the bottom of the tunnel half an hour before kick-off when Desmond White approached me and said he thought I was playing. He said I should go up to the dressing room. I go up to the dressing room and get a row from the trainer, Willie Johnstone, for not getting ready. It was unbelievable. Nobody had bothered to tell me I was playing. No wonder there were no cups in the cupboard.

You started off 1960-61 at right-half for the Hoops in the public trial when the big team was at Sedan. The team was Fallon; Donnelly and Upton; Jackson, Kurila and Cushley; Carmichael and Colrain; Hughes; Divers and Byrne.

Season 1960-61 was a disaster for me. I know I was injured for a while but I honestly can't remember why I only played one first team game that season. That was against Raith Rovers at Kirkcaldy, a 2-2 draw. I played right-half. The season was a great disappointment to me. One first team game. I cannot understand it.

Now, Mike, Celtic seemed to want to persevere with you at right-half both in the reserves and the big team.

I was delighted to be playing at right-half albeit mostly in the reserves. I was always going to be a better player at right-half.

Willie Fernie came home on 6 October 1960. Opinion is divided on whether he was a faster player or a slower player, one who had benefited from England or one who was the same as when he left or one not half as good. What did you think?

I think the main difference when Willie came back was that he did not run with the ball the way he had when he was younger. When he came back, he passed the ball to you much earlier and was always available to take it back. He had probably become a better team player.

Despite Jack Harkness's prophecy Celtic had taken only 19 points from 20 Scottish League games by 7 January 1961 and 'drastic action' was needed. Yet Celtic reached the Scottish Cup final versus Jock Stein's Dunfermline on 22 April, a 0-0 draw. How confident were you of the outcome of the replay?

Well, although Celtic were having a poor spell, I honestly thought they would have won the replay. History will say it was Dunfermline 'keeper's Eddie Connachan's final. And there was a terrible blunder by Haffey which gave Dunfermline the vital second.

You came back to the first team at Firhill in a game I will always remember, brilliant sunshine, 12 August 1961, the electric atmosphere game that Celtic won 3-2. You must remember that game!

I do remember that game vividly because in the first minute I ran a John Divers cutback into the net for the opening goal and then I got the winner with ten minutes to go. Firhill was a lucky ground for me.

Paddy Crerand was in a lot of trouble with suspensions and first of all the club tried John Kurila, then yourself at right-half. You reverted to inside-right and again you were scoring goals as inside man to Stevie Chalmers.

Paddy and me had been ordered off in a fight at Brockville in a Five-a-Side competition and Paddy had also been ordered-off in a Scotland game so along comes Bob Kelly and suspends Paddy for a month! It boggles the mind! So I played three games at right-half and felt I did really well but when Paddy came back I reverted to inside-right.

On 20 February 1962, you and Billy were fined £50 each plus a severe censure and a warning as to your future conduct for taking part in a bounce game in Lloret de Mar on 9 July 1961. How did the SFA ever get to hear you'd been breaking the rules?

We got caught because of a Celtic supporter who stumbled upon this game while on holiday. He asked Billy and me if he could have a picture taken with us. When the rumours started of an illegal game in Spain, the SFA had no evidence until this Judas sold a copy of the team photograph to the newspapers. We had to hold our hands up and plead guilty because when Harley, Hilley and Gray, the famous Third Lanark trio, who were pals of ours, asked us to join them in the game, we thought why not.

You played in the reserves versus Rangers at Ibrox in a forward line of Chalmers, Divers, Carroll, Jackson and Brogan on 8 September 1962. Did you remark young Gemmell's fine performance at left-back that day versus Alec Scott?

I remember very well when this young, gangly left-back joined Celtic and his early days in the reserves. But to be honest, I never visualised at that time what a wonderful attacking full-back he would became.

Two days later you played the whole 90 minutes at inside-left against the almighty Real Madrid followed by a lap of honour and a triumphal bus ride down into the town, to the Central Hotel, for the banquet.

Oh yes, this was a night I will never forget, 10 September 1962. The players of Real Madrid were my idols since I had watched them in that unforgettable game against Eintracht at Hampden in May 1960. I felt privileged to be on the same park as them. I thought we did very well. When we scored to make it 3-1, I had a goal disallowed which really upset me. I've a great picture of it in the house which I'm really proud of. We gave them a very hard time of it in the second half. I thought Alfredo di Stefano was the best all-round player I ever saw.

Then Valencia, the 4-2 defeat. I think you set up the two Celtic goals.

Oh yes. To have played in Celtic's first-ever European tie is a memory I cherish and it was a fantastic experience as we had hardly ever played against foreign opposition. There had been terrible thunder and lightning storms prior to the game but by the time we kicked-off – I think it was near 9 o'clock – it was melting hot with very high humidity which made it a very hard night for us because they were a quality side, then as now. But in fact, with the away goals rule prevailing nowadays, 4-2 would not have been a bad result at all.

For the return leg with Valencia, Celtic bought Bobby Craig. Did you feel your prospects as Celtic's inside-right had dimmed dramatically?

I knew my days at Celtic Park were numbered early into the 1962-63 season. Bob Kelly had gone off me and once that happened you were on your way so Bobby Craig was never the reason. It was hard to understand as season 1961-62 had been my best. I was older, although only turned 22, but I was fitter and stronger, my knowledge of the game was deeper and my confidence had soared. I felt I had served my apprenticeship.

Billy brought you back to Celtic in 1988 to scout in Europe. How successful was this period in your career?

I did match analysis for Billy when he came back as manager at Celtic for the second time. I gave him a report on each team they were playing against each Saturday. This job took me to places such as Berlin, Budapest and Cologne so it was a good experience in lots of ways.

How would you sum your career up, Mike?

To sum it up, I loved playing for Celtic. It was my boyhood dream and I was very sad to leave. But it's better to leave when you feel you're not welcome any more. The sad thing is, I played only two games for Celtic after my 23rd birthday. As I said earlier, you must serve an apprenticeship in football just like tradesmen who do a five years apprenticeship before becoming journeymen. In 1961-62 I felt like a journeyman. I played the most games in any season, 34, and scored the most goals, 18, so I felt I had served my time. I think Celtic did okay from me. I cost them £250 from Benburb plus a £20 signing-on fee and they sold me to St Johnstone for about £7,000. According to Pat Woods, the Celtic historian, I played 78 games for the first team and scored 32 goals which is a ratio of 41%, goals to games played. I feel quite proud of that.

Excluding Mike Jackson, what would be your all-time Celtic XI?

That's a hard one and I can't be sure because there are so many permutations that come to mind. I could opt for the team that won the European Cup in Lisbon and few could disagree because it's not just about the best players but how they blend as a team that matters. Then there's the bulk of the team that won 9 League titles, so it would be hard to go against them. However, in my opinion, Danny McGrain and Kenny Dalglish would have been the icing on the cake as pool members of the Lisbon side when they were at their prime. From my early years, I would like to add Bobby Collins, a man who was the mainspring of Don

Revie's emerging Leeds United and was also a magnificent player for Everton. He played well into his forties and had all the attributes for the modern game. I could also say what a sweeper George Connelly would have developed into with his control, vision and passing ability. Then there was the aggression of David Hay in a variety of positions and my old pal, Pat Crerand from Holyrood. It's results over a period of years that determine what makes a great team. So I'll go for the Lions plus McGrain, Dalglish, Hay, Crerand, Bobby Collins and Connelly as additions to that squad.

Mike Jackson, ten million thanks!

Thank you. I hope this helps you with the book.

Frank Haffey

Goalkeeper
1958-1964

Frank, to begin with, who were Campsie Black Watch?

Campsie Black Watch were a first class juvenile team run by a manager coach called Gerald Marley. He was a brilliant coach, manager and administrator. The last I heard he was still there in 1998!

Now didn't you have a connection with Maryhill Harp?

Well, I did and I didn't. I never actually played football for Maryhill Harp but I signed for them to cover myself in case I didn't make it at Celtic. I couldn't reinstate as a junior if I'd never been one.

How did you get to know that Celtic were taking an interest?

I never did. I was over a year with the club, about 18 years old, when Jimmy McGrory informed me Celtic had been keeping an eye on me since I was 12! I signed provisional for Celtic at half-time at Ibrox against Rangers reserves. We lost 1-0.

Frank, as a reserve to Dick Beattie, you were sharing a dressing-room with the likes of Tully, Sammy Wilson and Alex Byrne. That must have been some experience.

Oh, that was a big thrill. Do you know what Charlie told me?

What?

He said I would be the clown prince of Celtic FC after he left! I phone Alec Byrne every week or he rings me. He lives in South Australia. Of the three of them, Sammy was the quietest. Charlie never called me Frank. He always called me Francie.

Dick Beattie lost his place to you to let Motherwell in for a 3-3 draw at Parkhead on 2 January 1959. There were no goalie coaches in those days. Did you and he work out together?

Not really. I got on very well with Dick and Johnny but we did our thing and went our different ways. Charlie called me 'The Cub' after 'Tiger' Bonnar.

Two lapses of concentration and that was Dick Beattie out and Frank Haffey in.

Well, I've been coaching goalkeepers of all ages for many years and I still am. My coaching method is to ask these questions of my protégé. One: What happens if a goalie makes a mistake? Answer: It's a goal. Two: What happens if a goalie makes another mistake? Answer:

It's another goal. Three: What happens if a goalie makes three mistakes? Answer: He's lost three goals! The whole sum and substance of the lesson is that the goalie mustn't make any mistakes! I can count on the fingers of one hand how seldom my bacon was saved by one of my defenders.

This 3-3 game was a magnificent match so much so that Jack Harkness wrote in the Sunday Post that by New Year's Day 1961 Celtic would have the finest team they'd had for many years and one that would rank with the best in Britain.

There were certainly a lot of good players at Parkhead at the time.

Good players but a distinct lack of plan. Tell me, Frank, to go back to the spring of 1958, can you remember your debut, 4-1 against Third Lanark at Parkhead on 30 April? The team was Haffey; Meechan and Mochan; Smith, Evans and Peacock; Higgins and Jackson; Colrain; Divers and Auld.

Do you know, it's amazing but I have no clear memory of my debut game for Celtic. There are players I remember. I do remember Bertie Peacock. Bertie was the ultimate gentleman. He was a great player and a super person. I never heard him swear or say a bad word against anyone. When he was dropped finally for John Clark in the Cup-tie against Hibs in 1961, he wasn't told until half an hour before the game. Do you know what he said to me?

What?

He said, "I've stayed too long at the one club."

I know what he meant. What about Neilly Mochan at left-back?

Neilly was a great attacker but I think that as a forward he was getting slower hence the move back to a position where out-and-out speed was not called for.

I can't see Higgins and Auld as full-backs.

Maybe not but Neilly managed it. Johnny Higgins was a quiet poacher. Bertie Auld was a terrier.

This was a much-changed team from the one that had beaten Rangers 7-1 the previous 19 October: Beattie; Donnelly and Fallon; Fernie, Evans and Peacock; Tully and Collins; Billy McPhail; Wilson and Mochan.

Yet we were in the same season, 1957-58.

Now, Frank, you became Celtic's first-choice goalkeeper as of 21 January 1959, a 2-0 win over Kilmarnock in the League at Parkhead. The team read: Haffey; MacKay and Mochan; Smith, Evans and Peacock; Higgins and Jackson; Colrain; Divers and Auld. When you took over from Dick Beattie what happened? Did you commiserate with him and did he congratulate you? Or was it just one of those things?

It was just one of those things.

You had a few games on the trot then and one report I've read of Falkirk 3, Celtic 2 on 7 February 1959 queried whether Haffey was a better goalkeeper than Beattie. But this was

before the third round of the Scottish Cup at Parkhead on the last day of the month, 2-1 for Celtic when you had a magnificent game. Do you remember that one? Haffey; MacKay and Mochan; Smith, Evans and Peacock; McVittie and Jackson; Lochhead; Wilson and Divers.

That was my first Old Firm game. Oh, I remember it very well. I had a great save from Max Murray with about ten minutes to go but Celtic winning two-nil. Bobby Evans came up to me at the final whistle with his hand held out. He told me I was brilliant and said I had a great future ahead of me. I call him Bobby now but in those days he was rarely known as anything else except Dai. Dai because of his Welsh surname.

I never knew that! Now, you had a sore throat at the end of March and Dick Beattie played in the 3-0 League win over Hibs at Parkhead, a day when Dunky MacKay was described as the best defensive prospect in the country. What was it like to play behind Dunky?

Oh, to play behind Dunky was an absolute delight. Dunky was the first attacking full-back I had ever seen. An attacking defender can become an extra forward provided he has the ability to recover when the attack breaks down. Dunky could manage that no bother.

He got his first cap this season against England on 11 April 1959 when Bobby Evans led the Scottish team out at Wembley. He was the only man on the park not to wear shinpads. He wanted to go to England and he ended-up with a moribund Third Lanark. How was that?

I've no memory of Dunky's situation. He was like myself. He missed out on Jock Stein.

Were you a vocal goalkeeper, Frank? I've heard that Jock Stein was critical of his goalkeepers for not being vocal enough.

I think I was vocal enough. I was certainly as vocal as Dunky or Bobby Evans.

Frank, on 4 April 1959, Celtic meet St Mirren in the Scottish Cup semi-final at Hampden and it's a disaster: 4-0 for St Mirren, 3-0 at half-time.

The Hampden disaster against St Mirren? I can it recall it well but all I will say is that if a defender is on the attack, he should make sure he has enough pace to get back if the move breaks down. Bobby Evans was a great defender but had what I consider one bad fault: he loved the sliding tackle too much. The sliding tackle is okay if you win it. But if you make a sliding tackle and you miss, then you're lying on your back and you can't recover.

Now it was Haffey versus Rangers again on 2 May, in the Charity Cup, the semi-final, a 1-1 draw: Haffey; Donnelly and Mochan; MacKay, Evans and Peacock; Smith and McVittie; Byrne; Colrain and Auld. You had another great game.

We should have won that game.

You did win it! Bertie Peacock took Celtic into the final against Clyde on the toss of the coin. Frank, Scotland had just capped Dunky at right-back and Celtic play him at right-half. Eric Smith was probably a half-back born but Celtic play him outside-right. How did players feel being played out of their best position like this? Another previous example is Bobby Collins.

You're asking the wrong man! You're asking the goalie! I don't really know how outfield players felt being moved about like that. I suppose they were just glad to be in the team.

Now the new season 1959-60 and Bobby Carroll joins Celtic.

Ah yes, Bobby and I were good mates at Celtic. A wee while after he joined us, I was invited to a dinner dance in one of the Catholic parochial halls in the Gorbals. Wee Bobby was a non-Catholic but I asked him if he would like to come along. He said he would and I thought we would have a bit of a laugh. I told him that the presiding cleric was a canon, Canon Ball. So on the way to the event, Bobby asks me how he should address the canon. I said, "Don't worry, just stand up and say, Thank you, Canon Ball for the invitation. So this is what poor Bobby does and the place erupts. Anyway, after about ten minutes, a fellow came up to me and he said, "The canon would like to see you." So I went over and the canon winked at me. "Do you know", he said, "only Frank Haffey could have talked some poor innocent into calling me that."

Now, 1959-60, Frank. Celtic lost 2-1 at Kirkcaldy on Day One with Haffey; McNeill and Mochan; MacKay, Evans and Peacock; Smith and McVittie; Byrne; Colrain and Mackle. What sort of a right-back was Billy McNeill?

Billy didn't play too long at right-back. He was so mobile, I thought it was only a matter of time until he was placed in the middle of defence.

What about John Colrain?

John was a gifted player with an almighty shot but could not or would not head a ball. The joke was John didn't like to spoil his hair.

The season had no sooner started than Celtic had found the glory blend again according to the papers. Then you had a very serious accident at work. You backed into a lathe which tore the clothes off your back. You were lucky to escape with only bruises but now you were out of the Celtic first team and John Fallon was in.

Yes, I backed into this lathe and was saved from serious injury or worse by a fitter/turner name of Hughie McFarlane, an ardent Rangers fan, but a very nice fellow.

John Fallon began to show magnificent form and was selected reserve Scottish goalkeeper for Scotland versus Wales on 4 November. Did you ever have doubts about getting back into the first team? Did you ever think in terms of a transfer?

No, Celtic was the only team for me. I knew I would have to fight for my spot back and I did. But then it was poor John's turn. He dropped a heavy steel spring on his thigh at work and I got back into the side.

That was on 12 December 1959, when Laurie Leslie had a great game, Celtic 0, Airdrie 0. He was in miraculous form. But you too had another almighty game against Rangers on Ne'erday 1960. You were 'Haffey the Barrier, Haffey the Cat, Haffey the Hero', with a magnificent penalty kick save from Little high up in the postage stamp corner in the 60th minute.

I remember saving Billy's shot. That was the game Jimmy Millar got Rangers' winner in the last minute.

How did you rate Jimmy Millar?

Jimmy Millar was always dangerous. He was always busy and had a great shot.

Frank Haffey

Was he the most dangerous Ranger you played against?

I wouldn't say that. I was always very wary of Ralph Brand. He would try and talk the ball out of your hands.

Frank, Celtic beat Everton and Bobby Collins 1-0 on 27 January 1960 and then went down to Roker Park three days later and lost 7-1 to Sunderland. Can you remember these games?

Do you know, I can't recall playing versus Everton or at Sunderland. There's nothing there. Sorry.

What about when you played for Scotland against the Scottish League on 1 February?

I remember that. It was at Ibrox, just a two minutes walk from my home. It was a 2-2 draw.

Now for a sad event, Frank. Jock Stein left Celtic for Dunfermline on 13 March. Were you sorry to see Big Jock go?

Yes, that was some blow. I know for a fact Big Jock was sadly missed. We all felt it, all the lads he was leaving behind. I admired Jock as a great coach and also as a very fine person. He took a great interest in me. I remember him saying to me very early on, "Frank, if you don't lose a goal today, we won't get beat." Classic!

Well, 13 days after Jock's departure, Celtic played Stirling Albion in a 1-1 home draw and this was described by one of the papers as 'the worst entertainment in the East End of Glasgow for years'. The team was Haffey; MacKay and Kennedy; McNeill, Evans and Peacock; Smith and Colrain; Mochan; Divers and Conway.

There were games like that. It's as well I don't remember it.

How did you rate Jim Kennedy at left-back?

Jim Kennedy was mobile and very reliable, a man of very few mistakes.

What about Jim Conway?

Jim was another mover, a very fast centre-forward. To my mind, he was wasted on the wing.

But the astounding thing now is, Frank, on 9 April, bar one Scottish trial but without another representative honour to your name, you are chosen to play for Scotland versus England at Hampden. Surely that was a gut-crunching experience?

You know I was third choice? I think Spurs held on to Bill Brown for League duty if he wasn't injured and George Niven was definitely injured. I felt like Harry Lime, geddit?

And you saved a Bobby Charlton penalty?

Yes, but he had to retake it because Denis Law had one foot in the box. The retake went wide past my right post.

Was there a tactics talk before the game?

If there was one I can't remember it. I can remember the team: Me, Dunky and Caldow; Cumming, Bobby Evans and McCann; Leggat and Young; St John, Law and Weir.

You had a bad accident at Dundee just one week later.

Yes, Dunky kneed me in the groin at Dens Park and I was kept overnight in Dundee Hospital. Bobby Evans took over in goal after I got injured.

Bobby had been deputy goalkeeper for Celtic and Scotland all the way back to Willie Miller. Anyway, that was some finish to your first full season as Celtic's goalkeeper.

You know in all the years I was playing juvenile football, I never dreamt for a moment I would keep goal for Scotland.

Well, that's the thing. You keep goal for Scotland once against England of all people and there isn't another representative honour comes your way until England again the following 15 April, the 9-3 game. But back to 1960. Celtic played Sparta Rotterdam in a friendly at Parkhead on 14 May. Celtic wore numbered shorts for the first time provided by Jimmy Steele. He had a haberdasher's in Larkhall.

I remember Sparta. They wore a jersey in black and white stripes. I heard Jimmy Steele died last October. He was one of those guys you just loved to have around. He was funny, happy, smart, a real good guy.

What's this about you catching sunburn on Celtic's 1960 tour of Ireland and John Fallon having to be fetched across?

Do you know, that's another thing of which I have no memory, getting sunburned in Ireland. Maybe somebody else remembers.

On this Irish tour, Charlie Tully put three goals past you in quick succession for Limerick on 27 May 1960. Did he rub it in verbally?

Now I remember that, the three goals. Do you know what he said to me after the third?

What did he say?

He said, "I've still got it, Francie!" I've told you he always called me Francie. "I've still got it, Francie!"

John Hughes made his debut against Third Lanark in the Scottish League Cup on 13 August 1960. He had fantastic ball control, a terrific shot and yet on the big occasions he just could not get started.

Yeah, Yogi was a powerful player, very hard to pull down when he was on a run. I think John's basic trouble was he was a very shy type of lad.

On 15 August, in the Glasgow Cup, Celtic beat Rangers 4-2. You saved a Caldow penalty in the second half. Did you indulge in any sort of gamesmanship like Baxter at the other end to put the likes of Caldow off his shot?

I recall saving Eric's penalty just after half-time. No, I was always too busy trying to keep the ball out of my net to engage in any form of gamesmanship.

I ask because the kind of thing I'm talking about is when Rangers players conned Paddy Crerand out of a penalty goal on 8 September 1962. Davis placed it. Crerand placed it.

Baxter said something to Crerand. Crerand threw the ball at Baxter. The ref placed it. Ritchie saved.

I remember that. Paddy fell for it. He just got sucked in. Are you aware Paddy was my Best Man? He introduced me to my wife, Helen.

I didn't know that, Frank. I've got a picture of you and some other Celtic players and Denis Law at Paddy's wedding. So, was any of this kind of sledging going on when you were getting ready to face a penalty?

There was absolutely no sledging at all. I just hoped I would go the right way when the ball was hit.

Right, Frank, in the following match against Rangers at Ibrox which Celtic won 3-2, you broke your wrist in a collision with Billy McNeill.

That's a serious injury and yet I have no memory of it. I couldn't even tell you today which wrist it was.

You didn't come back until the last day of September when you turned out with the reserves: Haffey; Donnelly and O'Neill; Jackson, McNamee and Clark; Murdoch and Gallagher; Conway; Colrain and Hughes. Willie Fernie came home on 6 October. Were you glad to see him back? People thought he had slowed down. What did you think?

It was great to have Willie back. Willie had never slowed down. Willie was one of Celtic's fastest players but he had a very long stride and I think that's what might have given the impression he was slower. He certainly wasn't!

Frank, the 9-3 game at Wembley. Denis Law says you were singing in the bath as soon as it was over. Is that a fact?

It's a fact all right. The baths at Wembley are quite huge. I was just 22, I was still a Celtic player and I had my whole football career ahead of me. I could sing or I could melt into the deepest, darkest depression. I chose to sing.

But the point is, you did not play badly. The *Sunday Mail* and the *Sunday Post* the next day both gave you three stars out of five. That's a 60 per cent rating. I'll go to see any movie gets a three star rating. But it would take courage to go back to Scotland and face the Rangers lot and yet you'd had two Rangers backs in front of you, Shearer and Caldow who weren't a lot of use on the day.

Well, that's as maybe but I was in the bath and all around me was doom and gloom so I just started singing. Denis Law came over and that's when he said, "Dammit, big man, for a goalkeeper, you're a great singer."

Because you had some voice, Frank, didn't you? You're the lead on Celtic! Celtic! It still gets air time at Parkhead today.

Aye, with Sugar Ray Robinson on the drums. But don't get me wrong. I wasn't indifferent to what had happened to Scotland. 9-3 was a very sad situation and I could have sung all night but I was still shocked and stunned. I might have been trying to laugh it off, sing it off, but inside I was completely burned-up.

You played along with the photographers?

Yeah. I posed in front of Big Ben with the hands at three minutes to nine and under the platform nine sign at King's Cross.

But the débâcle was not down to you.

No, but I was the goalkeeper. It's always down to the goalkeeper. Back in Scotland, I had people following me round with cameras wanting me to pose in front of houses with the numbers nine and three. I had photographs of me taken all over Scotland.

Was this your way of dealing with it?

I suppose it was. And if people had a problem with that, that was their problem. It wasn't mine.

You were just the scapegoat. You had a fair game but you were the goalie of a poor side against a very good English team. I think the way you dealt with things, you should have got the George Cross, Frank. It would have broken manys a lesser man. And talking about a lesser man, do you know where I spent the night of the 9-3 game?

No. Where?

All alone in a haunted house on the Isle of Dogs.

Really?

Yeah, but I wasn't told it was haunted until the next day. I heard nothing. I slept soundly but I was told the staircase leading to the bedroom I was in was haunted. What with the 9-3 game and a ghost on the stairs, I'd never have got any sleep. I bet you'd have managed it easy.

Oh, I don't know about that.

Did you ever hear of Moacir Barbosa?

The Brazilian goalie? He lost the goal that gave Uruguay the 1950 World Cup.

He got ready for a cross and the guy shot instead. The Brazilians never forgave him. But you know what his attitude was?

What?

There were 11 of us in the team.

Good answer.

What about the Scottish Cup Final one week later against Jock Stein's Dunfermline? The team was Haffey; MacKay and Kennedy; Crerand, McNeill and Clark; Gallagher and Fernie; Hughes; Chalmers and Byrne. Were you at all nervous after the Wembley experience?

I was certainly nervous but I think we were beaten by a far better team. Jock knew our style of play and must have put it into Dunfermline's game.

Did Celtic have a tactical plan?

I can't recall a tactical plan for either game.

Frank Haffey

Frank, for the start of 1961-62, you were in the Western Infirmary with a skin problem. Was this Wembley and the Scottish Cup Final starting to catch up with you?

Oh no, nothing to do with it. I had a skin rash which had been troubling me long before Wembley or the Cup Final.

Frank Connor took over in goal. Did you know Frank well at all?

At that time, Frank was a very quiet man, a very nice person. I didn't know him all that well.

Billy Price was in the side at left-half. How did you rate him?

Billy Price was a very clever player who read the game very well.

They say he changed Celtic Ha-Ha-Ha into Celtic Cha-Cha-Cha.

I'm not so sure about that. But he was some player.

Do you remember the goal kick incident of 3 February 1962? You tried to cut the ball sharpish to Dunky MacKay and it went into the net. The look on your face made it obvious you thought you'd scored an own goal but the ref ordered it taken again.

That was the day I had collided with Dunky moments before and I was still a little dazed.

Frank, can you remember another awful Scottish Cup semi-final, again against St Mirren, this time at Ibrox, on 3 March 1962? Celtic had been having a good season but Dunky gifted a strong first-half wind to St Mirren who ran out winners 3-1. Did you wonder why he did this? Or did he know he'd done it? Willie Fernie was playing for St Mirren and there was a field invasion at 70 minutes.

I'm sorry, I suppose I should remember a day like that, but I just don't remember it at all. It's blocked out.

The team was Haffey; MacKay and Kennedy; Crerand, McNeill and Clark; Frank Brogan and Chalmers; Hughes; Divers and Byrne. Jimmy Johnstone was at Parkhead by this time. Did you know him well?

Oh yes. Jimmy and I were good friends. I called him Wee Man and he called me Big Man.

John Donnelly, the right-back of the 7-1 team left for Preston about this time. What was it like playing behind John?

John Donnelly was a very reliable full-back. He was never flashy but he was always safe.

In 1962, according to the papers, Rangers players were on £30 per week plus £5 appearance money. Celtic were on £26 per week and £10 appearance money. Does that sound accurate to you, Frank?

I've got a salary slip here for 23 July 1963. Look. My basic wage was £32 per week.

It just shows you, don't believe the papers. Now, Ian Young came in at right-back on 4 May 1962. Like John Donnelly, he's very much a mystery man. What did you think of Ian Young?

Ian was another quiet lad who didn't say much. He enjoyed his own company. He was a steady defender.

Bobby Murdoch made his debut on 11 August 1962. I was there that day and I thought he was definitely something special.

Bobby was a strong, strong player. He was only a youth but he could read the game like a veteran.

Frank, do you remember Real Madrid at Parkhead, on 10 September 1962? Real were at their zenith. I paid my six bob for Jewish Charities to stand behind your goal in the first half that night when Celtic lost 3-1 yet you were first class. I think it was your best ever game. You wore a green jersey that night as opposed to the normal yellow. The team was Haffey; MacKay and Kennedy; Crerand, McNeill and Price; Lennox and Gallagher; Hughes; Jackson and Brogan. Celtic lost and yet the 74,000 crowd demanded a lap of honour.

We were followed all the way down to the Central Hotel by 4,000 supporters. We had to wave from the windows. It was the greatest tribute paid to me by the Celtic fans just because I'd had a good game against Real Madrid. That reminds me, just when we were going to sit down and eat, Jimmy Johnstone was next to me. He looked at the table and said, "What do we do with all this cutlery, Big Man?" I told him to start from the outside and work his way in. It was just two years before I had asked the exact same question of Bobby Evans.

Now according to the papers again, you were too dehydrated to play against Valencia in Spain a fortnight later. And yet the rain had been pouring down!

I don't know about dehydrated but I'd had a raging cold for several days before we went to play Valencia.

Can you remember the brief impact of Bobby Craig? He was signed for the return with Valencia at Parkhead.

Bobby was meant to be our Messiah but he came and he went very quickly.

Ne'erday 1963 was 4-0 for Rangers at Ibrox, an awful day. Charlie Gallagher thought his career was over. How about you, Frank?

We were 1-0 down at half-time when Paddy and Sean had a blazing row in the dressing room. Paddy threw his shirt at Sean. We went out for the second half and got beat 4-0.

Just four days later Tommy Gemmell made his debut at left-back. How did you rate Big Tam?

Tommy Gemmell was like Dunky, an attacking full-back but more effective in that his final pass would as often as not result in a goal or if not, he would end up scoring himself.

Once again you played Rangers on your own in the Scottish Cup Final of 4 May 1963: Haffey; MacKay and Kennedy; McNamee, McNeill and Price; Johnstone and Murdoch; Hughes; Divers and Frank Brogan. A 1-1 draw. Any memories of this one?

I'll believe you when you say I had a good game but you know, I can't remember it at all.

Or why Jinky was dropped for the replay?

No. It's not there.

That's quite amazing, Frank, because that first game was one of your superlative performances. I think the papers took you back to Hampden on the Sunday to be photographed leaning against a goalpost in your day wear, a Hampden Belongs To Me sort of pose. And you don't remember?

I wish I could remember. I'd need to re-read the papers of the time.

After the horrendous start to the 1963-64 season, Celtic were being described as a 45-minute team especially against Rangers.

I can't understand that. We started training at 10 o'clock and never stopped running until 12 noon. We had lunch at Ferrari's restaurant and started back 2 pm until 4 pm.

Well, you were definitely fit. I'm quite surprised to learn there was an afternoon training schedule. Okay, Frank. On 25 October 1963, it was 9-0 against Airdrie and you took a penalty which might have made it ten. The fans were chanting for you, "Haf-fey! Haf-fey! Haf-fey!"

I recall the game against Airdrie very well. Roddie McKenzie made a great save. Billy McNeill asked me if I would like to take the penalty. I am the only goalkeeper to take a penalty kick for Celtic FC.

I'd never given that a thought until this moment! Frank, do you remember the circumstances of your ankle break in your last game for Celtic versus Partick Thistle in November 1963, in the Glasgow Cup at Firhill, a night of downpour?

No, it wasn't an ankle break. It was very badly damaged tendons. I had plaster on for six weeks. It happened ten minutes from half-time and I was on the treatment table. With two minutes to go, Jinky walks in. He and Ian Cowan, the other number 7, had both been sent off. They'd been fighting.

But I think they shook hands before they cleared the pitch. That was some game that night. It was regarded as a vindication of Scottish football. Willie Thornton said it made the continental stuff look like rubbish and Bob Kelly went into the Jags' dressing room to tell the Thistle players they had struck a blow for British football. But that's all by the by. Frank, why did you leave Celtic? In 1961, in the Wembley bath, you envisaged a career lasting until 1976, presumably all spent at Parkhead. Why did you go?

Well, I played a few reserve games to make my comeback. I was just married, I had just bought a house, we had just had a baby and guess what?

What?

Jimmy McGrory, the Celtic boss, asked to speak to me in his office and he told me Celtic were cutting my wages. I was dumbfounded. I asked him what about all the good years I had given Celtic especially the good performances against Rangers. He broke down and cried and said it wasn't his idea, it was Bob Kelly's.

The old, old story. So did Swindon come in for you?

I asked for a transfer because of the wage cut mainly but also because the club had just bought Ronnie Simpson. I needed more money to keep our house and keep up the standard of living that we had had before my injury. Swindon approached Celtic and I was happy with the offer they made me and just went south.

But, Frank, you only lasted a season down there. What went wrong?

Bert Head was the manager at Swindon and right from the start he and I did not hit it off. It was one of those things.

Your next move was Australia. Why Australia?

I had always fancied Australia and I got a very good offer from St George, Budapest. They offered me a house, a job, and very good wages. I was with them four seasons and then I moved to Hakoah, the Jewish team, for another five seasons. These were the happiest times of my career.

Frank, I'm sorry we've had to rush this but it's been a rare pleasure talking to you. I admired you as a goalkeeper and now I admire you a hundred times more for being so kind and affording your time. Thank you very much.

My pleasure. Thank you.

Bobby Carroll
Winger
1959-1963

Right, Bobby, you've got a Scottish Junior Cup medal, one of the great medals because you start off with about a million teams and you battle through, round after round, to the final.

1959 was the first time Meadow had won the Cup. We got to the semi-final in 1958 and lost to Shotts Bon Accord and in the second round of 1959, we met the Bon Accord again and thought we were out but we beat them 4-1 at Shotts and then went on to win the Cup. It was a big moment.

You played for the Meadow but you weren't an Ayrshire boy.

No, I was born in Killearn Street, Possilpark, in 1938, the youngest of a family. I was at East Keppoch Primary from 1943 to 1950 and at Possil Senior Secondary from 1950 to 1953.

Now how did you discover Celtic's interest in you?

Willie Cowan was Celtic's scout. He approached me at Irvine after a game, and a fortnight later I signed at Dalry station. The first night I went to training as a provisional is something I'll always remember. Willie Johnstone was the trainer and he said, "Just go out, there's players training, whoever's passing the tunnel, just join in with them." So I went out and passing the tunnel, just as I emerged, was Sammy Wilson. I joined in with Sammy. He said, "What are you doing?" I said, "I'm just here. I'm to join in with you." "Don't join in with me," he says, "this is all I do." And all Sammy did was two steps and bend on one side, two steps and bend on the other. "You'd better train with somebody that does training," he says. That was the very first time that I remember.

And did you find somebody else?

I did, yes, a group – I bumped into a group. In those days it was dark, no floodlights, you were running round a dark track, you know. There were lights on in the stand which helped you see a wee bit, but when you came down in front of the Jungle, you were almost in total darkness. I've got a memory of Jock Stein. I had just finished a stint and was taking off my tracksuit top when in bounded Jock. "Right, Carroll," he says, "get your hands up!" We stood facing each other, hands wide open and his were like shovels. We parried and slapped as hard as we could. Then one got through and I can feel the thud yet. I think it was his way of toughening us up.

Bobby, you made your debut in the League Cup on 12 August 1959, a Wednesday night, Celtic 1, Partick Thistle 2. So what was it like, your debut?

A great day. The only thing I felt was, I felt I was too soon in the first team because I'd just finished as a junior and I was thrown right into the Celtic first team. It wouldn't happen nowadays, I don't think. Then there was the slow handclap. It was my very first game and we got the slow handclap. I'd never known it before.

Did you find you were playing a different game from the one required of you at Irvine Meadow?

When Jock Stein came on the scene, Jock started to pull me back. When I played at Irvine Meadow, I used to stand close up to the full-back and burst through, get a start on the back. Jock pulled me back. He said, "All you're doing is marking the full-back. You're making his job easy," which probably was right. I mean, if the ball got played past the back, I was off. Jock wanted me to come away from the full-back, to make him mark me. But I also had to go back and mark the other winger. I never had to do that at Irvine Meadow. Jock expected me to go all that way back, rob the other winger, then burst past the full-back as well. Mind you, I always felt it was wrong. When I was standing down the line away from the full back, he was onto the ball as quick as I was. Dunky MacKay's job was to stall the winger. My job was to come in from the back and rob him. Jock was there as reserve team coach but when he moved into the first team side of it, then we started to have tactics coming in.

So you then had a rôle, Bobby, which was given you by Jock Stein? Was he using the blackboard at this time?

No. No, he would just talk to you. Tell you something he wanted you to try. He was still the second team coach. But he had his input there. Because we never practised throw-ins or free-kicks or corners. We did nothing. We never got told that such and such a left-back's completely one-sided, if you come inside him, you've got him, or that such and such a goalie's hopeless at corners. Nobody told you anything. You just went in on a Friday morning and if your name was up on the sheet, you went out and played. If you didn't play well, you were probably out of the team the next week. It's different nowadays. There was really no help given to you. You either did it, got on with the game, or you were hopeless, didn't play. But that was the time we were playing in. In those days if you were a good junior and you signed, then you went into the first team. You had two or three games and if you had a bad game you were out and somebody else got a shot and that's the way it was. Nobody ever said, "Come on and we'll practise with your left foot," or, "You're no good at heading, we've to improve that." Nothing like that. Not, as I say, until Jock came on the scene. One of the other things, I remember Jock was involved in, it involved me again, was that when Haffey got the ball, you know, when the ball was crossed from the right wing and Haffey picked it out of the air, I was getting it, I knew it was coming to me. And if it came from the left side, the left winger knew as soon as Haffey got it, zip! the ball was coming to him. It was coming into work then. Then Jock went away for his bit of experience at Dunfermline and when he came back, I was away by then.

What did it feel like to have Paddy Crerand behind you?

There were more passes coming from Paddy than there were from anybody else, believe it or not. Paddy had a great football brain even though he was young then. Paddy was like ourselves, only a boy, recently signed-up from the juniors. But Paddy was shouting at you, telling you where to be. If you didn't move into the right place, he'd give you a right rollicking. Paddy spoke more than some of the experienced players.

Bobby Carroll

Now, Bobby, your first Ne'erday game was at Parkhead on a Friday, 1960. And for this one, your position has been changed, you're playing centre-forward. Did you play centre-forward for Irvine Meadow?

No, never. I suppose they thought, if he scored all these goals at junior level, put him in at centre, see if he can do it here. We weren't scoring many goals at that time. That's about all I can put it down to.

But you're taking the park really with no theory as to how you are required to play centre-forward? You were just going to lie up on Bill Paterson, the centre-half?

Just play. Whatever. Nobody had told me to play any other way so I was just to play whatever way felt right myself. I did have the speed to play as a conventional centre.

Did Bertie Auld talk a lot?

Bertie spoke all the time! Bertie and I lived in the same area in Lambhill. I stayed just past him in the Cadder scheme. And Bertie was the first player at the park or one of the first to get a car. You've seen the film *Genevieve*? Well, the car in *Genevieve* was the same as Bertie's if it hadn't been for the running boards and the horn! So when Bertie got this car, he says, "I'll pick you up in the morning." That's how we went to the park in the morning. So I got into *Genevieve* and we went down to pick up Bobby Evans and Neilly Mochan. Neilly came off the train at Queen Street. Bobby Evans used to be waiting in his shop, doing his crossword. Bobby would come out of the shop and the four of us would away up to training.

Now, back to Ne'erday 1960. Big Frank Haffey had a magnificent game. He had some fantastic saves. Was Frank as good company as they say?

Frank was great company. Frank was the comedian of the team. And the singer. He used to sing, *Hey, Mister Blue.* He and Charlie Gallagher and I went on holiday one year. We went to Southend. Frank had a car, a second hand car. So we had a fortnight and we were coming back. We'd hardly any money left but we were coming through Gainsborough which is just the one big long street and we were starving. And we passed this great big hotel. Then next minute, "There's a chip shop!" But there's nowhere to stop. Anyway, Frank manages to turn the car round and we drive into the big hotel. The car park is at the back. I say, "Frank, what are you doing?" Because there's this doorman with the brown coat and the tile hat. "Just rely on me," says Frank. So we get out of the car, walk up to the doorman at the back door and he seems to be keeping an eye on us. Frank walks straight up, "Good afternoon! We're just going in for a spot of lunch." "Certainly, sir. Straight through here!" So in we go. The toilets were on the left-hand side. So we go in, wash, freshen up, then out the front door and along to the chip shop. We have our chips, then back to the hotel, in by the front door, out by the back. The doorman is still on duty. "Did you enjoy your meal, sir?" Frank pats him on the back. "Excellent lunch, my man. Our compliments to your chef." Into the car and off again for Scotland. That was Frank.

Right, Bobby, 27 January 1960, this great Floodlight Friendly against Everton, the first time Celtic had played the Toffees since 1938, and you scored the mother of all goals that night.

I don't remember my first goal for Celtic but that is the one goal that I do remember, the Everton one. I was two feet from the by-line. I just hit it first time. It hit the underside of the bar and dropped into the back of the net. I can see it happening to this day. It was one of these goals, I had to hit it, I just hit it first time. Jones, the left-back, might have thought it was going out but I knew I was going to catch it. I got to it and hit it first time. That was Celtic's first goal under the Celtic floodlights. You were talking there about tactics and I said there were none but I can think back to when we went to play Stirling Albion. I don't know if it was every time but I can remember this one time. It was the orange ball. Remember the orange ball? They had an orange ball and there was something in it, there was a pea in it or something. When you took a throw, it rattled. And I don't know if it was true, but it must have been true, because the ball was definitely heavier. I think they'd soaked it for a week before they played us and probably before they played Rangers as well. Trying to take a corner with that ball? It was almost impossible to get it into the penalty box. That was the only tactic in those days. Interfering with the orange ball. There was something that rattled. I don't whether they'd put a pea in it or not, but there was something that rattled. It was a tactic affecting play against us.

A cunning plan, eh? Now, on 19 April 1960, Airdrie 2, Celtic 5. Carroll is back at outside-right in the first team with Chalmers, Mochan, Divers and Gallagher. Charlie Gallagher is another one who seems to be getting moved all over the forward line. I know you were friends, but as a footballer, how much of an impact did Charlie make on you?

Aye, Charlie again was a smashing player. Charlie was a thinker. I used to compare Charlie with Johnny Haynes. I always felt Charlie was similar to Johnny Haynes, he had such a slick left foot and the way he fed the pass inside the full-back. But I never got to play with Charlie as my inside man. Charlie was always inside-left. He never came onto the right. When I went on the left wing, and I had a good run on the left wing, it was always Johnny Divers was my inside man. And probably my best football for Celtic was played on the left wing. But it was always Divers that was inside.

Right, Bobby, Charity Cup first round on 7 May 1960. Celtic and Clyde draw 3-3 and Clyde go out on the toss of the coin. Harry Haddock calls wrong. Now you played against Harry Haddock. He died just before Christmas 1998.

He was a great footballer and a great person. I met Harry quite a lot. On the park we just played our game. Other players threatened you. I got my share of threats, "I'll break your leg!" and that sort of thing. "Don't you dare try that again, sonny!" You know? But Harry was a gentleman and hard to play against. He was clever and he was fast, he had pace. Harry reckoned he played before his time. He had all the instincts of an attacking full-back but Pat Travers said if he hadn't passed the ball by the time he reached the centre line, he wouldn't be playing the following week. He couldn't go over the centre line. He had to get to get rid of it. But Harry was a great player. I never ever got to ask Harry but I can bet my bottom dollar he would have loved to play for Celtic. He'd have made a great Celtic full-back.

But his fame is with Clyde and none the worse for that. He was a great man and I was very sorry to hear he was dead. Bobby, you're coming up to Harry Haddock on the field. How are you going to get past him?

I'm going to push it past him and run!

But he knows you're going to push it past him!

Are you coming on to my time at St Mirren? I'll tell you something then. We'll resume this topic then.

Now, just pursuing things in a chronological order, on 19 May, you're over in Ireland for Derry City 0, Celtic 3.

John Hughes was funny on that trip or rather at the end of it. He was just a young boy coming into the team around that time. We were roommates. On the way back, we bought a few things for the folks at home. John was going then with the girl who became his wife. "I got her a watch," he said. So I said, "Are you going to declare it?" "No." So I said, "Where have you got it?" Then I noticed he was limping. He said, "I've got in my shoe." So we came up the Clyde. And did the boat not stop! It didn't come right up to the Broomielaw, it stopped somewhere. Maybe Whiteinch. You should have heard John! "Oh, you beauty! I'm getting off here!" And off he goes limping down the gangway, right into the hands of the Customs! But they never got the watch. To them, he was just a footballer with a limp. The rest of us got off at the Broomielaw. There wasn't a Customs man to be seen. Talking about Customs, there's a story about Willie Johnstone and the 1957 tour of America. Bob Kelly was against flying so they went out and back by sea. Anyway, when they came back, the bus picked them up and took them up to Celtic Park. The hampers were carried off the bus and into the dressing room and the directors got the hampers open. There was uncommon interest in the boot hamper but there was no boot hamper. Where's the boot hamper? The boot hamper was still on the docks at New York with the watches and the perfume and everything else that was stuffed into the boots! I don't know how true a story that was but it was still in circulation when I arrived. Willie Johnstone nearly got his books. He'd left the one hamper that mattered behind in the Big Apple!

Now, Bobby, at the start of the new season, another game that I have to ask you about, this Anglo-French Friendship Cup, on 6 August 1960, Sedan 3, Celtic 0.

We were outplayed. They were a very rough side. I think most of them were North Africans and they were hard as nails. The pitch was like concrete. It was roasting that day, temperature in the eighties and we were melting. We stayed in Rheims so it was a two hour journey to the game in sweltering heat. We were instructed not to drink the water. That was as much part of the reason as the heat. We turned up with nothing for the players to drink at half-time. I think quite a few of us took the field that day, both halves, quite dehydrated. We had to drink champagne. And I don't drink! So I had a few wee sips to wet my lips and that did me. By the time we got back to Rheims, you can imagine the state we were in, one way and the other! Sedan had given us some extra champagne to take with us. About half way back to Rheims, there's a shout, "Stop the bus! We need to go to the toilet!" So the driver stops, we get out, the champagne in the boot gets liberated and carried up to the back of the bus. A few of them were well under the weather the next morning, sore heads in all directions, but what on earth were we to do, there was nothing else to drink? It was bad that time. It was a poor show.

I wonder what was wrong with the water? The goals all came in a flurry, 21, 25, 29. You were up against a very physical team, heat and dehydration. And the crowd was 'howling'?

I don't remember the crowd. I tended not to hear the crowd. Even playing against Rangers in those days, 80,000, 86,000, once the game started, I didn't know there was anybody there. You get engrossed in the game and you don't realise. It's worse when there's a small crowd. When it's a small crowd all the insults come over plainly. You heard a big crowd when you came out onto the park at first. But once the whistle blew and the game got started, I used to get so lost in the game, there could have been nobody there. It was strange.

Now, 1 October 1960 against Airdrie. You are about to take a corner kick and a big black object, comes flying through the air and lands at your feet. Then a voice, "An' that makes two o' ye!"

No, that story's mistold. It landed in the penalty box. I was taking this corner and I stepped back to get my run-up and this thing, this black thing, came flying over out of the crowd behind me and landed in the penalty box. I took the corner and Johnny Divers headed over the bar. So while the ball is out of play, I go to have a look. I recognise the horseshoe shape, it's a black puddin' lying there and I'm still looking when the referee comes up. "What is it?" he says. "It's a black puddin'", I say. And right at that moment, the voice from the crowd, "Aye, Carroll, and that makes effin' 12 o' ye!" It was definitely 12 and it was in the penalty box, not at the corner flag.

Now Sedan came to Parkhead on 18 October 1960 for a 3-3 draw in the Friendship Cup. They were a goal up in the first minute. Was this an easier game than back on 6 August?

Not really. Again they kicked us off the park. It was a Scottish referee too but there was never any question of protection. There's a newspaper photograph, I'm in it, and the defender's almost sitting on my shoulders. It was a penalty, a definite penalty, but we never got a free-kick hardly. That was why we never won that game. The referee was definitely not in our favour.

He booked Hatchi of Sedan. Maybe that was the one sitting on your back! What was your temperament like, Bobby? Were you a quiet man?

Yeah. I think that was another part of my problem. I'd just take what was happening and try to carry on. I went to a funeral in Irvine. Afterwards in the hotel was the usual thing, drinks or tea and sandwiches. So not being a drinker, I just stuck to the tea and sandwiches. The following Tuesday, I was summoned to Jimmy McGrory's office. "Sit down. Where were you on Friday?" I say, "I was at a funeral in Irvine." He says, "Were you drunk?" I say, "No. Why are you saying that?" He says, "Well, there's a letter," and he threw a letter across to me, anonymous, not signed. I'd been in this hotel at half-past four on the Friday afternoon and I was steaming drunk. Because I was in the hotel and because there were people drinking a bit, then I was drunk as well. Yet he knew I was teetotal. You know the sort of thing I was saying earlier about no coaching and no tactics? That was no reflection on Jimmy McGrory. Jimmy McGrory was a great man, everyone had the utmost respect for him. But those were the times were living in.

Now, on 23 September, in a League match with Dundee United at Parkhead you moved to outside-left and began a rather fruitful partnership with John Divers. What about John Divers?

Yeah, John Divers. You had to get used to playing with John Divers because he was kind of hen-toed. John never hit the ball with the inside of his foot, it was always the outside. He would run with the ball at his foot tap-tap-tap and then, this time it was the bit heavier tap and you were getting the pass. You never knew when you were getting the pass with Johnny. With other players, they shape up when the pass is coming but Johnny hit it as it was spinning and the other thing is, because he was hitting it that way, the ball was coming at you on a spin so it took me two or three games to pick this up. I was getting shouted at from the Jungle, for not controlling the ball, as if the ball was too fast for me, until I suddenly twigged it, This fella's putting a spin on that! This is what it was. The ball was spinning and I'm trying to stop it and it's spinning off my foot. So then I learn, as soon as the ball comes to me, I just touch it like that, the ball goes spinning past the back, and I'm off! I worked it out in my favour at the finish-up. He was another very good player, John. My move to the left wing resulted in my best spell with Celtic. I was picked for the Scottish League against the Scotland XI at Hampden on 5 February 1962. The game ended in a two-goal draw and I managed to score one of the League's goals with a 20 yard shot. The right-back opposing me was Alex Hamilton of Dundee FC. He told me in later years he could not handle me. It's strange that some players become bogey players to others.

Now Bobby, you're back to outside-right on 3 February 1962 at Parkhead versus St Johnstone. Now this is the day when Frank Haffey tried to steer a free-kick smartish to Dunky MacKay and he put it in his own net!

It was actually a goal kick. Dunky was right-back. Frank was right-footed. The goal-kick was on the left-hand side of the goal. So when Frank came to take it, Dunky shouted for it. Dunky was an inborn footballer and he liked to play his football from the back. Frank looked up, hit it with his left foot, sclaffed it, the ball took a curl and ended up in the back of the net. His face went chalk white. But because the ball had not gone outside the area it was deemed not in play and he had to take it again. Poor Frank. I mind Charlie Gallagher and Frank and I, we were at a presentation at St Mary's Boys' Guild presenting medals and after we'd presented the medals, the boys were asking questions. And I don't think it was one of the boys, I think it was one of the men that were there, he said, "Mr Haffey, is it true your favourite song is *Nein, Nein, Fraulein*?" That was from a Celtic audience and apparently Frank got it like that all his life. We were at the game, the Celtic team and he had practically no cover. The two full-backs, they played wide to mark the wingers, Douglas and Charlton and England were bursting through the middle. As long as the Scottish backs marked the wingers, England were happy. Bobby Charlton was coming in for pot shots, Bobby Charlton with one of the hardest shots in the game.

But you've got to hand it to Frank. He did carry on. I mean, I'd probably have gone and hanged myself. But Haffey carries on! When did your face cease to fit at Parkhead, Bobby?

Do you remember St Mirren beat us 3-0 in the semi-final of the Cup? I was playing on the Monday before that when we beat St Mirren 5-0 at Love Street. I was told before the game started I wasn't playing in the Cup semi-final. I think it was Willie Johnstone actually gave me the news. "It doesn't matter how well you play to-night," he said. "You're not playing on Saturday." And that night against St Mirren was one of our best wins of the season. We went out and won 5-0 and I scored. I don't think you'd get that sort of thing happening nowadays either. There was a lack of professionalism there. I don't think it would happen nowadays.

Who was it, Bob Kelly?

No, I got on fine with Bob Kelly. I thought Bob Kelly was a good-going guy. I can remember him one day going in and talking to somebody in the foyer at Celtic and he was talking about TV. I can hear his words yet. He said, "Scotsport on TV will ruin Scottish football." He quoted the American scene, what had happened to sport in America, TV had taken over. He said, "If we allow TV to get a grip on Scottish football, they'll take over."

Bobby, you wanted to mention St Mirren earlier.

When I went to St Mirren, the rest of them were already all out. I got my kit on, went out the tunnel and Willie Fernie and John Wilson, the full-back were jogging past. So Willie said to me, "If you want to keep fit, join in with us. If you don't, the rest are over in the far corner there." So I looked over and the whole team's standing with their hands in their pockets. St Mirren was the only team I was with that gave you pockets in your tracksuit. So I joined in with Willie and Cockles but I said to them, "What's happening here?" Willie says, "They don't train. We're the only ones that train here." And I thought, "What have I come to here?" So we're going round past them and I could hear them talking. They're talking about *Sunday Night at the London Palladium* on TV the night before and what else was on the box. Then the trainer comes out, Jimmy McGarvey. Jimmy claps his hands, "Come on lads, couple of laps!" Jimmy was ever such a polite wee man. Immediately there was uproar. "Away you and eff off! Away back in there and treat somebody!"

They stayed there till we got a ball out and then had a game at the back of the goals. But you asked me earlier about Harry Haddock and how do you beat Harry Haddock. I spoke about John Wilson there. The early weeks when I was there, Celtic were coming to play us. Cockles says to me, "Tell me something, Bobby, see this man Johnstone, I can take Henderson of Rangers, but see Johnstone? How do I get the ball off him?" I said to him, "Lots of people would like to know that!" "Anyway", I said, "what's the problem?" "He comes up to me," he says, "and I know where he's going, I know he's going that way, but he still sends me the other way first! I know he's going to do it and I say to myself, I will not go. I say to myself, he's sending me that way but he's going to go this way. I won't take it so I go that way, my way, and he still goes the other way, his way. He's impossible." He's the one man, he said, that he couldn't play against, Jimmy Johnstone. Jinky.

Now, Bobby, 26 September 1962, against Valencia, in Spain in the Fairs Cities' Cup. Mestre of Valencia concedes an own goal in 29 and then the first Celtic player to actually score for Celtic in Europe is Bobby Carroll with a quarter of an hour to go.

I'm disputing the first one. I actually scored two. I know some newspapers gave it as an own goal but as far as I was concerned it was two goals to me. Mestre couldn't get out of the way and I claim both goals. It was going in. Although it hit the lad, it was going in anyway. He couldn't get clear. Both of these goals were made by Mike Jackson. Both of them came from the right wing. Mike was pushed down to the by-line and cut them back and I put them in. The other thing is, Mike and I were then dropped for the Saturday game against Raith Rovers!

Well, what's new? What was it like kicking off at so late at night?

It was strange, very strange.

You had problems with sleeping, didn't you, before a match?

Well I used to go to bed late. If I went to bed at 11 o'clock, half past 11, then I slept all night. I had no problem then. But I didn't dare go too early. I'd lie and I'd be thinking about the game.

Bobby, why St Mirren?

St Mirren promised me first team football. Can I tell you a story from my time with Dundee

United? We had just landed in Iceland. It was 12 o'clock at night broad daylight and the press were all taking photographs. We were just off the plane when I get the word, "There's a guy over there behind the fence seems to know you." I said, "What! In Iceland?" You know who it was?

Who?

The Reverend Jack!

The Lutheran Pastor? Great Celtic supporter!

Aye. His church was in the north of Iceland and he'd come down to spend the week with Dundee United. Do you remember Hugh Delaney, the chairman of the Celtic Supporters' Associations? The Reverend Jack took me into this shop and upstairs here is this artist painting this portrait of Hugh Delaney. The Reverend Jack says to me, "What do you think of that?" I say, "It's terrific. What are you doing it for?" He says, "I'm going to present it to him!"

I wonder where it is now?

I don't know. The Delaney family maybe.

Bobby, putting yourself on the bench, what about picking your all-time Celtic XI?

I think Simpson; McGrain, McNeill, Clark, Gemmell; Johnstone, Crerand, Auld, Tully; Dalglish and Wallace. How's that?

Not bad. Very good. Bobby, thank you very, very much. God bless. Safe home!

Thank you! Thank you!

Willie O'Neill
Left-back
1959-1969

At Celtic I was in the third team to begin with but my very first game was with the second team. The Ants went out of the Cup on the Saturday and I signed for Celtic on the Monday. I played on Tuesday in a reserve game against Clyde, I think it was. I got injured in my very first game – I was into the third team and I was in the third team for quite a while. My first game for the big team was the 1961 Cup Final replay. It must have been a year or so.

Willie, were you signed as a left-half or a left-back?

Left-half. I was never a left-back. And my right foot was a non-event.

You had the most astounding debut of any Celtic player I can think of, coming in for Jim Kennedy, stricken with appendicitis, for the Scottish Cup Final replay against Dunfermline on 26 April 1961. Jimmy McGrory said you had the temperament for the big time. When did you know you were playing and did you really have the big time temperament?

I was very quiet. You couldn't get me to talk. I used to sign autographs in wee toaty writing in case people thought I was big-headed. That was me. But I had the temperament. On the day that we played, we went for a meal. It was Wednesday, the thing that we would usually do if there was a Wednesday game. And then the players go out for a wee walk and then we'd get the bus and go to Hampden. Alec Byrne, he was told to take me and kind of calm me down, you know? So we were walking along and Alec was talking this and that and I'm saying what I think, and after five or ten minutes, "Listen," said Alec, "I was sent out to calm you down. You're calming me down!" It wasn't an intentional thing. I was very, very shy. Players go into the dressing-room and get all up-tight. That type of thing didn't bother me. When I got told I was in the team, it did hit me. The same as when I went home and the press were all around my door. I felt a wee bit fluttered. But the next day I was all right again, you know? There was the initial shock but then I was okay.

The team was Haffey; MacKay and O'Neill; Crerand, McNeill and Clark; Gallagher and Fernie; Hughes; Chalmers and Byrne. Six members of the 1967 squad. That replay is still a biting disappointment for Celtic fans of the time. Do you remember much of the actual game?

I don't know. I was under pressure to do well. It was my first game. Under pressure to do well, first and foremost. We wanted to win the Cup but when you lose two-nil, it pulls you down slightly. It was very hard to get beat. I mean, I read the paper next day giving me all this praise, all about Unlucky Willie, how I was supposed to have had a good game and all the rest of it. It didn't do me any good. We'd got beat. I'd rather have played badly and Celtic won. I still feel it.

Jim Kennedy was back in the big team for August 1961. You started partnering John Donnelly at full-back in the reserves. John Donnelly is one of the mystery men of Celtic.

Oh, John, aye. John was a good player. His name always comes up because of the 7-1 team. Nobody can remember who was right-back. John Donnelly was the right-back. John was a class player.

He lost his place to Dunky MacKay, didn't he?

Oh well, that was Dunky. Dunky was some player. It wouldn't have mattered who it was, Dunky was something else. Dunky was a great player. But Dunky was before his time, you know. He was an attacking full-back. And then you'd get Sean Fallon and Bob Kelly saying, "What's that full-back doing away up there?" It wasn't until Stein came in that things changed and full-backs were flying up the wings, half-a-mile a minute, getting up there, scoring goals, you know? John Donnelly was the same nature as myself, a very quiet boy. He'd just come in and do his thing and go away. If someone spoke to him, he'd listen and answer but you'd have to speak to him first. A bit like myself. I'd never start a conversation, you know. I'd wait till someone asked me something and then I'd unwind. I'd hear things being asked that I knew the answer to but I'd not say, I'd let someone else say.

By January 1962, Jimmy McGrory was telling us he would not stand for overconfidence at Celtic Park. Would you ascribe Celtic's basic inconsistency to overconfidence?

I wouldn't say overconfidence, no. The problem was largely Rangers' dominance. The pressure was getting more and more to the players. We took a lot of stick from the fans. A forward like Charlie Gallagher suffered a lot more than me. I would get away with it in defence, sort of thing. We all wanted to play but we needed a style to play in, a job to do which happened when Stein came. Stein would never ask someone to do something he couldn't do. He didn't ask Charlie to go out and kick. He wouldn't ask me to go running up the park because that wasn't my style. My style was to defend and pass it. He asked you to do whatever you were good at. And I don't think we had that before Jock Stein, you know.

Willie, we've mentioned Jimmy Johnstone. I think you and he became great pals. Had you known each other before Parkhead or just linked up when you got there?

No, we just linked up when we got there. I think probably by the time Jinky got to Parkhead I was starting to talk a wee bit, not loudish. There was a group there talk-talk-talk-talk but I was with a quiet bunch, "Hello, how are you today? How do you do?" Jinky and all the quiet boys were in my group.

I was at the Public Trial in August 1965 and Jinky came out with the Hoops for the second half. He could hardly stand because of something you'd said. Some joke you'd told him. I'm not asking you to remember that but the sight is fixed indelibly in my head.

I wish I could remember what it was!

The pair of you were still talking on the pitch and he could hardly stand whatever it was

you just said to him. What about trips by 'plane? I've heard you kept him distracted with O'Neill's distinctive brand of pawky, low-key, mordant humour.

He didn't like flying and I used to joke with him all the time. "I don't like the look of that wing, Jimmy, I wouldn't sit there if I were you. That wing's loose, this plane's a crate." I'd make a joke of it. He'd say, "Don't you! Don't you!" We'd get the banter going, we'd talk, instead of sitting there terrified to death. If you got him talking, then I would be laughing, "Och come on, wee man, I'm only kidding you, I'm only kidding you!" You know that stuff. And he'd say, "Ach, you're always at it." But he was talking. It took the pressure off him as well. Don't get me wrong, I was scared as well. Maybe not just as much as him but scared all the same.

Now you were still with the Whites for the Public Trial of 7 August 1962: Fallon; Young and O'Neill; Clark, Cushley and Price; Johnstone and Carroll; Rooney; Murdoch and Byrne. Ian Young was part of the big team of 1964 and 1965 but then virtually disappeared. What was Ian Young like as your full-back partner?

Ian did his job. He would go out and he would stop. He wasn't a great passer of the ball, he wasn't a great header of the ball but he knew his game, he did his job. If a man needed marking, he would mark him. He didn't play that cavalier stuff, he'd just stop him. He did the simple thing. He wouldn't try to thread a ball from here to there all the way through the play. He'd give it to Charlie or Bobby or give it to someone else. As I say, he did the simple thing. He was unfortunate but maybe not all that unfortunate, he got to the Cup Final in '65.

What about Billy Price? How did you rate Billy Price?

He was a good player, oh yes. One hundred per cent. I would say the directors signed him. If Jock Stein had signed him, he would have signed him to do a job. He would have worked something so that Billy could do it. It was unfortunate that he played for Celtic when he did. I remember Paddy Crerand said to me – we were going to Valencia, I think it was, yeah? They'd dropped Billy Price from left-half and put me in. I think they wanted somebody with more puff. Paddy said to me, "I hope they're not putting you in just to tackle people and kick the ball away." But I didn't do that anyway, you know? But I tell you this, he wouldn't give the ball away, Billy.

He was a very nice fellow. And a great big guy and all. But they were all great! I don't think there was a bad person at Parkhead. But Billy, aye, he was unfortunate he wasn't there when Stein was there.

What about Bobby Murdoch? When I first saw Bobby Murdoch I thought he was a feast for the eyes.

To me, Bobby was the best that I've seen at Parkhead. He did everything. He could see everything, do everything. He was there to help you, a great, great player.

Now, your temperament for the big time was invoked again when, as we've said, you got Billy Price's place against Valencia in Spain on 26 September 1962, the Fairs Cities' Cup tie, a 4-2 defeat? Were you put into that team as a defensive element?

Well, I suppose you could call it that but I was only a boy, youngish, compared with Billy. I was put in to chase these guys. He would have struggled. I would have thought that was the idea. But Billy was a great player, a better player than me, you know. But if you're over there, and these guys get by Billy – I'm not saying I was the fastest thing but I could work on it, you know? Whereas Billy wouldn't be able to do that. That was the idea.

After Valencia you began a run in the Celtic big team in place of Billy Price. This was about the time Paddy Crerand was being reckoned the best right-half in the world. What was it like being part of a half-back line, Crerand, McNeill and O'Neill?

Och, I was just happy to play. Paddy was great. Paddy was 200 per cent Celtic. He was always driving the people on around him and his cross-field passes were Paddy at his best. It didn't matter how far away you were, Paddy would get the ball and the pass was on its way – without even looking! That was Paddy. He was a master of the pass. But I would say Bobby had even more than that. Bobby had more than just the pass. Bobby had everything you need.

You move to left-back in place of Jim Kennedy. How were you for pace, Willie, because if you're transferred from half-back to full-back and you don't have the pace, are you ever going to make it?

I think if anything I read it better than pacewise. I would try to make the winger do what I wanted him to do. I knew where he was going. I don't mean that in a big-headed kind of way.

Who taught you that?

I had it to start off with but at times I was diving in. It became 50-50 whether I was going to get the ball or not. It was Big Jock, something he said. "You're not there to stop the winger. The winger's there to beat you. And if you dive in, he's beat you. If you go and confront him, then he's got to think about it." So if I don't dive in, then he's thinking about going there but he can't go there because I'm making him think about it. I'm not diving in. And it's right. It worked all the time, you know. And it finished up, I was showing wingers where to go and when to go. I don't want that to sound big-headed.

I know this sort of full-back play can be taught. I've seen it being taught.

To this age I've never been big-headed but I was coming up against wingers – he kicks the ball – I've got the ball – and he's still going on. That's how easy it was getting with certain players, you know. A good player like wee Willie Henderson, he said the same. He was talking about McNab and Cyril Knowles. He'd played against these guys, great full-backs but the one he couldn't get any change out of was me! But it was the same kind of thing. You were talking about pace. If you went tight with Willie, you got an extra yard for Willie – he was away. All he was going to do was hit it by you and he was away. But there was no way he was going to beat me because I'm holding off and he's got to find the pace to beat me. I thought a lot about my game. I never had a bad game against wee Willie. I always remember I was down the tunnel, the teams were going out, down the tunnel at Parkhead. I was sub. The two teams, wee Willie there. "How are you doing, big man?" "Hi, Willie, not bad." I've got the tracksuit on. He said, "You're getting a raw deal, big man. But you won't hear me complaining."

The reason I got dropped finally, I got dropped after Dundee United beat us 3-2 on Hogmanay 1966. Stein said to me, we're going to play runners rather than tacklers at full-back. And Gemmell had a bad game that day. He had a terrible game. So he brought Jim Craig in. And that was the reason. He came up to me and he said, "I want runners rather than tacklers." And Tommy Gemmell could run. Plus his shot. You couldn't beat that! He could hit them from 40, 50 yards.

Right, Willie. Paddy Crerand left for Manchester United in January 1963 and Bobby Carroll in February for St Mirren. Did the transfer of players affect you?

I would say not really because I was never really close to anybody then other than Jinky, Bobby Lennox, Bobby Murdoch. They didn't go. Nobody like that went. There were guys went maybe like myself who didn't make it regular in the first team. I was never really close to them, do you know what I mean? I think when people went away, I used to think, What does he want to leave Celtic for? There was no way I wanted to leave Celtic. It didn't matter what you did to me. I wanted to stay at Celtic Park. It was me, Lennox and Jinky. When you've seen one, you've seen three. Always together. Everybody got a laugh. Lennox was a joke a minute, Jinky was the same and I was their number three. We used to take the mickey out of all the big boys, you know? There was Big Billy. He'd call us daft kids and tell us to grow up but it was all good banter, all good stuff.

Celtic's left-back was now Tommy Gemmell and Jim Kennedy moved to left-half. March 1964 was a time of great excitement. Celtic won 3-0 and looked certs for the Cup Winners' Cup Final. But MTK won 4-0 at the Nep Stadium, Budapest. Did you travel to Budapest?

I did, yeah. Myself and Dunky, we were sitting on the bench that night. What came through my head – we were talking about Ian Young, yeah? Well, I thought Dunky would have been in that team because he was an attacking full-back but they didn't want attacking full-backs. I'm sitting looking at Ian Young and I'm thinking, This is Dunky MacKay sitting next to me. You should be on the park. Dunky was a great back! The trouble that night was, we had attacked at Parkhead and now we were trying to attack again.

You began to play for Jock Stein as of the very next game after the 1965 Cup Final, a 5-1 defeat at East End Park.

Everybody's attitude seemed to change the minute he came. As I said to you, you had that extra yard. You wanted to get into Celtic Park. Everybody wanted to get in. Once Stein came, training started at ten o'clock, everybody was in at nine o'clock. Training finished at 12, 12.30. You were still there at half-one, two o'clock. Or you left at one, you were back at two. Nobody wanted to leave. Everything just changed. Jock Stein. How it happened, I don't know. It happened to myself as well. You got fuelled-up. The man was something else.

Celtic reserves on 17 September 1965 were: Simpson; Craig and McCarron; Jim Brogan, Cushley and O'Neill; Connelly and Ayrton Inacio; Jimmy Quinn; Henry Quinn and Taylor. What about George Connelly?

We never saw the best of George Connelly. I think he could have reached the top. We never saw the best of him. By this time, I was just starting to come into the team and any game we went away to, Jock Stein would take maybe a couple of young boys. George used to room with me. He was the same as me, he was a quiet boy. As I say, he was a good player but we never saw the best of him. Another two or three years and he could have been sky high.

Now, what about this Brazilian trialist, Ayrton Inacio, one of Celtic's samba imports?

Inacio, yeah. A lot of skills but it was all fan dance stuff. I wouldn't say he couldn't play in the Celtic team, I wouldn't say that. Sometimes he flattered to deceive. He wasn't experienced. It was young boys coming over, trying to show-off kind of thing. But they had skills, oh, no doubt, great skills. You should have seen some of the things they would try to do in training. I saw one only the other day, the guy ran over the ball and whipped it over his head. They were doing that then! The Brazilians in training.

The Scottish weather didn't beat them?

No, I don't think so.

What about Jimmy Quinn, grandson of the Croy Express? He was left-sided like the mighty Quinn and just as fast. He became a left-back, didn't he?

Jimmy? He had bags of talent. His biggest asset was his pace. But he had skill, oh, he had skill all right. He was another one, bags of skill. I think maybe there were too many of them going around at the time, skilful boys. It was hard. Celtic had a reserve team with every one of them knocking at the door.

Willie, Celtic set out for Bermuda and the USA on 11 May 1966. Ian Young got injured and suddenly your hour had come: Gemmell and O'Neill were Jock Stein's choice of full-backs. Can you remember Bermuda and the start of things?

Oh yeah! Every day, every hour! Oh aye, it was tremendous. The fact that I was in the team, I was getting a run, that he had changed it, and straightaway things started to click for me. I mean it was some tour, there were a lot of half-decent teams we met like Spurs and Bayern. When I came off on any game of the tour, Neilly was there and he'd say to me, I wouldn't mind playing outside-left with you at left-back. I don't mean that big-headed either. That was the way we were playing. We were winning the ball and passing it, no hesitation. The tour was great for me. I remember I got injured, I think in the second last game or something. It was quite bad and I went to the hospital. Somebody else went and he got a heavy, heavy, heavy bandage. The guy said to me, "You'll be all right in a couple of weeks." And I said to Neilly, "Tell Jock I'm all right." But it was bad. It was that size. But Stein knew that. It was like an egg protruding. So we went in and caught the bus up to the next game. But the night before we were playing, Neilly came in and said, "The Boss wants to talk to you." So I went up the stair. He said, "How's your ankle?" I said, "I'm all right." He said, "Let's see you running." He's got me running up and down in the hotel. The sweat's pouring off me because I'm trying not to limp, you know. I don't know whether he saw the limp or not. "Are you sure you're all right?" he said. I said, "Aye." He says, "Tomorrow night's the second last game and you're doing not bad. I'm thinking of playing you at the start of the season. This could be your position at left-back." At the start of the season! He didn't need to say that to me, cripes! Then he said, "Are you sure you're all right?" Trying to tell me I'm not! That's what he wrote in the paper after the whole tour. He said, "Willie O'Neill played two games when lesser players would have quit." I could hardly run but I played. And it got me into the team at the start of the season.

You talk about half-decent teams, Willie, but this was an unbeaten tour with matches against Spurs, Bologna, Bayern and Atlas of Mexico.

Aye, not one easy game.

Back in Glasgow, Celtic beat Manchester United 4-1 but you were up against the young George Best and he had a great game, saving your reverence, Willie. Can you remember him on the day or was he just another class winger you dealt with?

Oh no, I remember George Best. He had a good game that day but I think a fit George Best would have murdered me. I think he was back from an operation, some bad injury. I think he'd been off for quite a while. That was his first game back. I think a really fit George Best would have torn the backside off me.

I know the Parkhead crowd was quite impressed. I don't think he was too well-known at the time or not so well-known to Scotland. His star was rising. Willie, you got a League Cup medal against Rangers at Hampden on 29 October 1966. Can you remember saving a certain goal when you cleared the ball off the line in the second half? If I'd been in your boots it would still wake me up at night. I'd still be having nightmares. It was so tight, I suppose you could as easily have put it in the net?

Aye, but there were no nightmares. Things had been going well for me since the start of the season and I was kind of halfway through it. The confidence was there. But when I say the confidence was there, I wasn't confident enough to kick it with that one.

Your right foot?

Yeah. The ball went by me and I went across and I stopped it with this one.

Which one?

My left. It was practically right on the line and I could have kicked at it with my right but I could have missed and I didn't want to take the chance with that one.

Did you never practise to try and develop your right foot?

I did try but it was always my left was my useful foot.

In the European Cup, you played against Zurich and Nantes. Did that qualify you for a medal when the Cup was won the following May?

No, the club struck medals for us. There were 12 medals on 25 May. The goalkeeper was the only sub. I think the manager got one. John Fallon got one although he didn't play. The club struck another four or five for us.

Do you have an outstanding memory of Lisbon on 25 May 1967? I mean, where were you? You weren't on the benches?

Oh no, we were away up in the stand. I think when we equalised, yeah. I remember when we lost the penalty, I felt deflated. This was going to be hard but when we got the equaliser, I took off into the air. I thought, We're going to do it here! Och, I mean, 2-1 flattered them. Bobby Murdoch again, he's tried here, he's tried there, tried here again, tried every position to break them down and the best of it is, we'd done it! Great. Tremendous.

Now you played at the Bernebeu Stadium, Real Madrid 0, Celtic 1 on 7 June 1967. What was

that for an experience, European Champions, Celtic, beating the great Real, the ex-Champions on their own turf? Did your mind go back at all to the 3-1 game at Parkhead five years before?

I think Jock had his mind made up – somebody said he wasn't going to play the Lions again in the one team but he did it again the following year. But see after that – that was the first game they played, was it not, after Lisbon?

It was.

Well, he changed the team. I went in at left-half, Tommy Gemmell was left-back and what else? – the team was changed about. Was John Clark right-half?

I've got it here: Fallon; Craig and Gemmell; Clark, McNeill and O'Neill; Johnstone and Murdoch; Wallace; Auld and Lennox.

Aye, that's it. It was tremendous. It was playing at the top, playing against him, Di Stefano. And it was packed, 125,000, 135,000, I think.

Still, Celtic have played to more than that.

Di Stefano nutmegged me. And I'd never been nutmegged in my life. So he's nutmegged me and Jinky and Lennox are on different wings and they're shouting across to each other, "He's nutmegged him! He's nutmegged him!" I was wondering, Have they got a bank on here or something? So we went in at half-time and I thought, "I'm going to get pelters here!" So I made sure I was last in and going in the door I still don't know what I'm going to say. So I went in and they're all there so I said, "Listen, before any of you say anything, is there one other player here can say he was nutmegged by the great Di Stefano?"

Willie, you travelled to Buenos Aires and Montevideo with Celtic for the World Championship?

I played in Buenos Aires. I wore the number 10 shorts. Bertie got injured in the League Cup Final against Dundee. We beat them 5-2. I came on as sub. We left on the Sunday after the game, went over there and Bertie was still injured. I was number ten. That was one of my best games. Although we got beat.

Can I just read you what Billy McNeill had to say not so long ago about the first game in Argentina: '…It was a sort of war. They messed us about in every respect, hotels, transportation, training facilities. The stadium was amazing, the atmosphere was fantastic, but all sorts of things were thrown on the pitch.'

It was terrible.

And about the game in Uruguay? 'What none of us had realised was that Uruguay and Argentina were such enemies. We were already wound up but then the Penarol lads who'd been in Glasgow came into our dressing room and wound us up even more. Unfortunately we snapped.' Have you anything to add to that?

I think that was what it was. Basically, instead of calming ourselves down, we just thought well, if that's the way you want it, you kick us, we kick you.

Instead of trying to catch them in the tackle, we were running about trying to kick them. To me, the first game when we there caused the second game. Oh dirty! They were animals. In the first game, we tried the right thing. We tried to play them. But it didn't matter what you did, they'd stand on your toes, spitting on you, anything they wanted to do, they were doing it. Even before the game started, getting the team photo taken, this guy's playing keepie-uppie in between the photographer and us and then when he'd finished, battering the ball at us. Terrible stuff. To me, we handled it that game. But it carried on to the next game. Everybody was fired-up about it, you know? By the time we got on there, then they started straightaway again, we couldn't handle it, you know?

It looked terribly bad on TV back here. I was down in England and they made a meal of it. Never mind what Sir Alf had called the Argentinians the year before, Celtic were Scottish hooligans exporting a hooligan brand of soccer.

Yeah, but when did you ever see Tommy Gemmell run up and kick someone or John Clark with his hands up?

I know. But it's an episode I still find very painful. Willie, you played in Buenos Aires and you got 45 minutes against Penarol in Glasgow. You still continue to play against class opposition like AC Milan in Jersey City in May 1968, against Kurt Hamrin at outside-right. It was against the rules but they stuck the great Omar Sivori on the pitch as a third substitute. All this class stuff! David Cattanach was your right-back. You were in the team that won the Toronto Cup against AC Milan on 1 June with Jim Brogan at right-back. Any memory of these games?

Not really. I think they passed in a blur.

You went down to Mexico and Celtic lost 3-2 against Necaxa. The game was played in an atmosphere so rarified the Celtic players had to have oxygen at half-time. Is that true?

Oh yes! I mean, you could get to where you wanted on the pitch but the minute you stopped, that was you, desperate for air. You could run the length of the pitch but once you got there, there was this siren sound in your lungs.

As bad as that?

Yeah.

Was the oxygen available from the start of the game? Did you know you would need it?

Oh aye! Because we'd trained before. We'd had two or three training sessions. We'd do wee sprints and you'd think we were all right but then the whee-whee-whee-whee sound would start in your chest. It was heavy stuff.

You played for Celtic against Carlisle in January 1969. Your other full-back was an all-time Celtic great-to-be: Danny McGrain. What did you think of Danny?

Oh, we saw Danny, we saw Kenny, we saw all these boys coming through. They were coming up and we thought we were getting old at 28, 29. You could see the class coming out of these boys. We had a training game that had started two or three seasons ago, Danny and Kenny and these boys used to be in the team playing the first team. And these games were getting harder and harder. You could see the talent emerging. I remember Jock Stein talking

– one of these same games – Kenny played a simple one-two, you know? Then he ballooned the ball over the bar. Miles over the bar! Big Jock turned round and said, "What a player he's going to be!" So I started looking. There were two or three or four reserves playing with Kenny. I started watching him after that. I began to think, dear God, the way I watched them play. They were all coming through around that time. You talk to John Gorman. He couldn't get in for the McGrains and Hays and all these people. He went down to Carlisle first and then he went to Spurs.

Willie O'Neill, thank you very much.

Charlie Gallagher
Inside-forward
1956-1970

I never really saw Jock Stein very much at all in the early days. I was with Celtic two nights a week and it was Sean Fallon took us for training. That's about 1956, I think. Willie Waddell had offered me terms with Kilmarnock. They were getting bigger and bigger every time but I kept telling him I wanted to play for Celtic. So at the end of, I think, possibly nine months, he said, "Well, I'm sorry, Charlie, I've done everything possible. Whether it was legal or illegal, he offered me the whole time that he had been putting offers to me. He offered me a lump sum. I signed for Celtic and I got nothing. I never got a single penny. I was a young, naïve, innocent boy, not knowing anything about football but the fact that I signed for Celtic was all I was interested in.

You played in the pre-season trial on the 4 August 1959. You played for the Whites in that great strip with green sleeves and the shamrock on the chest.

The political strip!

The team was Beattie; Donnachie and Kennedy; Clark, Kurila and Conroy; Gallagher and Chalmers; Lochhead; O'Hara and Divers. How was that, your first time stepping out before a big house at Celtic Park?

Oh, it was magnificent! I must have done reasonably well because when the season started, the League Cup got under way and Celtic were having a bad time and I played my first game on 22 August against Raith Rovers. I had a good game, so did Dan O'Hara and we won 1-0 at Celtic Park. Raith Rovers had a great team at the time. They were no pushovers.

Charlie, were you signed as an inside-forward or as a winger?

An inside-forward. This is Bob Kelly, with a bee in his head that I wasn't strong enough to play inside-forward yet in that first game against Raith Rovers, I had a great match at inside-left to Bertie Auld. Cyril Horne, who used to write then for the *Glasgow Herald*, said I was one of the best club debuts ever in his experience. Yet I had only two or three others games that season 1959-60 towards the end. I was a boy there, in the days of Evans, Peacock, Tully and the other giants. We trained and then we went up to the town. There was no training in the afternoon which to me was amazing. You were like a part-time team, you trained in the morning, finished at 12 o'clock and Celtic gave you lunch at Ferrari's restaurant at the top of Buchanan Street. Now we would go up there and you would go up the stairs and the dining-room was there and it was all Celtic. That part was the dining-room for us. We sat on the left hand side and all the first team players sat round the corner on the right hand side, divided, totally and utterly divided. In those days it was very, very them and us.

Charlie Gallagher

Charlie, you were a Kelly Kid.

I was a Kid. The first Kelly Kids I can remember were myself and a guy called Joe Logan, and another Roy Paton, we were the Glasgow boys. And then you'd get them coming in from Lanarkshire, Billy McNeill, John Clark, Bobby Murdoch. That was when we first met in early 1959-60 so we've known one another a long, long time. I think this is where the kind of camaraderie we had came from. Camaraderie, it's a great word nowadays, everybody uses this great word, but our camaraderie of the '65, '66, '67 era, it came from the fact that so many of us had been there so long, we all knew one another. All the wives knew one another, we knew one another's kids, we knew their first names, we were at one another's weddings. This is where the camaraderie of the Stein era came from, from the early 'sixties, not from the European Cup time, but long, long before. The only strangers were Joe McBride who was well known to us, Willie Wallace, who was known through football, and Ronnie. The rest were all brought-up through the system. I think the reserves won everything in 1959 and the club gave us each a Golden Shamrock. My medals are all on display at Celtic Park. The Glasgow Cup is the best medal of all the medals that's ever existed. And I've got five! The European Cup's a class medal as well. The kids around the corner would ask you, "Gonna show us your medals?" They'd say, "That's a cracker" about the European Cup but it was always the Glasgow Cup medal that caught their attention, the size of it, the feel of it, the coat of arms and it always glinted.

So Charlie, this bee in Bob Kelly's bonnet. But, saving your reverence, some people cannot play on the wing! It would require a miracle.

Do you remember the Glasgow Cup game against Rangers at Ibrox? The four – nothing game? August 1966. What I remember about that game is, I think big Yogi was down to play outside-left and Jock changed the team about quite a bit. It was obviously horses for courses in a lot of these games. So he rearranged the team before the start and big Yogi wasn't playing but I was playing at outside-left. Outside-left, I said to myself, Why the hell am I outside-left? And he came up to me at the start of the game and said, "You're named number 11, outside-left, but you will help us to win the game. If you don't get one kick of the ball, I'm not worried. I'm not in the least interested." So, why was that? Because Rangers play a marking system, full-backs follow the wingers. When Rangers were attacking, one of the backs covered the centre-half but mainly they were deputed to pick up the Celtic wingers. Kai Johansen was the right-back for Rangers. He was marking me. Stein said, "You start wandering. Johansen will follow you all over the park. Big Gemmell will be up and down that left wing where you are supposed to be." Wee Henderson, I think, was at outside-right and he seldom had a great game against Big Tam. So the match started and I started wandering and of course, Johansen started following me. Once he got into the middle of the park, he was lost. Everything was down that left wing, everything. So, the first half was about ten minutes started, we got a free-kick. I crossed the ball, big scramble, Big Billy scored a goal, 1-0. The second half Rangers changed a bit, Johansen went back to regular right-back. I started getting all the balls I could take. And I used them. We won 4-0. That was the first kind of tactical view that we'd seen from Jock Stein. He had noticed how Rangers played and he had changed the system. It was the middle of the week, a Tuesday or a Wednesday night, big, big attendance, Glasgow Cup. Nobody's interested in it nowadays or so they say, and we hammered them 4-0. I remember one of the goals we scored that night and it was a plan that had been used regularly when I was in the left midfield and Bobby Murdoch in the right midfield, that Stevie Chalmers would wander out to the wing, the centre-half would follow him and then a big long ball down the middle, Murdoch or me, and Bobby Lennox would just go wheeeek! Away in! We got our fourth goal like that that night. I got the ball and by this time Kai Johansen had forgotten all about me, sticking to his right-back position and I was running about free. I hit a long ball right down the middle and Bobby Lennox hit it past Ritchie. It's on a tape, it's on the '65 tape. It was a good night, it was a good night for me at outside-left. That was my experience of outside-left then. I was outside-left in number only.

Back to the Cup run of 1961 with you at outside-right.

I played in the Falkirk game, the Montrose game, the Raith Rovers game and against Hibs 1-1 at Parkhead, which was a 56,000 crowd.

And then you went to Easter Road and John Clark got the only goal in extra time before 39,243 with thousands locked-out.

We played that night at Easter Road and what I remember, they were actually sitting on the touchlines right round the park, something that would never be allowed nowadays. They were right round the field, sitting on the track, all the way round. It was one of the biggest crowds Easter Road had ever seen. Why, I don't know. Of course, it was the quarter-finals but that still doesn't explain the vast enthusiasm.

Tell me about Alec Byrne.

Alec Byrne was an enigma. He was one of the nicest guys you could ever know in your life. He would never say a bad word about anybody, never, ever say a bad word about anybody. He was a right, holy, good Catholic, a great Catholic. He's married with eight of a family, isn't he? He used to pick us up, he was one of the first people at Celtic Park with a vehicle. He lived in Greenock and he used to travel up, the old, old road right up through, right past Ibrox every morning, and he'd pick Paddy Crerand and me up at the corner of Crown Street and Ballater Street every single morning in an Austin A40 – a van! And he never had a bad word to say about anybody! And I think I've only seen him on one or two occasions when somebody would kick him on the park and he'd lose the head, because he was one of these players, he'd dribble, beat a player, then lose the ball but if somebody kicked him, then for ten seconds he'd lose the place but basically he was just a nice guy. Alec Byrne was a fantastic dribbler! I was never a dribbler so you don't know what dribblers think about. Wee Jinky would need to tell you why they dribble so much and never release the ball. Alec was the same. He'd never release the ball, he'd just dribble, dribble, lose it and that was it. But he was a good player. He was a good player to have in your team. That's a great player to have in your team, a dribbler, because he'll take the ball from one end of the park to the other. That's why Stein used Johnstone and Hughes so much. If you were under pressure, 1-0 up, 2-1 up, give the ball to Johnstone or Hughes. They'll take it up to the other lot's corner flag for you, they might lose it then, but they've taken the pressure off.

Charlie, a game that is still like a sword piercing my soul, the Scottish Cup final against Dunfermline?

Yeah. I remember things like that. The draw and the defeat? Jock Stein won the game as far as I'm concerned for Dunfermline that night. He negated us, everything we tried. I was having a good season that year. Paddy was behind me, Willie Fernie was inside, most of the play was always down the right wing. I always dropped back for the ball from Paddy or Willie and then used long balls to Stevie. That was our play, Paddy long balls, Willie Fernie a bit of dribbling, but Stein being the manager, obviously knew all of us from Celtic Park, he knew the way we played and I always remember the first game because I never kicked a ball in the first game. Willie Cunningham, the Irish international, was their captain. He stayed beside me or very close to me the whole game, and I never – I don't think I got a solitary kick of the ball the whole game. We missed a couple of chances. Big Yogi, I think, missed two or three chances and then of course, Eddie Connachan had a great game in goal for Dunfermline. The replay, I don't think we had the knowledge or we didn't have a manager or a coach with the brilliance to change tactics so we went out to play the same way and they did the exact same thing. To me, if we had a manager – I'm not decrying Jimmy McGrory whom I think everybody loved – we just didn't have the basic essentials to change games. Players – if it's left to the players – you always need a coach to change things. It's all right people talking about a captain there, you've got to get advice from the sidelines to do these things. Otherwise you just didn't think. Trouble is, not enough people were interested. We're going back a wee bit now but when I first went into the Celtic team in 1959, the players were not interested, they never spoke. I went into that dressing room, nobody spoke to you. Well, Best of luck, and that was it. There was nobody told you how to play. You were going into a team that was going out onto the park, 11 players, to kick a ball about. In the late Fifties, early Sixties, if you were inside-left, you went up and down this fixed path on the park, nobody dictated tactics because there were no tactics whatsoever. There were no tactics until Stein came to Celtic Park, none whatsoever. I don't know if you've spoken to anyone who played in the 1961 Cup Final but I would say that was what beat us, lack of tactics, because I think we had the better players. Better skills but just didn't know what to do.

Now skip to the 1962-63 season and there's this business of Johnny Divers allegedly turning up at Celtic Park for the League Cup opener versus Hearts on 11 August with no boots! He'd been playing for the Glasgow XI versus Manchester United at Hampden on 8 August and his boots are still AWOL from Parkhead. He's told he's out of the team and you are told to strip.

In those days pros carried their boots around with them. It was nothing like nowadays. Even the internationals carried them in a brown paper bag and that's how John Divers would have taken his to Hampden for the Manchester United game. What I remember about that day, horror of horrors, I'd had a big lunch! I wasn't playing so I thought, I'll just have the usual, whatever's going. I was still at home in '62, I was staying with my mum and dad. And knowing an Irish mother, I would have a good meal in me before I set off for the ground. I was up at Celtic Park at one o'clock, playing snooker et cetera but next thing Willie Johnstone came in to me and said, "You're playing." I said, "What!" He said, "John Divers has been dropped." It was only later the reason emerged that he'd forgotten his boots. But this was typical Bob Kelly. In those days he could have gone and played in somebody else's boots. Find somebody's boots the same size as yours. But I remember I scored a fantastic goal that day. I must have been 25, 30 yards out and I just hit one and it screamed into the net.

Some goal against a retreating defence.

Oh, it was a fantastic goal. It just went screaming in. It was a screamer.

Charlie, 13 October 1962, you've got a new left-wing partner, Frank Brogan.

Another good player. Frank was a good player. He was probably one of the greediest goalscorers that I've ever known in my life. He was one of these guys – the story used to go about the park whether its true or not – that when we trained, he actually counted the goals he scored at training and marked them into his wee book! He'd end-up the season having scored 180 goals!

Now Ne'erday 1963, Rangers 4, Celtic 0.

A terrible day. A terrible day. Paddy wanted his opinion, he wanted to be the person making the opinion. Sean came in and started making remarks. Paddy started shouting at Sean and said one or two things which to me should never have been said. Sean was in charge of the team that night. We were all bad but Paddy started shouting at Big Yogi. We got away to a bad start that day because it was a bad, bad park. The game never should have been played. Bob Kelly wanted the game off, Rangers wanted the game on. The referee went on the Rangers' side, Play the game. There was a snowstorm all through the match, they beat us 4-0 and Paddy and Sean started an argument. Paddy decried Sean's career as a player and said if Yogi ever played for Celtic again, that was the end of it for him. It was a terrific argument in the dressing-room after the game. And one of the reasons I remember it, I had to make my way down Broomloan Road to my sister's flat. She wasn't long married at that time and it was after the game, after the argument, we'd been beaten 4-0 and the snow was coming down. I got out of Ibrox that night, probably about an hour after the game, and I'd to go down Broomloan Road, I'd to go down Helen Street. My sister was having a wee party – they lived down at Govan Cross – and in those days, nobody stayed after the game. The supporters were all gone and I made my lonely way down, convinced this was the end of my career at Celtic because we were absolutely hammered. I will always remember. I went into this house, my sister was in it, and my brother-in-law. He's a fanatic and always has been a fanatical Celtic supporter. They said to me, "Have a drink, just forget about it." Mary was waiting, we weren't married at the time. I never drank in those days so I said no. It was the most horrible night of my life. Being beaten 4-0 at Ibrox on New Year's Day, the most important day in Scottish football. Making my lonely way down Helen Street, a place I'd never been in in my life before! A lonely town, if it hadn't been for my sister's house. A dark, dark New Year's Day. That's not one of my better stories and it's funny, it's one I've never told before now.

Charlie, I know you hate being reminded of your corner kicks.

No, no. No! I've changed my opinion about that because it's folklore now. It was just that I could take them with both feet from either side of the park. I wasn't as strong in my left but for somebody who was played predominantly at inside-left, I was right-footed.

Did somebody encourage you to become two-footed?

No, it just came naturally. I could kick with both feet.

What about the Public Trial on 4 August 1963? You've got a new outside-right partner and his name is Jimmy Johnstone.

Ah, wee Jinky! Wee Jinky was one of these players, that when you were in trouble, you give the ball to Jinky! Early on in his career he was a very weak player physically and I think the majority of people didn't think he would make it because he had no strength. He was good on the ball but he didn't last a game then all of a sudden he started getting big, no, not bigger, he never got bigger, but he started to put on weight, he got stronger. Now whether he did it in training or not, I don't know. But all of a sudden, once he got into the team, played regular, he was very, very strong and that was always our outlet. When you're in trouble, give the ball to Jinky! I think I've told you before about the corner flag, get the ball down to their end, wee Jinky dribbling people. He was incredible. In training, a ball for Jinky, a ball for Yogi, a ball for the rest of us, that was the cry. You could never get the ball off him in training. Incredible!

In 1964 Celtic beat MTK Budapest 3-0 at Parkhead in the first leg of the semi-final of the Cup-Winners' Cup then went to Hungary and lost it 4-0.

Ah, but that again was down to lack of planning. Again, back to no tactics. If we had had a coach who could say to us, Right, play a defensive game – but Bob Kelly, I always remember, 3-0 up, Celtic had to go out and play an attacking game to impress them, the Scots in Europe. 4-0. The team is absolutely unchanged in Budapest from the one that won at Parkhead. It's exactly the same team. In those days, if you'd played a defensive side, you'd have won. We went there to throw a 3-0 lead away. That was a pure and utter farce.

Charlie, Bertie Auld comes back to Celtic on 14 January 1965. Gallagher and Auld make up the left-wing against Hearts on 16th. There's a huge roar when his name is announced and another roar when he appears on the field.

Wee Bertie was a character. Wee Bertie's one of these guys, I don't think many people could dislike him. He was one of these guys, a typical Glaswegian, I'll not say a hard man. A gallus character. Even to this day, he's still the same way. You could not dislike the guy! He was coming to take my position but there was no way I could not like the wee fellow. Just a nice guy. I liked Bertie very, very much. My wife liked him great. I remember the time Mary and I were getting married, we were walking down Buchanan Street. Somebody ran past her, stole her handbag and I started chasing. It was wee Bertie! Him running down Buchanan Street with a lady's handbag in his hand and me after him!

After Bertie, Jock Stein comes home on 8 March 1965. In the Scottish Cup Final against Dunfermline on 24 April, Celtic book the wind yet they go in at half-time 2-1 down.

Well, from what I remember, big Stein told us not too worry because we had played reasonably well. We had played reasonably well in the first half.

Is that a lot of help being told that sort of thing?

Oh yeah! They'd scored just before the interval. They went in front early on then I had a shot from about 35 yards again, it hit the crossbar, bounced away up in the air and came back down. Wee Bertie was running in, he nodded it into the net. Whether it was going in or not, nobody knows but wee Bertie put it in. That brought us back into the game. Just before half-time they had scored but what I do remember is big Stein telling us at half-time not to worry, to keep playing the same way and we'd get in front. And I think personally, after being beaten four years previously by Dunfermline, I think most of us would have been worried about it but he was the type of manager who could calm you down in those circumstances. We scored seven minutes after the re-start which obviously made it more than a level game at 2-2. The second goal from my memory and from watching it – I've got it on tape – I'd got the ball at the half-way line. I threaded it through to Lennox, then wee Bobby cut it back and Bertie scored. And after that, I think – it's all right saying it after the event – it was just a case of when? Because we did all the attacking, it was Celtic attacking all the time.

Were you deputed to take the corners?

I did take most of the corners at both sides anyway, in those days. It just so happened, I think – wee Jinky wasn't playing that day – when wee Jinky was playing on the right he never took a corner, he was never strong enough to get the ball across. I took most of the corners and I was fortunate on the right wing, I was taking them with my right foot and they were outswingers. Although I say I was two-footed, I still took all corners with my right foot which was the stronger. And on the right wing they were outswingers for players running in, as in the famous Vojvodina game, but on the left wing, they were always cutting in, and in the 1965 Cup final, I took the famous corner on the left with my right foot and it's an inswinger here. Big Billy's got a great photograph in his pub above his bar and it's taken from the press box or the old Hampden stand, me taking the corner, big Billy heading it in. Billy's got it as a big, big blow-up on his bar. Because that was the start of everything.

Apart from the agonising nine minutes until the final whistle.

Ach, agonising for the supporters, but on the park, we knew we'd done it.

Charlie, 3 January 1966, just three years and a couple of days after your walk down Helen Street, Celtic 5, Rangers 1. Gallagher scores Celtic's third goal.

It's funny, I always seem to score great goals. I never seem to score poor goals. I scored a great goal that day, a very foggy day. Rangers scored early on in the game, Davy Wilson, first two minutes. We hammered them the first half, shooting towards the Rangers' end. Nothing. One-nil, half-time. The second half, we ran out, scored five. I think the only worry we had that day was the fog, it could have been called-off. I don't think the Rangers' supporters knew that the goals were going in at the Celtic end, apart from the roars. We scored them all at the right end for our supporters. It was just magic, magic. I scored a great goal from the edge of the box. I remember the fourth goal, Bobby Murdoch scored it. Free kick. I took the free-kick. Tiny Wharton jumped up. The ball passed under his legs and Bobby stuck it in the net.

Did you travel to Tbilisi?

I travelled to Tbilisi, yes, the 1-1 draw.

You were part of that terrible marathon to get home?

Oh, that was a nightmare, that was the one that ended up in Stockholm. Mary and the other wives were getting bulletins all the time. Mary had taken this big abscess and she says they all thought she was weeping but it was the pain in her face. It was the year before Paul was born.

You couldn't take off in Stockholm.

We never got back till the Friday night until near 11.

Charlie Gallagher

And yet Stein turned you out for a training session? In front of 500 fans!

Oh, I think that was a public relations exercise because they realised – they'd been told – that we were still playing on the Saturday. The Scottish League had refused to postpone the game against Hearts. I think this was big Stein's way of saying, "Right, stuff you, we're going to be martyrs," and had us out. It must have been near enough one o'clock in the morning when we finished our training session at Celtic Park. We got beaten on Saturday – we only got beaten 3-2, Hearts at Tynecastle. I don't know if we'd a weakened team out that day or not. That was a nightmare. Never mind the bulletins, they had no idea what was happening over here. But big Kelly gave us a bonus. For keeping our spirits up in the face of such adversity. It was Aer Lingus and we travelled from Tbilisi to Moscow, then from Moscow. They were trying to land somewhere and they couldn't land, and of course, the character of the team showed, big Gemmell, wee Jinky, Bertie Auld, they started sing-songs! Everybody joined in, the supporters and the directors and the press. I think the press commented, although it was a kind of a dangerous flight, which was an understatement, the players had kept everyone's spirits up. Big Nobs gave us a bonus. I think it was a fiver or a tenner for being so happy, looking on the bright side of life! As against the time in South America when he fined everybody, we all got fined, £250, even if we weren't playing in the games!

Now Jinky is in trouble for not adhering to the pre-match plan in the 1-1 draw versus St Mirren on Guy Fawkes' Day 1966. So there was now a definite pre-match plan each time?

Oh yes, it was pre-match plans now, all the time. From those days on, from the time that Stein came we had a pre-match plan because on the Friday, big Stein used to have a big notice-board, we had a big, big board, and it was all these wee men, not men, wee stickers, and that was their team, and he told us how they were going to play. He knew about how they were going to play, and we were told how we were going to play. It was up to them to worry about us. He told us how to play every game. Pre-match plans were very much in vogue.

Now, Charlie, because your parents come from Donegal, you are picked to play for the Republic of Ireland against Turkey in Ankara on 22 February. Stein gives you the ball to lead Celtic out in the Cup against Elgin at Parkhead on the 18th.

Sean Fallon got me that cap. It was on one of the trips abroad. He knew my parents were from Gweedore and he asked me would I be interested in an Irish cap. I was taken by surprise but of course I said yes. He said, "Leave it with me." Next thing I heard, he told me I might need an Irish passport. I was the first Scots-born Irishman to qualify under the grannie rule except that it was my parents who were native Irish. John Dempsey of Chelsea had already played for the Republic but he was London-born. He was a chirpy cockney. I was broad Glasgow.

Were you stripped at Lisbon, Charlie?

No, there was only one stripped, the goalkeeper, John Fallon. There was a substitute goalkeeper allowed in those days. We were all sitting away up where Big Billy was eventually presented with the Cup. It took us a long time to get to the dressing-room after the game. We had to fight our way through the fans. We had blazers on to authorise, to verify, that we were part of the squad. By this time they were all going daft before we could get in. I remember going out training on the park before the game and the crowd all there, watching us. At Prague in the semi-final we were all on the bench but not at Lisbon. Big Stein said, "Right, all sit on the bench," because we were getting pelted with things, they were really throwing things. It was Dukla in the semi-final, wasn't it? I travelled to South America and we got pelted that night as well, like Ronnie Simpson. Just sitting there, it was terrible. That was the first game in Buenos Aires. They recognised us from our blazers and we started getting all sorts of rubbish thrown at us. God knows where they got it from. Then the game in Montevideo, the replay, wasn't it? Ha, that was a nightmare as well. All the things happening on the park.

You won the Scottish League for Celtic as Auld's replacement in '67-68 but that's the end of it, isn't it, Charlie?

I started in '68-69 and I got a bad cartilage injury. For '69-70 I was fit again but Stein told me if I found a club, he'd give me a free transfer but I said no. I didn't want another club. So he wouldn't play me. The way I finished with Stein, I said, "I'll take a free transfer if you'll give me my wages till the end of the season," which any manager would have done. He wouldn't do it, so I said, "Tough, I'll stick it out." But he wouldn't play me in any of the teams. You see where that chair is? I sat there for six weeks after Celtic let me go. I just could not cope with it. Then one day Mary pushed a paint brush in my hand. "Get on with it!" I had one pot of paint. It was lime green. And everything I touched turned to lime green. The bunker was lime green, the fence was lime green, the clothes poles were lime green, everything out there that did not move was lime green.

Your lime green period!

Come on, you've got a game to catch. It's a wet, wet night. Jump in the car. I'll drop you off at Parkhead.

Thank you very much, Charlie. You really are a star.

Bobby Lennox
Forward
1961-1978-1980

Bobby, I want to ask you about Celtic post-Lisbon and post-Montevideo. Looking back, how would you sum up the Celts of that era?

There was always the feeling about that team, no matter how we played, we could win. It was just confidence in each other's ability, I think. You looked at the back and thought Billy and John won't give anything much away. Bobby'll dominate with his passing. Wee Jimmy'll do something, Wispy'll get goals, Stevie'll get goals. Billy'll come up for a corner, Bertie Auld'll score, we were scoring goals from everywhere.

Now, Bobby, before they went out to the Argentine for the World Club Championship, Celtic were already eliminated from the European Cup in the preliminary round against Dinamo Kiev at Parkhead on 20 September 1967. Dinamo were 2-0 up at half-time. What went wrong?

Well, what happened, the boys at the back made a couple of mistakes and the boys at the back were terrific players, they were great defenders but there were a couple of mistakes made early in the game which happens because we're all human beings. So we were two goals down but we got one back in Glasgow and I still felt we would go to Russia and win. And I scored a goal in Russia to bring us level when we were down to ten men. Billy scored a goal that got chalked-off and I wouldn't know why. Big Yogi scored, he dribbled round the goalkeeper and put it in the net – that got chalked-off, I don't know why. There was a corner kick in the dying seconds, everybody into their box, the ball was cleared up the park, they ran away and made it 1-1. So we were our own worst enemy. But we played well in Russia. We really played very well in Russia. We were human beings, we made mistakes and we got punished for them.

Now, Bobby, moving on a couple of years, Celtic beat Rangers 4-0 in the Scottish Cup Final on 26 April 1969. You might have thought before the game, 1-0 for Celtic, 2-1 for Celtic. Had you any idea it might be 4-0?

No, because we went down to Troon before that Cup Final – I'm quite sure it was Troon we were at – and Yogi's not going to play and Jimmy's not going to play. Both boys were suspended. I think people thought I might play wide on one side and Stevie play wide on the other or whatever but Big Jock put George wide and Bertie wide and Steve and I just poised, you know, between them. It worked a treat. Two goals in the last minute of the first half, that was the game over. It was a great performance. And when Big Billy scored in the first minute, we'd got a goal and that was the team settled. It was great.

Now Feyenoord in the second European Cup Final in Milan on 6 May 1970? Had the two victories over Leeds home and away taken their toll the way they say consecutive hard fights can take it out of the best of boxers?

Every tie was like a European Cup Final. I think, probably at the back of our minds we thought, We've beaten Leeds, that's us! But to be fair, Feyenoord on the night, Feyenoord were brilliant. They were really, really brilliant. They played really, really well. The only thing I would say about the game, when Tommy scored the goal – it was an evening game – if we had held the lead until the half-time whistle and got in the dressing-room one up, I think it might have made a big difference. It might have deflated them and given us a lift. But the equaliser came quite quickly and that unsettled us again, I think, you know?

Had you had any warning to beware Feyenoord? I know Sean Fallon had seen them play and thought these were no pushovers.

I think everybody thought if we played to our best we would win the European Cup. I don't think there was anyone ever came to us and said, "This player is great and that player is great, they do this and they do that." I think we all thought, from the top to the bottom, if we play well – and at that level, you can't play badly and win – if we played to our full potential, we would win the European Cup.

Move into 1971 and Celtic now had two buzz bombs in the team, yourself and Tommy Callaghan. You were a striker but how did Big Jock exploit Tommy's speed?

I don't know that Tom was a sprinter. He was more of a runner with a long, loping stride working from the back to the front, turning defence into attack. He was more of a carrier of the ball, big Tid. He'd go from back to front carrying the ball. He had a great kind of double shuffle, you know, which was very deceiving. I think he was more one to go the distance rather than a sprinter. He was a great team player, big Tid. A lot of people thought he was this and that and the other but he was a great players' player, big Tid. He was a lovely man, a lovely guy. I think he was like me when I first went to Celtic Park. I came from Saltcoats which was a million miles from Glasgow in those days and Tid came from Fife and he'd lived in Fife all his life. He scored a wonderful goal on his debut against Partick Thistle. And I think when you do things like that, sometimes they're hard to live up to. I think it took Tommy quite a wee while to settle actually. But he was a good player for the club.

Now, saving your reverence, Bobby, it's around this time that people are saying as they always do that Celtic are no longer the team they were. We're four years on from Lisbon. Even manager Stein seems to feel the old spirit is not there in certain games and he calls for Monday morning training sessions. Did you feel something was missing?

I think that 1967 team was split up far too soon. I think what happened was, Kenny and Danny and George and Davie were starting to break through but I think we probably would have been better keeping the good older professionals at the Park longer and it may have helped the young boys come through. I think the team was split up far too soon. I really do.

Kenny Dalglish made his debut in 1968. What impression did he make on you?

Kenny made a big, big impression on everyone in training. Before he got into the team he was the type of boy that could come and train with the first team and not be overawed. Kenny would never be overawed although he had great respect for the guys. He could train with the first team and that was his level, he was fine there, he was confident and comfortable there. Before he ever played in the team, we knew Kenny could play. Danny was the same, and George, and Davie. But Kenny was the one you always thought, "He'll be a player!" The difference with those boys is, Danny apart, they all came through and they all left. We all came through and were desperate to stay.

19 April 1972 was the night Dixie missed his penalty against Inter in the semi-final shoot-out of the European Cup at Parkhead. You took so many successful penalties for Celtic, why were you not on the roster that night? It was Deans, Craig, Johnstone, McCluskey, Murdoch. Were you hurt?

No. I'd never taken a penalty for Celtic before that night. Never. We went to Methil one day and we missed three penalty kicks. I was on the bench so Big Jock said to me, "If there's another penalty kick, you're taking it!" But it was said more in agitation than anything. So we went to Motherwell in the Scottish Cup, a week or two later, I think. And in the dressing-room Big Billy said, "See you're taking the penalty kicks today, Wee Man?" I said, "No bother! No bother!" I was putting my boots on and Big Jock said, "Good on you, you're feeling confident." But I was only kidding Big Billy on. And that's how I got landed with the penalties. The following week we played Aberdeen in a very important League game in Glasgow. We got a penalty kick late on in the game and Bobby Clark's down injured, getting treatment, and I've got the ball and this is my first penalty kick. And even my best pal in all the world walks across and he says, "Bobby, let somebody else take it."

This is Jimmy Johnstone?

Yeah. Because I'd never taken a penalty and I'm waiting ages to take this one. I took a few steps and stuck it away in the corner. And that was the first of my penalties. I could never hit them like Tommy. I didn't miss a lot. I quite liked taking them.

You were never a day's trouble to Jock Stein but was there ever a time you felt like putting in for a transfer yourself?

Once. I think I was scoring a few goals and I'd been playing quite well. I hurt both my feet, believe it or not, and I got injections in each of them on the Wednesday. It was just a pain and it went away, it was fine, it was great. I said I was fine and I did my training and passed a fitness test et cetera. We were playing at Dunfermline on Saturday. I walked into the dressing-room and we were all sitting and he came in and read out the team, Scottish Cup-tie. And I was out. Not a word said. Just the team. And we got beaten two-nothing by Dunfermline on the Saturday. I was really disappointed. I mean, I was left out of the team a lot. But at that time I was really, really disappointed. I said to my dad when I got home, "I think I'll go in and see what's happening. I think I'll ask for a transfer." He said, "Watch what you're doing. You do whatever you think but watch what you're doing." So on Monday I drove to Glasgow and wandered in, walked in the front door but I never said anything. On the Tuesday I did the same. On the Friday morning I was walking out the Park and there was a wee window at the Park and Jock was at it. He said, "You're very quiet." I said I wanted to be quiet 'cos inside I was on the bubble, you know? He said, "Are you disappointed you were left out last week?" I said, "I don't know why I was left out last week." He said, "You're in tomorrow. Away you go!" And that was it. He must have realised I was so quiet it was out of character. I really couldn't believe he had left me out. I really couldn't believe it. I'm not saying I was one of the better players but when you're enjoying a really good spell and the team's going well, all of a sudden to be left out and then get beaten two-nil! It was as if he was saying, We thought we could win without you so we gave you a rest last week. Yet Big Jock was not very bad at saying to you, "Look, you're not playing tomorrow, we're leaving you out, blah-blah-blah." But he never said a thing. And you're standing in the dressing-room and all the boys looking at you and you're thinking what's going on?

Right, Bobby. Now Stevie Chalmers held Celtic's post-War scoring record of 241 goals until you beat it with a penalty at Boghead on 24 November 1973. Is it true you were unaware how close you were to a new record?

I remember the penalty, aye. But I didn't know about the record. I didn't know. I think I scored my 250th at Airdrie and I only knew that because people had been talking about 240-odd goals at Dumbarton! But that penalty at Boghead, it was typical, it was up at the top end, it was a wet, miserable day. I scored with the penalty and I think it was time-up. Somebody came in and said, "Great, Wee Man! That's you second highest goalscorer in the club!" I had no idea. I'm going to have my photograph taken tomorrow with McCoist because he's equalled my record in the League Cup, 60-odd goals or something. And I only knew that after McCoist scored the goal. Nobody ever said, "You're the highest goalscorer in the League Cup." You find out these things when somebody's just about to beat you!

Bobby, you were booked for the first time in the domestic game on Ne'erday 1974 against Clyde. Even then you claimed an accidental collision but the SFA suspended you for a week on 29 January.

I got booked against Clyde – stupid! The ball's gone for a throw-in and Harry Glasgow and I – I think it was Harry Glasgow – George was on the ball – gave me a shove. It was never a foul! And big Willie McVie, the Clyde centre-half, jumped on the two of us and we all fell – you know the way the track has a dip at Shawfield – we just fell down there. We got back up, pushing and shoving, and the ref comes across and he books me and then he books Harry Glasgow. So I said, "What are you booking us for?" "Oh," he said, "you didn't give the ball back." "But," I said, "it was our throw-in, what are you booking me for?" It was big McVie that caused it. Harry and I should never have got booked. Getting booked just wasn't in my nature. I didn't see any need to get up and run after somebody and have a kick. Maybe it was cowardice, I'm not sure. I'd get up and get on with it.

So you didn't suffer from red mist?

No. No. I think I was fortunate I didn't get that. Wee Jimmy walked four or five times but as soon as a thing like that is finished, you think, I wish I hadn't done that. So maybe I took a second or two longer to react, I don't know. I'm not saying I didn't get really mad a few times or agitated and I'd probably get up and argue a few times but I think it would need to be something serious for me to get really agitated. Perhaps I just lay out on the grass a second or two longer.

Who's the referee that you admire the most?

Tiny Wharton was great. Hugh Phillips was really good. I never got involved with the referees, to be fair, so I never bothered too much about them.

Bobby Lennox

You never shook the referee's hand coming off?

I never shook their hand, no. But as I became older, as I became an older player at the club, I really gave referees a hard time of it, shouting and bawling and ranting and raving. I think I got away with that because I was a kind of older statesman at the club. I used to say to the guys in the reserve team, "Don't call the referee a silly old so-and-so. Say, excuse me, Mr John or Mr Archie – if you approach them the right way, they're not going to book you for talking to them!" I used to overdo it in the last season of my career but I got away with it because I was one of the older ones, you know?

So you didn't say, Excuse me, Mr Archie?

No! Once a referee knows you, that sort of approach can only cause him problems.

What do squad players do on a big European night like the first game against Atletico? Do they go down to the dressing room at half-time to gee the team on?

Oh no, you don't go into the dressing-room. They've got all they want in the dressing-room, the players, Big Jock, shy away from it. If I was on the bench for a big game or any game at that time, I liked to spend my whole time behind the goal, jogging about, getting a good loosen-up. And at half-time, if I'd sweated through my shirt, I'd get another dry one on and get back out because I remember a game against Aberdeen one time, early in the substitution thing. I came off the bench late in the game but it took me five or ten minutes to get my second wind, to get myself going and then it was time-up in five minutes. So, I thought, this'll never happen again, I'll spend my time behind the goal, jogging about, wee sprints, running back and across behind the goal. When I had to go on, I was ready to go on. I still see guys loosening-up and I don't think the way they're going about it is right. They don't spend enough time – I know they've got to do a bit of stretching, that's fine, but I say, Get yourselves running, get your second wind, get yourselves sweating and when you go on the field, you're fit for any play.

You played against Atletico in Madrid. How was that for a night to remember?

The whole trip was fraught with danger. Big Jock was going to get shot, Wee Jimmy was going to get killed. I remember we went to our rooms that day, there were police all about and soldiers. We'd arrived in the hotel, lovely hotel, big gardens and a wee brae round about it and the police wandering about there. Wee Jimmy shut the curtains right away. Nobody was going to see into our room. Then he picks up an apple. I said, "What are you doing? They didn't just say they were going to shoot you, they said they were going to kill you! How do you know that's not poisoned?" So from that moment on, he never touched a bite.

Bobby Charlton played centre-forward for Celtic in Ron Yeats' testimonial on 13 May 1974. I don't know if it was this occasion or another but he said he'd have got another ten years out of his career if he'd always had Bobby Lennox to play with. What was it you were doing for him?

I think he was able to find me and I had a couple of cut-backs enabled him to score goals, that sort of thing. He invited me and Stevie down to play in I forget what testimonial it was. I scored three goals. This was down at Liverpool. He picked me up, took me over to Liverpool and he and I and his wife went back to Manchester after the game. He was thrilled to discover he was the most-capped Celtic player ever. So going back in the car he was saying to his wife, "Do you know who Celtic's most-capped player is? It's me!" He had to sign for Celtic to play in the Ron Yeats game.

Do you remember missing a penalty that was important then but which nobody remembers now? Against Rangers in the shoot-out after a 2-2 draw in the Drybrough Cup Final on 3 August 1974? You missed Celtic's first but Denis Connaghan saved the day for Celtic.

We played well in that game but when the final whistle went we all went to the halfway line and I was the penalty-kicker at the time. So I said to Billy, "I'll take the last one, Big Man, no problem," just in case I was needed and I was the most experienced. "No," he said, "Go and give us a good start." I said, "Fair enough." Now this is going to sound like an excuse but it's not. We then walked the whole length of the ground, me and the referee and the goalkeeper. It seemed to take ages. I put the ball down and the referee said, "Hold on a minute," and he went to have a word with the goalkeeper. And it seemed to be ages. And I'm knocking it in here, and I'm knocking it in there and at the last second I changed my mind. And you don't do that! If I'd been taking a penalty kick later on in the roster, I'd have run from the halfway line, put the ball down, taken my penalty. From Billy saying, "No, give us a good start, Wee Man," until I took my penalty kick, it must have been four or five minutes. Then Big Denis saves two, so it was great.

Jock Stein threatened to throw in the towel if Celtic's bigots did not stop their sectarian chants. Did you feel sympathy for Big Jock or should he just have ignored this sort of thing?

I don't think you can ignore the bigots' chants. I think, when you go to Celtic Park and you hear the songs that they've got, there's no need to sing anything else except Celtic songs. When we were playing, *Ob-la-di, Ob-la-da, We Are Sailing, You'll Never Walk Alone*, anything that came out, it would get sung at Celtic Park. I don't think there's any place or any need for party songs. I was a player and I can't tell you how it felt, the mass of colour and the fans singing *Over and Over* and *Hail! Hail!* Really great.

Do you remember the European Cup tie versus Olympiakos Piraeus in Greece? You were sent off for a tackle with four minutes to go.

That sending-off – again this might sound like me making excuses – but it was the stupidest thing ever! We were getting beat two-nil and I went on and I'm playing wide. Number Ten, he was a good player, a really good player, took free-kicks et cetera. And he got a free-kick about 25 yards out in their inside-right position. So the boy's got his left foot over the ball and I started closing him because the linesman's flagging for a substitution. This guy has a looney kind of smile and we're looking across and waiting and the referee comes from the far side of the field to me and books me for not retreating at the free-kick. I said, "There's a substitution being made!" "No! No! Free-kick!" He said he had blown his whistle to order me to retreat. And I had never heard him! And that's a fact. I'm standing waiting for this substitution. So minutes later, the ball got put up the right and the right-back has gone to cross it. And I came out and he's crossed it and I blocked it. The ball's got clear but he's gone over and he's screaming. And the ref came right across the park, yellow card, and he's put me off. To be fair, Big Jock came into the dressing-room and told me the sending-off was a joke. I can't believe you've been sent off the field. But you didn't get booked for nothing the first time. I said, "But Boss, they were making a substitution." "But you knew the free-kick had been given." "Boss, I didn't even think!" If I had known they were lining-up the free-kick I wouldn't have been standing over the ball to stop them taking it. I was standing over the ball because that's where I was standing waiting for the guy to come on. If I had heard the whistle or seen the flag being waved on the touchline, I'd have stepped back. He gave the ref respect for booking me at the free-kick but no respect for sending me off for the tackle. It was some night. There were rockets going off and a very noisy crowd but that's to be expected.

Jinky got a free transfer on 9 June 1975. Who were your best pals now at Parkhead?

Danny and Tommy. Danny and I were really close. And Big Roy and I became very, very close. He was from down here, just up the road. Roy was a good player and when he wasn't playing well, he was still hounding you on. I took Roy when he was 15 to Celtic Park. I've always felt that young guys should go to the factory before they become football players because young guys, once they go up to Celtic Park or any football ground, they think they're made from the day and hour they walk in. When I was reserve team coach, I had guys coming to Celtic Park at nine o'clock in the morning, young guys, and leaving at three in the afternoon. Now some of them would live near first-teamers and I'd get asked, "I live near Charlie Nicholas or Derek Whyte. Can I come in with them in the morning?" I would say, "Your job is to be in here on time and get stuff ready". And then they would say, "You know, I stay near Tom MacAdam. Could I leave at 12 o'clock and go home with him?" See if they worked in a factory for a year? They'd appreciate coming in at nine o'clock in the morning and away out at three. And that's why I think some of them don't make it. They hear first-team players telling tall stories about I'm getting this amount of money or that and they think, Maybe I should be getting that! But they've never kicked a ball! And I feel young guys between 15 and 18 need to be sorted out. So anyway, going back to Roy. Roy was staying in Ardrossan which is a mile and a half, maybe two miles, but I'd say to Roy, "I'll get you at Saltcoats station. Get the bus from Ardrossan, I'll get you there." I wasn't going to go to Ardrossan although it was only up the road. And then when Roy got a car, he would come and pick me up. But in the early days, he got the bus in here from Ardrossan. It didn't do him any harm. And Roy and I became really close friends. We went everywhere together. And I've always been really close with Danny as well.

You broke your leg in a clash with John Greig on 24 November 1976 at Ibrox.

I went behind the goals and then I came back on. I was thinking of the manager. If I walk in tomorrow morning, he's going to think I'm acting here. I came back on and I did a bit of stamping on it, then I did it harder and then I thought, I'm not right. I signalled down to them and he took me off. At half-time, John Clark – I think John was in charge of the second team at the time – John Clark and I went to hospital. I'd had a lot sorer injuries than that one, injuries that didn't involve breaks but had been sorer. When we got to the hospital there were two wee nurses who said, "If you stay the night we'll be able to do this and that," and the next thing Wee John got on the 'phone straight away and 'phoned Dr Abrahmi. He was the specialist. He got straight down to the hospital, I got the plaster on my ankle and Roy and his dad came from Ibrox and got me down the road.

1977-78 was an awful season for Celtic without Dalglish, Stanton, Conn and Danny McGrain.

I couldn't get in the team. No matter how bad they were playing, I was out of the team that year. There were one or two clubs came in for me that year to see if I would go. I know Big Jock said I was injured but he came to me one day and asked me how I would like to go to America. I told him I didn't know what to say. It was a long, hard conversation. I was the only player who had played every season with Jock Stein as a manager. So he must have thought highly of me that I was the one he had kept all that time. He said he would let me go eventually but America was the place to go. I don't think he wanted me to go to a Scottish club anyway. So as I always say to Catherine when we talk about America, we met this guy from Houston within a few days – and I was away within about two weeks or so. I thoroughly enjoyed it. Catherine loved it. They wanted me to stay but I said no, I've had my five or six months, I'm going home. They wanted me to come back the next year but I said I'd need to go back to Scotland and play to get fit to come back here. Then they wanted me to scout. But when I came back, Big Jock had chucked it and Billy was the manager and the first person who 'phoned was Big Jock. He said, "Billy's short of experienced players. I know I was the one who let you go but if you go back for six weeks then Billy can sort it out." Then Billy 'phoned and I talked to the gaffer and of course, I was absolutely delighted. So I went to the Park and the six weeks turned into a season and then Billy said, "Look, I'd love to sign you next season but maybe just to use you on the bench as we've done the last few months and bring on the young players." And that's how it came about. And I played a lot of games again.

You were Billy's colleague from the days of the Lions. Did he go to you for advice?

No. Oh no. He was the manager. I was a player. The thing I did find difficult, I mean, I had known Billy since I was 17 and he was Caesar, you know, and John was Luggy and no matter what, I would shout, "Listen, Caesar – Boss!" I found it very difficult, not because of disrespect because Billy was the greatest guy in the world and Billy and I were really close. It was just very difficult. I was at the back of the bus one day and I said something about Caesar. So he said to the other guys, "Look, Bobby's obviously got a problem with this but what you've got to understand, in his case, it's not a problem." But I got over it and Boss began to come out more and more and more. But it wasn't disrespect, I just found it hard. It was like someone changing their name! I mean, if Danny McGrain were to say to me, "Now start calling me John" – how hard would I find that?

You had one great night when Celtic won the League 4-2 against Rangers at Parkhead on 21 May 1979.

Ah, that was a great night!

And you came on in the 66th minute.

When we were down to ten men.

Big Billy spoke of 'ten men doing extraordinary things'.

I think wee Doylie was sent off and Big Billy took Mike Conroy off and put me on. It was one each or 2-1 at the time, I can't remember. I think it was one each at the time and then Bobby Russell scored. You know the strange things you remember. The corner came in and it got hit. It kind of passed me here on the thigh. I heard the noise and I knew it was in the net. I knew it had that force. But the boys were great that day. And then the third goal, an own goal and I could feel it on the park that night that Rangers weren't up for it. Although we were down to ten men, I felt we'd got plenty of room, the boys were running by them. Although we were playing really well, Rangers weren't up for it. But it was a great night. I've got a great photograph somewhere of after the game. Wee Jimmy came down to the corridor and he's got his jacket and shirt and tie on and I've got just my shorts, cuddling each other. That was a great night, yeah. That was the night the television cameras went on strike. There's no film of that game.

Bobby, if you left yourself out, what would your all-time Celtic team be? Would it be the Lions?

It would have to be the Lions. I know Danny was a wonderful player and Kenny was a wonderful player and Roy was great and Henrik Larsson's wonderful but we were the team and sometimes you're better with a team than a lot of gifted individuals.

Who's going to take Lennox's place?

My wife Catherine?

Would she want to play? You've got to stick someone in there. A male. We just need a name.

I don't know.

It could be Patsy Gallacher. It doesn't need to be a modern. Or Jimmy McGrory.

Jimmy McGrory, right enough. He scored the goals. Put him in the middle. Bertie wide and Jimmy McGrory. Something like that.

All right, Bobby. You've been very kind to us. Thank you very much.

Not at all. Not at all.

Denis Connaghan
Goalkeeper
1971-1977

I was born in the Gorbals in January 1945 and went to school at St John's, Portugal Street as an Irish speaker. I'd been staying with my grandparents in Donegal.

Who commended you to Celtic?

John Murphy had a lot to do with running the Under-Eighteen team at Holyrood in 1963 but it was Davie Doig persuaded me to be a goalkeeper.

It was Sean Fallon who signed me. I played a couple of games for RanCel juveniles and landed-up playing junior with Yoker Athletic.

What was the junior game like for a dramatic change from schools football?

Rough. It was a great grounding. It toughened you up especially from a goalkeeping aspect. Then it was still allowed to challenge the goalie and the goalie had to learn how to take tackles, how to take shoulder charges and everything else. It was a totally different ballgame from nowadays.

Now, Denis, Celtic freed you in 1964. Why?

When I signed for Celtic as a provisional there were several senior goalkeepers at the Park. Into 1963-64, there were two other young goalkeepers signed-up. The summer of 1964 I asked permission to go to my older sister's wedding in America. Now that might have caused them to misconstrue that I was going to emigrate but I can't see it. I think it was just with the volume of goalkeepers, they had to unload some. I came back and I rejoined Yoker. We didn't have a good team at Yoker, we had a reasonable team, and I think at that stage Rob Roy had just won the Scottish Junior Cup but it was one of my first games back and we beat them 1-0. It was as if we had won the Cup! That set us off on a good footing and I really looked forward to my Saturdays. Tremendous!

Why did you transfer to Renfrew in '65?

To get money for my holidays! I think they offered me a signing-on fee of £25 or something. That was the sole reason.

Who signed you for the Buddies in 1966?

Doug Millward. He'd come up from Ipswich, he'd played under Alf Ramsey. I went along and he spoke to me. He told me what his plans were and but he wasn't there long. Jim Thorburn was the main goalkeeper, just the two of us. He said if I proved I was up to the mark there'd be no problems in getting a game. Within a matter of a few months, I was in the first team.

Denis Connaghan

Denis, you were in America from April 1967 until December 1967. How did that come about? How was this done?

It was Doug Millward again. He had agreed to go and manage Baltimore Bays. He told me one night he had signed a good team. So I joked he hadn't signed a good goalkeeper, not yet. Next thing Alec Wright was asking me how serious I was. Doug and I sat down and discussed the situation. I got an agreement but it was kept very hush-hush. That was the first year of American professional football. We were signed players, representing a city and we flew all over America to play matches, a great experience. One of my teammates was Dennis Viollet of Manchester United who survived the Munich air disaster. Dennis died fairly recently. I saw America at the club's expense. I enjoyed my eight months there.

Were St Mirren glad to see you back?

Well, they must have been because they came to the airport to pick me up! I decided to stay in Scotland and re-sign for them.

Denis, 12 February 1969 was Ronnie Simpson's nemesis at Shawfield. Did you learn anything from watching a 'keeper like Ronnie Simpson or were there other goalies that you used to watch?

I wouldn't say there was a particular favourite. Ronnie was a very good goalkeeper, an instinctive goalkeeper. He probably never had command of the 18-yard box to the extent that certain goalkeepers do but he didn't need to when he had someone like Billy McNeill in front of him. In a one-on-one situation, Ronnie was immense, he could shut down people one-on-one. That's what really pulled me, that's what I was impressed with, and that's what really I tried to work on but also with Ronnie being smaller and stockier, what's very often easier to do is to work on your angles whereas I should have tried to be more commanding in the air and I indeed should have been more commanding in the air. But really, I was very impressed with Ronnie what he achieved and coming in at that late stage in his career. What he achieved from going to Celtic Park in the space of four or five years was absolutely incredible. He would probably have said he was a bit unlucky collecting that injury. It proved so difficult for him to get over, he was forced to retire. It was just unfortunate because he'd have got another couple of years out of his career at the top. There's other goalkeepers I can remember. I can remember Johnny Bonnar at Parkhead, Bobby Brown that played with Rangers and Scotland. I never saw too much of them apart from reading about them in the papers. Johnny Bonnar and Dick Beattie were the sort of goalkeepers I remember.

Were you a noisy goalkeeper?

I wasn't averse to doing a bit of shouting but in front of 4-5,000 at Love Street, prior to Parkhead, it was always easier to make yourself heard. You go to Celtic Park or Ibrox Park and you play in front of 50-60,000, the crowds they were pulling in in those days, you think you're shouting the way you normally do but the difference in the size of the crowd and the volume of the noise was entirely something else and unfortunately I proved to my cost that I wasn't compensating for this and we lost goals as a result. I always liked to get involved and do a lot of shouting and sometimes it would result in eruptions during the course of the play because some players don't like the goalkeeper shouting at them. They like shouting at the goalkeeper when he makes a mistake but if the goalkeeper sees an outfield player making a mistake, he's not allowed to shout at him! I've had fall-outs with players in the course of the game because I'm shouting from 40 or 50 yards away. I've seen them do something wrong or not chase somebody and they don't like that. But if I drop a corner kick and I'm getting the ball out of the back of the net, they're shouting at me and I'm expected to take it! But the goalkeeper's facing the play. He can see the play as it develops. It's only natural he should warn his teammates. If somebody's doing a blind side run across the defence and he's coming from behind the defender, the goalkeeper can see that and it's his job to shout a warning. And all of a sudden he's aware of it and he can do something about it. It's the same for me. I'm going for a cross ball and the defender will shout, Nobody near you, Big Man! It works both ways. You've always got to be talking to one another on the park and warn people about what's going on round about them. It's a big bit of the game.

You had the young Gordon McQueen in front of you. Could you see his potential then as a great centre-half for Leeds, Manchester United and Scotland?

I saw him when he first came to St Mirren, a big, big, raw boy of 18. In the air he was absolutely immense, big long strides, very one-footed, left-footed. But there was just something about him. You could see if he was given his chance – and just like myself, he was given his chance early at St Mirren – he was given his chance within a matter of no time at all – and you could see the potential for him to do well was there. I thought he had the makings of a top-class centre-half and I was more than happy to see the Big Man go on and achieve things and fulfil his potential. He had the height and he proved he could use it when you think of the number of goals he scored in later years, you know, from set positions. He was a very good listener. He was a learner. I was very pleased to see the Big Man going. There again, I'd fallen out with him and all. There was a game at Love Street and this free-kick and I shouted, "Go to your left, Gord, Big Man!" And of course he moves to the right and they score. I was shouting at him," Do you not know your expletive deleted left hand from your right?" I was out of the box and then it dawned on me – this is only a young boy. These things happen. That was one mistake he made. The rest of him was all potential.

Celtic lost the League Cup Final 4-1 against Partick Thistle on 23 October 1971 and you were signed on Monday 25. Can you tell me the circumstances of that transfer?

This was kind of ongoing for about six months, this transfer. There were rumours backwards and forwards linking me with Celtic. But nothing materialised and then the disaster happened against Partick Thistle and I was told on the Saturday night that Big Jock would like to sign me but I just took it as what had gone on before. I said, "Aye, I've heard it." But sure enough on the Monday morning he 'phoned me at work to see if he could meet me and I agreed to see him at Rouken Glen in the car park but then he 'phoned me back to cancel. He said, "We'll just meet at Love Street and that, you know?" He took over the St Mirren boardroom and that was it. I think he felt Rouken Glen was too public. He obviously knew my feelings and aspirations and all of that but as I talked to him, I knew he was wanting something in terms of performance and you'd obviously have to produce the goods for him. It wasn't a question of going along and being another number. If he was going to sign me, I'd need to produce the goods. It didn't always work out but on the whole, I thoroughly enjoyed my spell there. He didn't have to do a hard sell on me because I already knew him indirectly. I'd been to school with his son-in-law and I'd met him already a few times. I was delighted at the time and it was just a pity my signing arose out of Celtic losing a Cup Final 4-1. I was playing that day and I couldn't believe it when it was announced over the tannoy, the half-time score, "Celtic nothing, Partick Thistle four"! At Celtic then we could have played the outfield with a team of goalkeepers at five-a-side. We might not have scored many but we'd have kept them out. But it was always a bugbear with Big Jock, goalkeepers. He hated them, Eugene. He would say to me, "When I die, Denis, I want to come back as a Celtic goalkeeper. It's the easiest job under the sun. All Celtic do is attack all day. You've got nothing to do." I suppose it was true. They certainly attacked all day. But when that scenario happens your concentration has got to be a lot sharper, you've got to be on your toes and everything else. He certainly loved taking goalies for training. Goalies were his weakness and he tended to blame his goalies perhaps overmuch because he was always looking for the new Ronnie Simpson. But Ronnie made his mistakes as well but the thing about Ronnie, he was a past master at putting the blame on someone else. If it was a bad goal, he was already shouting at someone else before they could shout at him!

You made your debut with a broken nose. How did this happen?

It was just an accident that happened in training. We were training at Celtic Park in the morning and I was going out to do a wee bit for the company I worked with in the afternoon. It was just a total accident, a clash with Louie Macari. I don't know whether his knee caught me or whatever. He just caught me on the bridge of the nose and just cracked it. But there was no way I was going to miss the game because of a broken nose! No, all they did was put a wee plaster over the top of it and let it set. You see people wearing a plaster nowadays for breathing exercise so maybe I was one of the first! He had just nicked the top, it wasn't exactly a full-scale fracture. It would have been different if I had caught his shin. Twenty-four hours later I was black and blue here and then the club doctor had a look and said, "I think you've probably cracked a wee bone at the top." It wasn't as if my nose was squashed all over my face. I had the plaster on and I was fit to play.

You're supposed to have admitted showing no real form for Celtic since signing from St Mirren. When you were dropped or rested was it explained to you or did you just see your name down for the reserves on the team sheet?

It was. Big Jock didn't change a team a lot. If you weren't playing well and as a goalkeeper, it was doing silly things. You didn't need to lose a goal, it was maybe just you were doing one or two things – you had dropped a cross ball or something else – he would likely get on to you and say, "Big Man, you need a rest, you're not producing the goods." The first time I was out of the team was through an injury. Big Jock always was kind of loyal to players that came in. If you came in and were producing the goods and suppose you cost £100,000 and were just bought and you were injured and were out of the team and the person who took your place was playing well, Jock was generally pretty loyal to the players that had come in and were filling the positions. You would usually find out the reason why you were out. There was a team sheet but you were made aware of it if you were being dropped because you'd be in on Friday for a light work-out and he'd take you aside and tell you, I'm leaving you out tomorrow because of this, that and the next thing. So you weren't caught cold. There's nothing worse than turning up on a Saturday and walking into the dressing-room and discovering you're not in the team. You'd be made aware of what the situation was. And you'd obviously be aware yourself that you hadn't been as convincing as you ought to have been, that you'd made a few bloomers although you might have got away with it.

You were at Stirling the day Jock invaded the terracing and asked for the party songs to cease. Do you remember that day, 12 August 1972?

It wasn't the first time that Jock had done that. Jock detested that carry-on and it wasn't the first time that day at Annfield. That day he actually went physically into the crowd. Other times I've seen him come so far up the touchline, mostly at away games. And I've seen him shouting, "Denis!" And he'd tell me to tell that mob behind the goal to squash their chants and that. So you had to turn round to the crowd and tell them, "Look, Big Jock's raging at you! You better cut out those things that you're saying." I saw him do it at Liverpool once during a testimonial match, coming up the touchline and doing the same thing. He was a great man for presenting the proper image of the club and let's face it, Big Jock wasn't a Catholic so he didn't like these sectarian things at the best of times albeit his heart was at Celtic Park so he knew the scenario. Celtic was being degraded. It was like what my father used to say, "What's the point of singing these songs to the other end or whatever end you want to sing them to when you're going to work beside that same person the following Monday, you know? Why do you give in to that extent about his colour or his religion or anything else and then you forget about it when you come off the terracing and you go to work on a Monday and the same fellow is standing beside you?" Big Jock did not like it at all and he tried to stamp it out as much as humanly possible. He went onto the terracing that day and it made the front page of the newspapers but I've seen him do it a few times. Actually quite a few Celtic goalkeepers have been in the same situation and Big Jock has told them to tell that lot behind the goals to stop it. It was Ron Yeats' testimonial at Liverpool 1974, when he told me, "Go on, tell them to shut up!" So I turned round and said, "Big Jock's going to be up the terracing at you! You'll need to calm down. Cut out the sectarian songs." And to give the crowd their due, you know, they took cognizance of the fact because they had so much respect for him and everything else and it certainly worked. But a place like Stirling where it was virtually all Celtic supporters in the crowd and only about a couple of hundred Stirling Albion supporters, he certainly didn't think twice about going in among them and making his feelings known because of what was being said that day. He felt he wasn't getting his message across and the only way was to go himself and do it.

You came back to play in the Scottish Cup-tie draw against Motherwell on 10 March 1974. And what was incredible, you still had to play in a losing Celtic side.

I never realised it was as long as that! I had my first defeat against Partick Thistle but I thought it was long before that. I'm about two and a half years down the line!

Motherwell tried to put an end to your roll but you had a fantastic game in the replay at Fir Park on 13 March, blocking at point-blank range, turning screamers over the bar.

Celtic played Motherwell in the first game on the Sunday, two-each at Parkhead. I never knew I was playing that day. Ally Hunter was injured but I knew nothing about it. I turned-up and was told I was playing in the Cup-tie and was kept in for the replay. At Fir Park I had one save from big Jimbo Muir. I don't know how I got to it. It was completely out of this world. We won 1-0 and got through to the semi-final. I remember someone saying in the dressing-room afterwards, "That's it, you'll be back in again, Big Man," but I didn't want to tempt fate but it worked out quite well, Eugene.

Do you remember the match against Basle at Parkhead on 20 March 1974? Celtic were 2-0 up but it was 2-2 at half-time. Stein warned his players the game had to be won all over again. Celtic took it 4-2 in extra time and moved into the European Cup semi-final. I think you were now in your finest phase as a Celtic goalkeeper.

I remember it! I remember this first game as well over there because I was third choice goalkeeper and I was left behind here and I watched the game at the STV studios. Celtic lost 3-2 and I wondered, What's going to happen? And all of a sudden I was thrown in for the second leg. It was 2-2 at the end of the game at Parkhead and I was sitting wondering what was going to happen and Big Jock was hammering into us left, right and centre, but then Tommy Callaghan and Stevie Murray scored for us.

In extra time.

In extra time. I had a ground shot to save in the last few minutes or something and Big Jock said to me, "I was praying that you would just stay down there for the last two minutes." I said, "I wish I could have." He said "I was wanting you to take all the time you could, getting up and that." It was a long hard slog getting through that game but Celtic made it hard for themselves, first to get the goals that made it 4-3 on aggregate and then to go behind 4-5. We caused our own problems.

Denis, your hour of glory cometh. The home tie in the European Cup semi-final against Atletico Madrid.

It certainly wasn't a night for football. All they did, they were out to stop Celtic playing in every way that they possibly could. They wanted to stop Celtic playing. Wee Jinky was black and blue from the waist down, virtually. There were one or two other players were very much in the same boat. Their manager had sent out virtually seven or eight players of his first team squad with three or four hatchet men and a couple of subs with never any intention of playing a game of football. And yet they were a good side but in that first game they didn't intend to play football at all. They were trying to stop the game at every juncture. I went to throw the ball out and one of their forwards – it might have been the Argentinian, Ayala – he actually caught it in his hands. He stuck his two hands up to block the throw and ended-up getting booked for it. They just stopped the flow of the game at every opportunity. They wouldn't allow us to play at all. They certainly did football no favours that night at all. On top of everything, there was argy-bargy coming off the park as well, one or two players looking for the retribution they hadn't dared take earlier.

Was there a post-match banquet?

There was not, no. Neither at Parkhead nor over there. After these sort of games there might have been a bit of socialising in Glasgow but certainly when we were over in Madrid, we left straight for the airport. I do remember – was it Calderón, their president – the one I think their stadium was named after? He came to the airport to speak to Big Jock and Desmond White but neither of the two of them would get off the plane to speak to him. He actually came to the airport to apologise because we had just got washed, changed and onto the bus. They wouldn't speak to him. They said, "No, just forget it." We stayed at the hotel with an armed guard at the hotel. Nobody was allowed out on their own which we always did on European ties wherever we were, Hungary, everywhere else, no matter where it was, Germany. In European ties, you had your own free time and you wanted to see the country or the city you were in. We loved nothing better than to walk about the town centre, go and say hello. In every one of these places there were things to see, massive cathedrals and everything else, but the one place that I have never seen is Madrid. I'd have loved to have seen it but we were not allowed out for our own safety. Those armed guards were patrolling about. There was reputedly a death threat out on Jimmy Johnstone. So that was the atmosphere. It was pure hatred during the game. I've played in Old Firm games and it was that type of thing, you know, venom. And they were firing staples and everything else during the game. I picked up quite a few staples during the game, staples for cabling et cetera. If these things had hit me, they would have done a fair bit of damage. I showed them to the referee. He just shrugged his shoulders and put them in his pocket. He just totally disregarded it. It was pure hatred. We never saw anything of Madrid. We went to the training ground and then straight back to the hotel. We never saw anything apart from sitting at the poolside at the hotel.

Yet that was the game of your life. You kept the animals at bay until 12 minutes from time.

Ah, it was probably one of my better games for Celtic but unfortunately I didn't keep them out for the whole 90 minutes. It was great to get the chance to play in the two legs of the European Cup semi-final, having been on the bench for an earlier one. Big Jock had sussed out how they were going to play and pointed out the dangerous areas like free-kicks and all that. They had a great big player – I forget his name – who could bend free-kicks and we practised them with everyone else how much he might bend them and Jock would warn me, "Denis, don't go to the side of the wall, get into the middle of the wall." He went into it very, very deep. So fortunately I played well for the 80 minutes and then they got their goal. But we had one or two chances in that game as well and if we'd sneaked a goal it would have made quite a bit of difference. But our luck ran out at the end. If they'd played against us at Parkhead the way they played in Madrid we'd have been in with a chance but that first game they just totally stopped us playing football.

At Hampden on 4 May 1974 you were the Celtic goalie when the Scottish Cup was won 3-0 against Dundee United and their tyro centre forward, Andy Gray.

I never knew till just before we left Seamill to go to the Final whether or not I was in the team. Big Jock still had not made up his mind. Ally had played a couple of League games and he hadn't made up his mind as to who was going to play in goal. We went into the team talk and he hadn't announced the team. That was half-past twelve on the Cup Final day. You don't pre-empt things, you don't take things for granted, Eugene, especially not with Big Jock. I had come back into the team but always at the back of your mind was, Was he satisfied? Was he happy? I remember we were all sitting on seats like this and Jock with his big scratch pad and everything else, showing us how Dundee were going to play and how we would play and then he read out the team. He said, "We're going to play Denis in goal," and it was just like this weight coming off my shoulders. God, I thought, I'm going to get a chance at last! First thing I did was 'phone the wife, "I'm playing in the Cup Final today! Tell my mum and dad!" Big Billy said, "It was your performance against Atletico swung it in your favour." Big Jock said, "I couldn't have left you out after your performance in Madrid. But as I say it was only a couple of hours before kick-off and it's unnerving. Ally and I were sitting together during the team talk and you're trying to be nice to each other but deep down, each of you is saying, I hope I'm playing! I don't want to lose out again.

You were still first choice when the new season began 1974-75. Celtic were leading Airdrie 4-1 in the Drybrough Cup. Instead of hoofing clearances, you were doing a lot of tactical throwing. Airdrie got their second goal when you made to throw and forgot to let go of the ball. Or did you see it differently?

Oh, I'll never live it down! It keeps coming up! The *Sun* continually – Worst Own Goals – the *Scottish Sun*. I'm top of the list!

Denis, I wouldn't have asked you if I'd known!

Every time there's a stupid own goal in Scotland invariably they run a What's the Worst or Best Own Goal You've Seen? and I've been in the papers now about seven times and I've topped it five. I can remember it to this day and I can remember what I said after it and everything else. I got the ball. Okay, pre-season Big Jock – he was never a great lover of the Drybrough Cup. He used it as a build-up and everything else towards the main thing, getting fit for the League. This was the first round and we were away to Airdrie at Broomfield and we were coasting 4-1, I think you said. So I got the ball and Danny McGrain shouted for it. He was playing at left-back at that time and he turned his back and went to run and as I went to throw it, I saw a forward moving to shut down my throw to Danny. I tried to stop myself. I was going to overarm it and obviously the ball was loose. I tried to check myself and as I tried to stop I threw it in the net. If I had been 30 yards – but for a goalie to throw in his own net from 12 yards! I cannot argue with the framers of opinion in *The Sun*. I mean you can score an own goal, you can touch a ball into your own net from a corner kick. You're only a yard or two out but I'm 12 yards out. So Danny shouted, I started to throw it and I saw the boy coming to cut it off and at that moment I lost control. And I really must have chased the ball. I should have stood and it wouldn't really have been so bad. That's what the other players said at the time. I ran after the ball into the back of the net to try and get it. And sure enough, front page in the *Sunday Mail*, "What Is Big Jock Laughing At? See Sports Pages." And on the sports pages, "Big Jock Laughs As Denis Scores O.G." You know, I get asked about this every so often, "Do you remember the day you threw that ba' in the net?" And I always answer by saying, "How can I ever forget it? But can you remember what happened the following week?" And people will look at you with a blank stare. They can never remember that the following week, in midweek, you had beaten Dundee in extra time to get to the Final and all of a sudden the Drybrough Cup became important to Big Jock because it was Rangers. It was a fabulous day, scorching sunshine and that was the experiment of no offside between the two 18 yard lines. They extended the 18 yard lines to the touchlines and you couldn't be offside in the space between. So the ball was played from end to end and the middle of the park was missed out virtually. And players were dying on their feet because it was a scorching hot day, as I say. It was August and really, really warm and it went to penalty kicks. We played well. Rangers got an o.g. for their second goal, it deflected in off Pat McCluskey who played really well. Big Stewart Kennedy was in goal for them and he played really well. And it went to penalty kicks. Bobby Lennox missed our first one and I would have bet my last penny on Bobby scoring. He was the penalty-kick taker at the club and, you know, I saved one from Tommy McLean. And then the second one was from Derek Parlane and he thundered his. I can still remember it. I mean, it was a Tommy Gemmell-type thing. He just came up and he put everything into it. Fortunately, I dived the right way, to my right- hand side and I managed to knock it away. Then wee Jimmy scored with the winning penalty – the ninth one – and we won 4-2. Quintin Young was supposed to be taking the last kick for Rangers and a few of the boys had bet him that I'd save that one as well but he never got a chance to prove them wrong. So I had had an eventful seven days!

Right, Denis, excluding Connaghan, have you picked your all-time Celtic team?

I can't see past Ronnie in goal. At right-back I would have Jim Craig. At left-back I would need to put Davie Hay. Big Billy at centre-half, I think. George Connelly for – it's a crying shame. John Clark was a fabulous reader of the play but George Connelly had so much to offer the game and it's a crying shame what happened. Bobby Murdoch. Stevie Murray.

You rated Stevie Murray?

Oh yes, an immense player. I thought Stevie was a great player. Let's see, left hand side of the park I need to put Tommy Callaghan. Wee Jimmy. And I'd need to put in Kenny. I hate leaving out Dixie. And Bobby Lennox would be outside-left. That's 4-3-3 formation.

All right, Denis, thank you very much.

That's not a problem, Eugene. I've thoroughly enjoyed my walk down memory lane.

Dixie Deans

Striker
1971-1976

Dixie, where were you born and when?

I was born in Linwood, Eugene, in 1946.

Which schools did you go to?

I went to Linwood Primary and when I left there I went to Johnstone High.

I'm told you don't like Dixie as a name.

No, that's a lot of baloney, I don't know where that came from. I'm known as Dixie, I like Dixie, I don't mind at all being called Dixie. I'm John to various people but I was Dixie to the fans and the fans loved me as Dixie and I had a great rapport with the fans. So where it came from I don't know but it's all a lot of baloney!

Now you went from Neilston Juniors almost straight into the Motherwell first team.

I was a matter of weeks and then I got a chance in the first team.

You were one of Jock Stein's shock signings. How did he persuade you Parkhead was the place for you?

I don't think Jock had to sell himself at all. I was so honoured. It didn't take me long to sign the paper.

Did he promise you a first team place?

Well, more or less. In various ways it was indicated I'd be in the first team right away. I played one reserve game on the Thursday evening and I played in the first team on the Saturday and that was me, I was in the first team from Day One.

You had four weeks of a suspension outstanding.

I was under a six weeks suspension, that's a fact.

Dixie, in your first game with Celtic, you scored the fifth goal in a 5-1 win versus Partick Thistle at Firhill. Can I remind you of the team? Connaghan, Hay, Quinn, Callaghan, McNeill, Connelly, Johnstone, Dalglish, Deans, Macari and Hood.

That's not a bad team!

Was it different from playing with Motherwell?

Well yeah, the fans alone, the big crowd, it was tremendous, and Celtic was the name of course, Celtic, Rangers. When you were at school all kids wanted to go to Parkhead or Ibrox. So it was a boyhood dream.

This business of being ordered off so often with Motherwell. Did Stein encourage you to be a patient player, wait for your chances? Was there any sort of input of that sort?

I was always very confident of scoring goals. That was no problem for me. I knew was I was going to score. I just didn't know when I was going to score.

Were you ineligible for the first leg of the European Cup tie against Ujpest Dosza in Hungary 8 March 1972?

No, no. I went to that game but I injured my shoulder on the training ground in Hungary. Over there. I was playing in that game, actually, but I got injured in training the night before the game.

Now Stein said that considering the age of the side it was probably Celtic's best European Cup display since Lisbon. The 2-1 win out there.

Well, that's hard to believe because I wasn't playing!

This is the night that Liz Taylor and Richard Burton threw the party for the travelling Celtic fans. Were you there?

No, we didn't get seeing them, Eugene. We knew there was a party but we didn't get going. Big Jock was a party pooper, you know, he wouldn't allow us to go, and anyway, there was this big game coming up on the Saturday at Aberdeen in the League so they took us straight home after the game. I think the flight was going out about ten minutes after the game, that sort of thing.

On 11 March 1972, the 1-1 draw with Aberdeen and Stein takes Dalglish off because he says he is exhausted after such a long, long season and him still a boy.

Yeah. I don't know why Kenny was exhausted because I did most of his running. But Kenny used to get red in the face and do a lot of puffing and blowing so maybe that was it.

Was this a way of coddling a player do you think?

Jock was always keeping an eye on players who might have had too much to drink, too much booze, which didn't apply in Kenny's case because he wasn't a drinker. Jock knew when you'd had too much or when you were a bit tired here and there or when you were jaded. But I could well believe that by the month of March, Kenny would be a tired man. But he wasn't exactly a late bird and a boozer. He wasn't the man for a couple of drinks, unlike myself. But there was something up and Big Jock knew that so he took him off.

Scoring goals with your left foot. This was supposed to be your weak leg. Did you practise with both feet?

I suppose I did. Everybody's got one foot stronger than the other. Some people can use both but I wasn't too clever with the other one. In situations, it got you there and you nabbed a few goals with it. There were times you had no alternative, you had to use it and you did so. Now and again you got the odd screamer into the back of the net.

Did you go to San Siro for the semi-final of the European Cup against Inter Milan, 5 April 1972?

Yeah. I was there. Evan Williams had a tremendous game that night. We drew nothing each. I was on the bench that night. We knew it was going to be a tough game with the accent on the defensive. Jock told us before the start how the game would go and we'd do well if we got a result.

I've got here, George Connelly wouldn't give Boninsegna a kick.

George had a wonderful game. I remember that very well.

And Tommy Callaghan running all over the park.

Yeah, they were the two grafters that night.

Had you any expectation of coming off the bench?

Well, the kind of game it was, there weren't going to be a lot of chances and the way Milan played in those days, we knew it wasn't going to be the kind of game for a striker. But as the game went on and on, I thought I might have come on. I could see we were maybe going to get a goal out of this but it was a draw in the end and a draw was a good result in those days away from home. It was a wonderful game and the second leg, of course, I don't have to tell you about that.

I'll ask you about that in a minute! On Wednesday 12 April 1972, Celtic beat Kilmarnock 3-1 in the Scottish Cup semi-final, you scored twice and the papers said, "Deans Hits Form." But you had hardly been off form since you joined Celtic?

No. No. Not then because I was a regular scorer. But you know what papers are like. I was disappointed not to play against Inter Milan in Italy but Jock explained to me and I accepted it.

Do you remember winning the seven-in-a-row at Bayview on 15 April?

Was that the 2-2 game?

No, it was 3-0 for Celtic and you scored twice. Jock Stein said, "It won't happen again in my lifetime."

And it didn't, did it?

The business of the penalty kick against Inter, what I want to ask about it, is it true there was a competition at Seamill so that Celtic knew their five in the event of a penalty shoot-out and you won, you scored 100 per cent?

Yeah. I was banging them in from all angles then. There was a bunch of pressmen that day at the training ground and wee Jimmy was crossing them in and Bobby Lennox putting them over and I was banging them in from all angles. I hadn't missed one. I remember cracking to the pressmen, "How can this man keep me out of the team?" Big Jock heard this and quipped back, "Quite easily." But that was all part of the banter on the training field. He pulled me aside and he made me sub and again it was as if he was going to put me on in the second half and I was going to win the game for him, tire the Italians out a wee bit, put a bit of pressure on them but it didn't quite work out that way. But it was a wonderful game and the Italians being the Italians they were in those days, it was a great game and unfortunately it went to penalty kicks and as you know, Eugene, I put mine over the bar.

Did you change your mind how you were going to place it?

I think maybe I did. Sometimes you imagine things. Whether I did or not I can never be sure.

The very next game you were at home to Motherwell and you must have had the most loving relationship with the Celtic fans of any player of the modern era. There was deafening applause as Celtic came out and I think your name was chanted virtually from beginning to end. And they wanted you to take Bobby Murdoch's second penalty.

I remember that game as it was yesterday. I was a bit concerned, of course, how the fans would react and I think it showed. I remember Jock pulled me aside that night and also the next day and he assured me more or less that the fans would be on my side. There was nothing to worry about. But you wouldn't have a mind if you didn't worry and it was still at the back of my mind on the Saturday. I ran out onto the park before the game to loosen up and I got a standing ovation! I scored two goals in that game. We were awarded a penalty kick and the crowd roared for me to take it. And I waved to them as much as to say, "Oh no! No, no." You know? They chanted my name and they chanted my name. I think we won 4-2 that day. But I had a great rapport, relationship with the crowd, Eugene, as we said earlier. It was tremendous, it was wonderful and that put me back on the track, you know, and we went on to win the Cup that year and the League.

Now Dixie the Dancer, 6 May 1972, the Scottish Cup Final, Celtic six, Hibs one. You can't have imagined how that game was going to establish your name in Celtic lore.

That's right! Because Hibs were a wonderful team at the time and they were favourites to win that game which was unusual. We went out and there was this tremendous – the night before the game I could hardly sleep because I was thinking, Am I going to be playing? and Will I score? – and all that sort of thing. But you never knew how Jock would plan a game and who he would leave out. But I played and I scored a hat-trick which was a boyhood dream, not just because I was playing for Celtic but to go to Hampden in a Final, in my first Final and score a hat-trick.

Dixie, a young player of this time by whom my father used to swear, Brian McLaughlin? He thought he was the greatest thing ever.

Brian? Brian looked a great prospect but he got a bad injury. Willie McVie, the centre-half of Motherwell. He came back but he wasn't quite himself, I don't think. He was a good player but no one knows how far he might have gone. These things happen to young boys. You've got a great prospect, a new Kenny Dalglish or Jimmy Johnstone or whatever, but you never know if they're going to make it or not. Brian came back but as I say, he was never the same man. It was a shame what happened to him. But that's football.

You played in Bobby Charlton's testimonial at Old Trafford on Monday, 18 September 1972.

There was a dinner afterwards and Harold Wilson pulled me over and told me he had recommended me to Huddersfield. I was glad the deal hadn't come off because I had ended-up at Celtic Park.

How were you with referees? Did you ever find yourself thinking, Oh hell, not him again?

Well, I can tell you I was always glad that Tiny Wharton was in charge. He was a very good referee. He was a good man and very well-respected man, a big man, a giant of a man. You knew how far you could go with him. There were quite a few like Tiny but probably not as good. He was a wonderful man and you could talk to him and, as I say, you knew how far you could go. He'd run alongside you and say, "Enough of that, Mister Deans!" I remember I.D. Foote, Ian Foote. He sent me off three times, Ian Foote. The second time was for absolutely nothing as far as I could see yet he was always recognised as a good referee. I got my marching orders three times from him.

So when you took the field with him in charge?

Aye, well it was always at the back of your mind of course with the few games that I had him that it's going to happen again and this guy's got it in for me or whatever and you'd get a bit paranoid. But then, that's what it's all about.

Right, Dixie, the celebration of the seven-in-a-row on 13 November 1972, Jock got a record player and Jean got a diamond bracelet.

And we got 50 quid.

You got 50 quid?

That was it. I do think Jock deserved a lot more than a record player. But that was those days and that was how it was.

When you beat Hearts on 18 November 1972 in the League, a newspaper put it: 'Johnstone on song! Celtic on song!' That must have been a wonderful feeling.

We were fabulous in the dressing-room. I would say the whole Celtic team at that time was a team of characters. But once you were outside and over the line, it was heads down and professional stuff then, you know? Jock was a great motivator, of course, but there were games where you had to motivate yourself and it wasn't too hard to do that when you were playing with a team like Celtic. We were up for every game. It might not always have looked like it a couple of games, bad games or whatever. We had players who did the business and we did the business on the training field no matter how we lived off of it. We did the business and Jock made sure we did it. When it came time to play 90 minutes, we were up for it.

You were a great header of the ball, Dixie. Joe Aitchison said you had elastic legs. How did you get up so high?

Yeah, I was good in the air, Eugene.

What about when you were up against a big centre-half?

It wasn't a problem. I used to love a high ball coming down. Evan Williams was a great drop kicker of the ball. He used to punt them up there and I used to rise and I used to love rising above the centre-half and knocking them on for Kenny or Macari. I got a great kick out of that. One of my good assets in the game was in the air and I scored a few goals like that in the air. I was tremendous in the air and it didn't matter how big they were. Billy McNeill was six foot two, three, and I could always get above him!

Did you talk a lot to the opposition?

Aye, I was a niggler. I must have been because I was a great grafter and I didn't go down so easy. I could tackle and I could go in hard. I could take it and I could also give it. Centre-halves and half-backs and full-backs don't like players like that. This is the olden times you know! I used to do a bit of talking during the game and I've seen some comments make the paper when, you know, you might get a reporter coming up to the players' room. I remember one game we played Hibernian at Celtic Park and we beat them 5-0. And I scored three. It was a League game. And the following week we were to play them in the League Cup Final. I remember the headlines in the paper that week: 'Hibs' Defence Has Found A Way To Stop Deans.' Of course, I'm out on Saturday, the Cup Final, and I say, "Have you found a way to stop me? What are you going to do?" And I went on like that. And I scored a hat-trick that day. And after I scored the first one, I remember I went up to John Blackley and a couple of the other players, John Brownlie, "I thought you found a way to stop me? That's only one. There's more to come…" Stuff like that. And of course they're in the huff. But you've got them thinking. They're not that confident any more. But I think we gave Jock a lot of worries. There were one or two characters in the team who went off the boil a wee bit. He'd be worrying what I was up to or wee Jinky. It wouldn't happen the night before a game but a couple of nights before, who knows where we might be out enjoying ourselves! I couldn't believe it when he passed away that night. I was down there in Cardiff. I thought it was jubilation at the trackside. He was like a father to us, Jock. He was everybody's father. You know, he dropped me but I didn't hold that against him. He was doing his job. I could call him all this and all that but I brought it on myself probably.

Do you remember battle stations at Broomfield on 27 January 1973? Derek Whitefield pushed Connelly over in the box with a minute to go and McCann scored the winner for Airdrie. Celtic were incensed. Big Jock came down out of the stand despite a recent heart attack just in time to stop Jinky grappling with Airdrie trainer, Ian Reid. Sean Fallon confronted the referee and McNeill refused Whiteford's handshake. Where were you in all this?

I was probably punching somebody. No, I remember the incident but I don't remember a great deal of the detail. Airdrie were a team of kickers and hookers. As a matter of fact I was talking about them just a couple of days ago. I was along with Bobby Murdoch and we were talking about Airdrie's team in the old days, Paul Jonquin at the back and all those – they would kick the head off you! They had all these hard men at the back and I used to surprise them because I was hard myself so it didn't really bother me. I could look after myself, you know? I can't exactly remember what happened that day but I remember that day.

Two points lost in the race for the eight-in-a-row. This game was Ali Hunter's debut. How did you rate Ali in Celtic's quest for the new Ronnie Simpson?

He was capped for Scotland and yeah, he had a few good games at Celtic Park. He let things get to him.

To get back to the goalkeepers, it's often said that goalkeepers were Jock's Achilles' heel.

Well, there was a problem with goalkeepers. He certainly overworked them. We used to stand back and watch some days and he had them in the sandpits and he put them through it. When I joined Celtic there was Denis Connaghan, Evan Williams, Tom Lally, Gordon Marshall senior and John Fallon was still there. There were five or six or seven goalkeepers. The trouble is, the focus is always on the goalkeeper. He makes a bloomer and the ball ends up in the back of the net. I make a bloomer and we still win 1-0. Yeah, he had a problem with goalkeepers and I don't think he liked them, as you say. Maybe he was a bit hard on them, I don't know.

The race for the League was very tight in '73. Celtic had dropped 6 points in seven matches, they were evens for the title and Rangers were 6-4. Did this tension communicate itself to the dressing-room?

There was a wee bit of pressure on us. We were dropping points here and there and losing games we should never have lost but we were pretty confident of going on to win the eight-in-a row. We were always confident of winning the title. At the end of the day, that's what it's all about, getting there.

Celtic beat Dundee United 3-0 after extra time in the Scottish Cup semi-final replay on 11 April 1973. It looked as if Harry Hood was coming on to play extra time in your place but there was a rush of Celtic players to the dug-out. Stein said later, that they wanted to tell me that Deans had got over his cramp. That must have been some compliment! They wanted you to stay on.

Yeah! They wanted me to stay on. I said, "I'm all right! I'm all right! I got a bit of cramp." Cramp just comes on to you, Eugene, and then it disappears. You know? It was dreadful for a wee minute. I felt it coming back and I held on, held on, but you can only hold on for so long, you can't go 60 minutes with it. Then it was okay and I knew it was okay so that was them running to the touchline to say, The wee man's all right!

You came off against Arbroath on 21 April 1973 and got a huge ovation. This is still the race for the eight-in-a row. I mean, I've said this to you before, how did it feel to be loved?

Yeah, tremendous. I don't think I wanted to come off. I'd scored a couple of goals or I'd scored one goal and you know yourself when you've played well or you've played badly. But it was a tactical thing, the game was won and I think Jock was trying to protect me, didn't want me injured. But I wanted to play on. If you'd played badly, some of the games you wanted off. I regret the bad games I had for the club. I could have got abuse but the fans never gave me abuse at all. I had a fantastic rapport and that exists to this day. All the punters that come into the pub. I love them for it. It's great support. Fantastic.

The eight-in-a row was won at Easter Road on 26 April 1973. McNeill booked to play upslope in the first half. Celtic won 3-0 and you opened the scoring in 22 minutes. What was the Easter Road ground like to play on?

A great ground to play on but it was backs to the wall when Hibs were playing down that hill. I loved playing there.

Did that slope not bother you as a striker?

No. No. But as I say, it was at the back of your mind that when Hibs were coming down, you knew that you were going to be under pressure. If you ask me did I prefer playing downslope as a striker, of course I did. But I could still cope with uphill. On the eight-in-a-row day, I scored against the slope and I also scored with it in the second half too, a header from Callaghan, I think it was. Two that day.

The League was won by a point from Rangers. Did you sleep that night?

Probably not. I wasn't a great sleeper. I was one for sitting up and having a smoke in those days as Billy McNeill would tell you. I used to room with Billy when we were away. I was a smoker and I was always up late at night.

Jock tried to get me off smoking. A few players smoked and he tried to get us off it. It's one of those things, I'm off it now. I haven't smoked these last two years. I used to be a heavy smoker. Jock knew that. It didn't bother me then. It was only later in life not in my twenties or thirties. In our team I was the only one mad enough or man enough to smoke in front of Jock. Most players that smoked would smoke behind Jock's back but Jock knew who the smokers were. I was never as bad as some. Billy Bremner was a chain smoker. Billy was an 80-a-day man.

He died from a heart attack, didn't he?

He did, yeah. Then there was the Brazilian – was it Socrates? – he was a 100-a-day man. Tommy Callaghan was a big smoker. There were surprising ones that you wouldn't think. Denis Connaghan was a smoker. Yeah, there were a few smokers about. In those days you didn't know it was affecting you. I still had my wind when Kenny was puffed-out and he didn't smoke!

According to the papers, Jock wanted a running half-back so he signed Stevie Murray from Dundee and let Murdoch go. Were you sorry to see Bobby leave?

Oh yes, one of the finest half-backs I've ever seen, Bobby. Yes, so Bobby left and went to Middlesbrough. Stevie was a good player but he was never a Bobby Murdoch. There was only one Bobby, wasn't there? Stevie came in and he did a job for the club.

On 17 November 1973, you score six against Partick Thistle in a 7-0 win and you set Bobby Lennox up for the other goal. Both sides autographed the match ball for you. Have you still got it?

Oh yes, I've still got it. I don't give that sort of thing away and I don't want to lose it. I'll never forget that day, it was wonderful. A great game and to score six in any game, even if it's only a pub game, that's always something. But this was a professional game against the Scotland goalkeeper, Alan Rough. I put it to Alan every time I see him, who was the guy put six past him?

Now you missed the League Cup semi-final at Hampden, 3-1 against Rangers on Wednesday, 5 December 1973. Harry Hood got a hat-trick. The ground was described as a frozen waste. Would that sort of pitch have suited you, Dixie?

Jock didn't think I could hold my feet on a pitch like that. I remember that day and I was very disappointed not to be picked. Frosty grounds, no one can play on them really. But some players can hold their feet better than others. So Jock opted for Harry and I think Kenny Dalglish. He opted for the players of his choice and I wasn't the one for banging the door and arguing with Jock. But I was disappointed not to be playing. I liked hard pitches, soft pitches. But that day, if I remember rightly, it was icy on top.

At the end of 1973, you were on a terrific roll. There was a period during which you played 190 minutes football and scored ten goals which was almost an average of a goal every 20 minutes!

I remember that.

Did you every see much of Jimmy McGrory around Parkhead?

Jimmy was always about, yeah. I remember when I scored the six, he said he was calling to get me off and he came to see me after the game that day. He shook my hand and said the sweat was running off him, he couldn't bear it, he thought I was going to break his record. I had a laugh with him and said I should have. He was a lovely man. I don't know how the other players got on with him but he'd look out of his office and see me and say, "How are you, Dixie? How are you getting on?" Just a lovely man. I don't think he ever raised his voice.

Right. Now, Dixie, a great game at Easter Road on 23 February 1974. You scored twice in a 4-2 win. My notes say it was the day when Danny McGrain emerged as the complete footballer.

Well Danny really was. He was one of the world's greatest and when you think of what he had to overcome, the diabetes, the ankle injury, the cracked skull. A magnificent footballer and a great man. I remember that game you're talking about very well.

He was the Quality Street Kid who stayed. Now the night of horrors, 10 April 1974, Celtic 0, Atletico Madrid 0, the European Cup semi-final first leg. You were the one Celtic player booked.

Well, what can you say about a game like that, Eugene? Ah, it was ridiculous. The game should have been abandoned, it should have been stopped. It was definitely the worst game I ever played in. You should have seen the state of Jinky that night, he was black and blue. It was just a total shambles. The game should have been abandoned and it didn't get abandoned. They had three men sent off, five booked and two warned. We were made to go to Madrid. We should never have been made to go there after what had happened at Parkhead. They tried to stop me from playing in the second game over there because I got booked in the first game. I started the second game but I got taken off. We were all terrified. We never played at all. We went there – Big Jock more or less told us before we went, the lads were going to uphold the good name of Celtic. We knew we were going to go there and get beat. We knew that. But play? We didn't want to play, we were terrified. It was just a matter of upholding the good name of Celtic as Jock said when he told us we were going to Madrid. But we should never have been allowed to go there. We should have been awarded the tie. They played about and looked a good team because we didn't dare show any heart. Wee Jimmy Johnstone had been threatened he would be shot. I blame the press for that.

The British press?

Our own press, aye. That sort of thing should never have been reported. The pressure that put on, someone in the crowd with a gun. We lost two-nil but we never played. There was only one result expected, a win for Atletico.

And yet you held out till 12 minutes to go. Denis Connaghan had a great game that night.

Denis did, yeah.

No pasarán. Dixie, without wanting to pry into your personal affairs, what is this mystery illness that lands you up in the Alexandra Infirmary 10 May 1974?

This is after Madrid. I had a pain in my back and my heel but when I came home this night, I went to a place in Glasgow, a pub, to have a couple of drinks and I was standing there. I was standing with a vodka in my hand but my hand was like this, shaking all over the place. I was with a couple of my pals so I said to one of the boys, "Going to hold that drink a minute?" And he thought I was joking. I just couldn't do anything to make the shaking stop. Then I was starting to sweat. I had another drink after. I thought, Maybe another drink will settle me down. But I'm holding on to the bar with one hand. I had my car that night and in those days you used to take a chance with drink-drive, you know? Most of them did, didn't they? Anyway, I did. So I said, "I'm going away, I'm going home." I was starting to faint but I drove the car with the shaking and everything. I got home anyway and I went to hospital the next morning and I was kept in. My whole face was blown-up, my back, and they'd taken blood samples blah-blah-blah but to this day they still don't know what it was. They reckoned it was Madrid, they reckoned it was something from the pool, you know, when I was in the swimming pool. But they don't know what it was exactly even to this day. I was talking to one of the medical people not so long ago and they still haven't found an explanation.

It just went away?

Weeks later, I was in the hospital and oh, it was terrible, I was lying there, I didn't know what was wrong with me, I was asking, What do you think I've got? And then it was gone, just vanished.

Thank you very much, Dixie.

My pleasure. Thank you, Eugene.

Was it easy fitting in at Celtic?

I was made welcome right away. There was a good crowd of us there, a great atmosphere, and great guidance from McGrain. He was a very strong captain and a very well-respected man. He made guys wear the uniform. You know? I used to call him my third eye. That's a term I used to use in coaching. If you're behind me, you're my third eye. I need to worry a lot less about what's in front of me. So Danny would shout, "Right! Left! Back! Sit in! Forward!" – you know? He made you feel secure. You could go forward and maybe make mistakes. You got stick from time to time but the guy that didn't buy the ticket never won the raffle. There's too much in football nowadays about not giving it away. McNeill always gave me the freedom to create. He would say it's easy to pull down a wall, it takes a craftsman to build it.

On 12 January 1980 you played against George Best on Hibs' left in a 1-1 draw at Easter Road, a Scottish League match. Did you skin him or did he skin you?

I'll never forget that game because from the kick-off I went straight to him and he dipped his shoulder and put the ball through my legs. He nutmegged me in four seconds and I could not believe it! He nutmegged me and he made his pass and then he looked back at me as much as to say, "Sorry, son, what else could I do?" Anyway, I stayed away from him for the rest of the game. He had such fantastic skill.

One week later at Aberdeen you collected a knee injury that was going to need an operation. What was the problem?

It was actually something that had been there, for quite a while. It's a part of the bone that flakes off the patella and I'll give Big Billy his due, he let me play with it up until we played Real Madrid. And just prior, he said, "You're really doing yourself damage." And the surgeon then, Mr Abrahmi – George Abrahmi was the Celtic surgeon then, very, very good – he said, "Look, it's just like a wee pea, it's sore but it's insignificant." Things like that, so I felt I could play through it but Big Billy said I was hirpling and he was putting me in for the operation. When I woke up – I was in the Bon Secours in Glasgow, the sisters – when I woke up there was this scar, well, the big bandage first of all when I felt my knee. When they came to change the dressing, I could not believe it, the number of stitches, about 50 stitches! Anyway, Mr Abrahmi came and I was still a bit high and he said, "Do not fear. Believe me, that will heal just as quick as any normal wound. What I did was, when I was inside, I made sure that everything was intact. I made sure your cartilages were fine and everything like brand new. That will heal satisfactorily." His word was right but I was really frightened. I was only in the hospital for five days. I was determined, I was very determined to get back out to Parkhead. Celtic were playing down at Kilmarnock and I managed to get myself to Kilmarnock although I probably really shouldn't have been out of the house. I told Big Billy that wee Scottie – Brian Scott – had had a look at me so he asked wee Scottie and he said, "Aye, he's doing all right." I was up at the ground on Sunday just doing my exercises and the replay against Real Madrid in the European Cup was on the Wednesday. Big Billy asked me did I want to go. Actually Scotty took the stitches out, he took them out on the Monday, and Celtic took me with them. That was the 3-0 game. George McCluskey wasn't fit for that game but he declared himself fit. George should have scored in the first couple of minutes. It would have made all the difference.

Now Frank McGarvey watched the first Real Madrid game, the two-nil win at Parkhead. Were you aware that he was about to sign for Celtic?

No, no idea! None at all. There wasn't as much press as there is now but Big Billy was very conscious of stealing the headlines prior to a big game. That's what he did with me. I signed on a Friday and Big Billy stole the headlines before the game with Rangers on the Saturday. You got the back page to yourself, you know?

What was wee Frank like as a colleague?

McGarvey? Inexplicable! Nobody knew when Frank was about! Frank was just unbelievable. Frank was just Frank. I remember they were winding Frank up on a pre-season tour in Germany. They were winding Frank up, him and Johnny Doyle, about who The Man was. Up to now, Doyle was The Man. Doyle was The Man who kept the young fellows in control. He'd go into their dressing-room and take on five or six of them at a time, slap them about. Character-building you could call it, a bit of character-building. They all loved him but Doyle was The Man. If any of the reserves were out of order, John would sort them out. But now the word was going about that Frank was now The Man. They were kidding Doylie on that Frank was The new Man. The guy behind this was Vic Davidson. Victor was comical. He'd sit back and never take a poke himself, he just wanted people to explode over one another. So we were sitting playing cards or something and Victor starts, "Aye, Doylie, you've lost it now, McGarvey is The Man." So McGarvey likes this, he's going away with a pouted chest. So anyway, the two of them start wrestling on the couch. They were in a clinch for three and a half hours! I'm not exaggerating. Neither of them would give way, neither would give way. Victor's just sitting there still winding it up," Aye, he's getting you there, wee Doylie." Big Billy came by about two or three times and they were still at it. He said, "But they're taking so much out of each other!" And all over who was The Man!

I didn't feel Celtic had any chance at all in the 1980 Cup Final against Rangers. There was no centre-half, was there? They had to play Mike Conroy. You must have watched that game?

I watched it, yeah. See when you're not involved – I was a wee bit disappointed in that game because I'd come back from injury and I'm sure Big Billy put Bobby Lennox on the bench when I really felt he could have put me. I knew I was up for it. He put Bobby Lennox on the bench and Bobby got the medal.

You were back in the big team when Ayr United put Celtic out of the Drybrough Cup. The man in the number nine shorts was Nicholas. How did you feel about Charlie?

The Kid? He was special, there was no doubt about that. We used to play this game, we called it the Mad Mentals, the Mad Mental Game, 25 a-side, you know? It improved your touch, you had to have good control, you had to do something quick with the ball or else you got crowded off it, bounced off it. It was instead of the traditional 11-a-side or five-a-side. Billy would play, wee John Clark would play, they would play on either side so as to lend their experience! Twenty-two-a-side or 25-a-side. It was difficult playing in these big matches but this kid stood out all the time. He scored some spectacular goals and he would glide past people on this crowded pitch. It was obvious then he was a very special player. He was a great player and he scored some special goals. And it's funny, playing with players of his calibre, I always found brilliant – easy, for want of a better word. To play with guys like that, you just sort of clicked, all the moves just sort of gelled. Joe Harper was in that sort of league as well. And Tommy Burns. There were certain ones, you just sort of knew for sure what kind of pass they wanted or what kind of ball they were going to give to you.